MILES FROM HOME...

miles from help

She was perfectly capable of changing a flat. But today she was dressed for a luncheon — and the tire *was* muddy — the jack smeared with grease. Then (it seemed like a miracle to her) — a Texaco tank truck drove up. The driver stopped — and changed the tire for her.

This is a typical example of the willing cooperation which inspires every Texaco employee, on the road or at a Texaco Service Station. Even if you drive in only for air, or a windshield to be cleaned — Texaco welcomes you. Feel free to stop, not only for "dry" Texaco-Ethyl Gasoline and Texaco Motor Oil, but also for any service you desire. THE TEXAS COMPANY · *Texaco Petroleum Products*

TEXACO
GASOLINE...MOTOR OIL

WEIRD HIGHWAY

HIGHWAY

Illinois

Route 66 History & Hauntings, Legends & Lore

This Book is Published By:
Whitechapel Press
American Hauntings Ink
Jacksonville, Illinois | 1-888-446-7859
Visit us on the Internet at http://www.whitechapelpress.com

First Edition – October 2015
ISBN: 1-892523-97-3

Printed in the United States of America

INTRODUCTION

There is no greater highway in American history than Route 66 – the legendary "Mother Road" – which began in downtown Chicago and stretched all of the way to the Pacific Ocean. For millions of people, it represents a treasure trove of memories and a link to the days of two–lane highways, family vacations, lunches at roadside tables, and greasy–spoon diners that ceased to exist decades ago. For many, it conjures up images of souvenir shops, tourist traps, cozy motor courts, and cheesy roadside attractions that have since crumbled into dust. To others, Route 66 makes them think of rusty steel bridges, flickering neon signs, classic cars, and drive–in theaters. To others, the highway holds stories of ghosts, haunted hotels, roadside spirits, mysterious vanishings, and bewildering anomalies, too.

It's America's most famous highway – even though officially it no longer exists.

Route 66 began simply to meet the needs of a growing nation. It gained both fame and infamy during the Dust Bowl days of the Great Depression, as the highway became an escape route for the thousands of families who moved westward from Oklahoma, Texas, and Arkansas. It was the migrants and travelers, seeking salvation from the drought, whose plight was immortalized in John Steinbeck's *Grapes of Wrath*. In the book, he called Route 66 "the mother road, the road of flight." The nickname stuck and for many years, Route 66 was seen as a passage to hope for struggling "Okies" and those who were down on their luck. During World War II, Route 66 became a military conduit, providing a fast-moving passage for men, munitions, and equipment to move about the country. The continuous convoys kept the highway busy and the pockets of roadside merchants filled. In spite of this, however, Route 66, a road designed for civilian travel, paid the price in wear and tear caused by the military vehicles. It eventually weakened and began to decline, a development that did not go unnoticed in Washington. By this time, officials were already considering a wider and faster highway system that could handle the toughest traffic demands. By the time the war ended, the demise of Route 66, although still years away, had become inevitable.

For a few years, though, a return to peace time brought new prosperity and a tourism boom to America. Spurred on by Bobby Troup's musical hit "Get Your Kicks on Route 66," people were anxious to travel the country and the merchants of the highway cashed in. As traffic on the road increased, new businesses sprang up and an explosion of tourist traps, curio shops, and neon signs began to appear in just about every town on Route 66's path. Motor courts became "motels," diners became "restaurants," and general stores changed into "trading posts." Hundreds of new billboards helped to spread the word about these booming businesses.

It was an era of good times that we now look back on with nostalgia, but it was never meant to last. By the middle 1950s, the interstates were making their way west and over the next 15 years, Route 66 began to vanish. It was ripped up, downgraded, and re-aligned and the hundreds of towns that were dependent on the highway's traffic were slowly strangled in the process. Many of them became literal ghost towns, fading reminders of the days that once were. By the end of the 1960s, with the damage done, "America's Main Street" had ceased to be a through route to California. It was not officially decommissioned, though, until the stubborn citizens of Williams, Arizona, the last town to be bypassed, lost a legal battle to stop it in 1984.

Although long stretches of Route 66 still remain today, most of it is a hard to define mix of original roadbed, access roads, abandoned fragments, and lost highways. It has been re-configured in so many ways that even diehard travelers can sometimes become lost and turned around as they try and follow the road's often lonely miles.

Almost everyone who dreams of the glory days of Route 66 have ventured out onto at least one section of the Mother Road, looking for old alignments and often finding broken pavement and dead ends. In other places, we can often find true gems of the road, offering little-known places and sites to adventurers, sometimes found by tracing the rows of rickety telephone poles and reliable railroad tracks that Route 66 usually shadowed. For those who become lost and wonder if they are still on the old road, we watch for abandoned stores, broken and dead neon signs for businesses that have long since vanished, and even creaky motor courts that sometimes still eke out a living from travelers that are now few and far between. The past still manages to be present – however elusively – along the remains of Route 66.

I can honestly say that I'm one of those who has ventured out in search of Route 66, following it all of the way from my home state of Illinois to the West Coast. It was a trip that helped to cement my love for the road, for weird places, ghostly highway tales, unusual people, and eccentric sites, all of which eventually led to this series of books. It began merely as a collection of ghost stories from the path of the highway, but it turned into much more than that. With all of the books that I have written over the years, I have yet to pen a title that is not filled with history, strange facts, and curious wonders. My volumes about Route 66 are no exception. Soon after I started the series, I began to realize that it was a weird road trip of all of the oddness that the highway had – and still manages -- to offer. This is truly a chronicle of the weird – ghost stories, monsters, haunted places, quirky hotels, abandoned places, favorite diners, forgotten spots, classic roadside attractions, and just about anything that left me chucking, a little unnerved, or just scratching my head in confusion. It's the nostalgia of Route 66, mixed with the dark side of the highway's legends and lore. The series has a little of everything, including, abandoned drive-ins, oddball trading posts, UDO landing sites, spook lights, giant spacemen, and just about everything else that makes us still fascinated with Route 66 today.

I had a great time writing these books and I hope you have a great time reading them. I have to confess, though, that the series will end with a little sadness. Once completed, it's like closing the door on something that really doesn't exist anymore. Or does it?

It was once said that the whole world traveled down Route 66, but it's not that way anymore. It's a lost part of American history, but while gone, it is certainly not forgotten. Any other American highway would have become ancient history a long time ago, but there is something about this road that has remained within our collective imagination. What is it about this particular highway that conjures up so many ghosts of days gone by? No one can say for sure, but few can deny that Route 66 is more than just some old roadway. Route 66 is a trip back in time to a weird, lonely, and magical place in American history and if you plan it just right, it's one you can still recapture. Doing so is as easy as turning your steering wheel, taking a little time, and leaving the mind-numbing miles of the interstate behind. Just follow the road signs back to an era when you could still "get your kicks on Route 66."

I can promise you that you won't be sorry that you did.

Troy Taylor
Fall 2015

HIGHWAY TO THE WEST
The History of Route 66

*The Automobile Club of America has set out to secure a macadamized road from
New York to San Francisco. As yet, it is too soon to figure out how many millions it
would cost to build 3,500 miles of good macadam road across mountains and
prairies, but it is not too early to remark that the automobile promises to be a strong
and valuable ally of the bicycle in the great missionary work of securing better
country roads throughout the United States.*
"Automobiles and Good Roads," Chicago Tribune, March 26, 1900

The cross-country highway that eventually became Route 66 was years in the
making. It began with the rise in popularity of the American automobile and with the
demand they created for new roads. As automobiles slowly grabbed hold of the
American imagination, enthusiasts quickly realized how limited they were when it
came to decent roads on which to drive them. By 1902, an outcry was raised in
Chicago when representatives from the nine largest automobile clubs in the country
met to combine forces and to start making plans for a national network of highways
that would cross the entire country. They met at the Chicago Coliseum during the
much–ballyhooed run of the Chicago Auto Show with the idea of launching a new
organization through which they could lobby for their goal.

The new organization became the American Automobile Association (AAA), and loyal to its members, AAA made its first order of business the promotion of a transcontinental road that would stretch from New York to California. This was the beginning of all of the "highways" to come and the start of a long journey toward a system that was designed to connect all of America's towns and cities by road, from east to west, north to south, and all points in between.

By the time of the Chicago meeting in 1902, there were about 11,000 automobiles in America. All of them were rambling about to their best of their ability on muddy tracks and dirt trails, their drivers desperate for good roads to drive on. Within five years, the number of drivers looking for decent roads had increased to an amazing 300,000. They clamored for new roads, and the more autos that were purchased, the louder the hue and cry became. Harry Radford, president of the Cartercar Motorcar Company of Pontiac, Michigan, wrote, "It is my notion, and facts bear me out, that the motor driven vehicle has done more than any other agency toward improved highways."

Throughout the early 1900s, the new-fangled motor cars puttered their way into the hearts of those who longed to be free from the days of horses and bicycles. Of course, the main obstacle in the early days was money. With price tags of anywhere from $650 to $5,000, automobiles of the era were still considered a luxury. In those days, a good horse and wagon cost only about $200, which made many wonder why they should waste the money on a machine that had to be restricted to recreational use. There just weren't enough decent roads to drive them on. Common sense suggested that people should invest their hard-earned dollars in a reliable horse and wagon instead.

But common sense had little to do with the demand for the new motor cars. Much to the surprise of automobile manufacturers, people went crazy for cars. None of the fledgling auto makers could keep up with demand and often ran six months behind in filling orders. Once America's business sector realized the potential of the automobile, demand increased even more. Automobiles were bringing prosperity to the country and the need for bigger, better roads became paramount. Transportation was providing Americans with the means to obtain better goods and, at the same time, was making it possible for farmers and small companies to make their goods available to a wider range of customers. In addition, Americans would soon be able to travel farther than most had ever dreamed, allowing them to see and experience their country firsthand. It was truly the beginning of a new era.

America now had the vehicles with which to travel and now they only needed the roads to take them where they wanted to go. As it had been with the railroads in the nineteenth century, there were a handful of visionaries who saw what America needed for her future. There was no question about it – America's first transcontinental highway had to be built.

Motoring Across America

Thanks to the American Automobile Association, the idea of the coast-to-coast highway soon came to the attention of the general public. Slowly, average Americans began to realize what it would mean to travel freely from one end of the country to the other if, of course, there was ever a practical method to do so. People began to hunger for such a method and soon it seemed to be on the minds of everyone.

Well, almost everyone... Because, as it is with every new idea, there were the naysayers who claimed that such an endeavor was impossible. A highway of that sort, they claimed, could hardly be profitable. It would bankrupt the government! It was a shortsighted opinion, but it did have some validity. No one had ever attempted a building project of such grand design. In those days, it seemed as impossible as sending a man to the moon. Who would build it? How would it work? Where would the money come from to build so many miles of road? No one knew it at the time, but a mountain of commerce was already forming to support the transcontinental highway.

But work still needed to be done to make the idea of the long-distance route seem feasible to the public. Ordinary people had to make the journey – or at least try to make it – before it became clear that just about anyone could manage it. If a handful of adventurous motorists survived the journey, there would be no turning back on plans to make the highway a reality.

In the fall of 1910, four largely forgotten young men from Chicago departed on a mission to prove that it was possible to travel across the country by motor car. They would travel west by train and then return to Chicago in their motor car by way of Southern California, Arizona, and the Santa Fe Trail. Their idea was to show they could drive (if "driving" can really describe their venture across unpaved terrain) from San Francisco to Chicago and make the Middle Western path along the old settler's trails the most feasible coast-to-coast route.

The crew was made up of several intrepid automobile enthusiasts: H. Pomy, J. Rew, W.H. Aldrich, and B. Lackey. They equipped their Stearns motor car with all of the equipment and supplies necessary for such a trip, including three spare tires, six water bags, a soldering outfit and blow torch, an axe, hand-saw, brace and bits, 350 feet of rope, a pinch bar, shovel, two pulleys, an eight-foot "dead man" for rigging a block and tackle, and 40 feet of canvas. It was a full load and with the four crewmen, the auto weighed in at almost 6,000 pounds. Dressed in driving coats and with their eyes protected by goggles, they gallantly set out on the adventure of a lifetime.

They departed from San Francisco and the first leg of the trip was largely uneventful. The trip was trouble-free until they reached the arid region of Southern California. Under the baking sun at Needles, they hit the Colorado River and had to figure out how to cross it. There were no commercial roadways or bridges so they had to try and make it over on a crude ferry. It was just the first of hardships that they had to face. There were no motor lodges or hotels and few restaurants along the dirt roads where they could stop and eat. They had only dusty bedrolls, the hard ground, and whatever they could cook around the campfire.

After crossing the Colorado, the men decided to drive along an existing freight road, which had originally been built to connect the mines of California with the rest of the country. Before long, though, they were in "trackless" country. There were no trains, wagons, or other cars to be found. They were on their own and, as night fell, they had to drive using an acetylene searchlight by which to see. The trip was no longer a lark; it had gotten serious.

Somewhere between Hackberry and Peach Springs, Arizona, they made a wrong turn and got lost. They plowed on ahead until they found a man camping out in the wilderness. He told them that they had gotten off path and were within a few miles of the Grand Canyon. He advised them to backtrack about 20 miles and look for a trail with a right turn – otherwise they were going to have a really hard time getting across the canyon! They set back off in the direction from which they came and, using the searchlight, eventually stumbled onto a cattle trail. Bleary-eyed from lack of sleep, they continued on and finally rolled into Peach Springs around 2:00 a.m.

The crew pressed on, following the railroad tracks over steep ground and through rugged terrain. They passed through Williams the next day, followed by dangerous Diablo Canyon. At Winslow, they encountered the Shevlin River and Rew, who drove most of the time, shot through the raging water at 35 miles an hour. Water rushed into the engine compartment, but the heavy motor car barreled over to the opposite shore before sputtering to a stop. Once they dried everything out, they were on their way again.

The next river they crossed was the Puerco River, which the locals called the "Porky." According to Rew, "The Porky runs through a canyon, with the railroad high up on one bank above the washout level. It is sometimes thirty or forty feet deep and at time so incrusted in spots as to make swift negotiation possible. The surface of the arroyo where not incrusted is fine sand, which will stall a car when dry and sink it when wet. It took us eight hours to get out of that hole."

They made it through and continued on to Albuquerque and then Gallup, where the men stayed in a comfortable hotel, which offered, they said "A flop, a splash and three squares." After that, things went much smoother and they made it back to Chicago. Despite the difficulties they encountered, they all agreed that their route – following the old pioneer trails – was the most practical route for a highway that would connect the east and west. Unfortunately, their trip was not widely publicized and it would take another year before the promise of the highway route reached the public at large.

At that time, Thomas Wilby, special agent for the Office of Public Roads, set off on his own headline-making journey across the country. He traveled nearly 9,000 miles in just 105 days and concurred with the Chicagoans who made the cross-country journey the year before. He wrote: "A National Highway for auto travelers was the most feasible across the Middle Western route... it is along historical and fascinating trails where real activity is shown in the good roads movement. There is such a wealth of scenic and historic features that the completed highway will veritably prove to be one of the wonders of the world."

Pomy, Rew, Aldrich and Lackey were already aware of what Wilby had written. None of them ever received fame and fortune after their brave trip, but they were content in the fact that they were the first to travel what would eventually become the path of the country's most legendary highway.

Father of Route 66

Long before his dream of Route 66 was turned into reality, Cyrus Avery had a passion for roads. He longed for an America with good, state-to-state motorways that travelers could use with ease and would not have to constantly worry about getting lost.

No one knows where his passion for highways began. Avery had been born in Stevensville, Pennsylvania, in 1871, and when he was a teenager, his family moved west to what was then the Indian Territory of Oklahoma. After graduation from William Jewell College in Liberty, Missouri, Avery married Essie McClelland and moved back to Oklahoma, where they lived for the rest of their lives.

Avery's interest in roads began with the Ozark Trails: an unorganized system of roads that connected to St. Louis, Missouri, to Amarillo, Texas. He was impressed with work being done by some of the local highways advocacy groups, especially the Good Roads movement in Missouri, and in 1907, he moved from Vinita, Oklahoma, to Tulsa, where he began his climb to national prominence.

Living in Tulsa, he invested in the oil industry and became very aware of how roads affected his and other businesses. Five years later, he sought out and secured the post of county commissioner. He wanted the job for one reason – it gave him the opportunity to observe the need for an improved system of highways. And it also gave him a platform from which to promote the idea of improving roads throughout the state of Oklahoma.

One of his first acts was to devise an effective method for maintaining the current roads. His solution was the "split-log-drag" method, where horses were used to drag large split logs up and down the road, usually after a good rain. This smoothed out the roadway, tamped down the dirt path, prevented potholes, and kept the road fairly smooth – unless it was driven over after it rained, of course. When that happened, the road turned into a muddy, rutted mess. Even so, the public appreciated his efforts and he was dubbed the "Father of Good Roads" in Tulsa County.

In 1913, William Hope Harvey, the businessman, author, politician, and social thinker who established a famous Arkansas health resort called Monte Ne, sent out an invitation to "organize a delegation of commercial clubs, good roads and automobile associations" with the goal of forming a new Ozark Trails organization. Avery was one of the first on the invitation list and he gladly accepted the responsibility.

Thanks to Avery's presence, the group quickly gained notoriety and became an effective force for change. In 1914, an article appeared in the *Oklahoman* that stated, "The Ozark Trails Association, embracing the states of Missouri,

Cyrus Avery

Kansas, Arkansas and Oklahoma, is one of the strongest and most active good roads organizations west of the Mississippi River." In just a short time, the group had the enthusiastic support of both road boosters and Oklahoma state leaders.

The association planned its second annual convention in May 1914, and soon began looking for locations for the host city. Aware of the influence that the group might bring to whatever city hosted the event, various road associations along the trails competed vigorously to try and get the meeting held in their town. But there was no contest – Avery's hometown of Tulsa received the honor.

William Hope Harvey, who was now the president of the Ozark Trails Association, wanted to create a spectacle and get as much publicity as possible, so he traveled to the meeting in an unusual way – on foot! He traveled from his home in Arkansas and brought with him a supply of paint and brushes, giving all of the Ozark Trail markers along his route a fresh coat of paint. When necessary, he even installed new signs on the existing telegraph poles found along the route.

On May 15, Harvey walked into Vinita, Oklahoma, on what would soon be Route 66. After a foot soak, he joined Avery and a growing number of Ozark Trail enthusiasts who were already in town. Together, they walked to Tulsa, repairing and replacing road markers all of the way into the city.

A few weeks later, the newly marked Ozark Trail saw a revitalized campaign of roadwork and improvements and the method most commonly used was Avery's split-log-drag system.

Bolstered by his success with the Ozark Trails, Avery began to be appointed to various offices and positions. First, he joined the board of directors of the Northeast Oklahoma Chamber of Commerce. Then, he became the founder and president of the Albert Pike Highway Association. Next, the Associated Highways of America elected him as its president in 1921. Finally, in February 1924, he was named as the Oklahoma Highway Commissioner, a position that would make him nationally known – and lead to the creation of Route 66.

Toward the end of 1924, Avery was recruited by the U.S. Bureau of Public Roads to help develop a new system of interstate highways. Avery accepted the Bureau's offer and throughout 1925 worked with a committee to connect hundreds of existing roads into a nationwide network. It was the dawn of the American automobile. Cars had finally become available to the average person and families were taking to the road like never before. They wanted to travel and Cyrus Avery was one of the people who helped them to do it.

Avery was given broad authority and made sure that one of the chosen routes, designed with the backing of officials in Illinois and Missouri, cut directly across his home state of Oklahoma as part of a Chicago to Los Angeles thoroughfare. When first presented, this unconventional route was not well received. Avery dug up every bit of supporting evidence that he could find, including the opinion of Thomas Wilby, who had pushed for the same route as early as 1911. It took months for Avery to overcome the committee's reluctance and even when they finally accepted it, there was more disagreement, this time over the proposed numbering assignments.

While U.S. Route 60 was Avery's first choice, he was immediately challenged by the governor of Kentucky, who demanded the more prestigious zero-ending number for a highway across his state, which had been tentatively listed as U.S. 62. As the argument escalated, the governor went a step further and stated that the Kentucky highway, which started in Newport News, Virginia, should connect with Avery's route in Springfield, Missouri, to create a true east-west highway called Route 60. This would break up Avery's route and leave the stretch between Springfield and Chicago demoted to "branch" status. This was an idea that Avery refused to consider. The debate raged into 1926 when Avery realized that he needed to reach a settlement over the issue before upcoming elections at home jeopardized his political appointment. In a hasty resolution, he deferred to Kentucky and opted for number 66, a number his chief engineer, John Page, inadvertently discovered had not been assigned to anything. Avery liked the sound of the double sixes and found that it was an acceptable alternative. At last, with everyone satisfied, Washington finally granted approval and Route 66 was designated on November 11, 1926.

To help promote the new highway, Avery organized the U.S. 66 Highway Association shortly after leaving office, and through its efforts, Route 66 was soon entrenched as America's premiere highway. Avery passed away in 1963 at the age of

90 and will always be remembered as the man who created the legendary "America's Main Street."

Building the Mother Road

Despite an ongoing debate about the constitutionality of the federal government intervening in the road-building efforts of individual states, the Federal Aid Road Act was passed in 1916. At a White House ceremony that was attended by representatives from farm organizations, the American Automobile Association, the American Association of State Highway Officials, and members of Congress, President Wilson signed the bill into law.

George Diehl, president of AAA, was determined to see that American roads were paved. He told reporters, "The majority of states have provided for definite systems of state highways, which they are constructing as rapidly as available means permit. Every effort should be directed now toward having federal funds apply on these state systems and not frittered away on countless little disconnected local roads."

There was a lot at stake with the new program. It allotted $150 million to be spent over a five-year period, and how the money was spread out was to be decided by the secretary of agriculture. The states were all required to match the federal funds they were given. The money was distributed quickly and, almost as if by magic, turned into roads. Progress was swift and by October 20, there were 17,369 miles of road under some form of construction. As the new roads came together, the dream of a national highway was becoming a reality.

By 1926, roads across the state lines were about two-thirds improved. By that time, more than 25 states boasted continuously improved roads over their entire length. In fact, the 1920s are still seen today as the "golden era" of American road-building. Work was being carried out in every state in the union and new, paved roads were rapidly appearing.

As the national highway, which would soon be Route 66, came into being, the days of a motorist finding his way by luck were coming to a close. The open road was out there, calling to the American traveler, and tourists gladly accepted the invitation to drive. The first choice for motorists before Route 66 was the Old Trails Highway, which had been established in 1912 as a coast-to-coast series of roads that extended from New York to Los Angeles. It was made up of roads that followed many of America's most historic trails including, Braddock's Road, Cumberland Road (or National Pike), Boone's Lick Road, the old Santa Fe Trail, and the Grand Canyon Route. Signs were few and far between, but many enterprising organizations and publishers put out maps and guidebooks to help motorists find their way. The *New York Times* extolled the virtues of the Old Trails Road, "It traverses mountains, plain and forest, and is rich in varied scenery, while offering splendid road conditions and very little desert country."

Tourist routes like the National Old Trails Road were far more "civilized" than they had been in the days when four young Chicagoans braved life and limb to traverse the unpaved stretches of the country. By 1924, motorists were assured that it was no longer necessary to carry a large supply of gasoline with them since "gasoline stations are found along the road." Furthermore, hotel accommodations and automobile campgrounds could be found in just about every city and small town. Where the dusty trails were once slow and treacherous, the new paved roads allowed for a speed of at least 18 miles per hour. At one time, a coast-to-coast trip took months. By the 1920s, it could be enjoyed in only 20 to 30 days.

Motoring could still be an adventure, though. Experts still had many recommendations for long distance trips, including no less than one set of skid chains, a good horn for use on mountain curves, one set of tools, a jack, good cutting pliers, four extra tire tubes, three spark plugs, a water jug or canteen, one flashlight, an axe, a small shovel, radiator hose connections, lamp bulbs, and a tow rope or cable.

By later in the 1920s, however, much of the earlier sense of danger had vanished. Adventurous drivers had been replaced by a more subdued motoring class, which was exemplified by families who took vacations by car. These new tourists sought both adventure and the open road, but were not looking for the same sort of thrills as their highway predecessors. Even so, while tamer than ever before, the highways still had a sense of mystery about them. With no exit signs to guide them, nor billboards or signs that promised food, gas and lodging, scores of motorists truly embraced the unknown. Touring by car could still be seen as an exploration into new and uncharted territory.

But change was coming, as was Route 66.

On New Year's Day, 1927, the U.S. Bureau of Public Roads announced a new road-marking system that would forever change the way that the American public navigated the nation's roads. Uniform marking for U.S. highways had arrived, announced the *New York Times,* and now 80,000 miles of highway would be marked in a manner resembling a giant checkerboard to link section to section and connect each section to the other.

The days of remembering trail names, color marks, insignias, and other various designations were over. Instead, a simple black-and-white shield with bold, black numbers would provide all of the information that a motorist would need. At the time, there were 22 states with identification shields already in place and 20 additional states were preparing the roadways for the 1927 automobile touring system.

For the first time, motorists could determine – simply by looking at a highway number – which road they were traveling on and which direction they were going. The beauty of this new system was in its simple numbering scheme: Main transcontinental received even numbers from 10 to 90, in multiples of 10. North-to-south routes were designated with odd numbers such as 1, 21 and 31.

The single exception to the multiple of 10 numbering rule was U.S. Highway 66. This glaring anomaly did not escape the attention of a *New York Times* journalist who correctly predicted that "No. 66 is a highway that is expected to prove of great importance."

The numbering system was an instant success and it created a brand new market for road maps, guidebooks, and every conceivable kind of tourist literature and advertising. Familiar names were still used to describe the best routes in all of these publications, but the new official highway numbers were added for clarity. For example, one guidebook stated, "The recommended route is the National Old Trails Road, as it has been known for years. This is now a combination of United States Routes 40, 50, 350, 85 and 66."

As the new guidebooks and maps flooded the market, it spurred a renewed wanderlust in Americans who promptly demanded – and began taking – longer vacations. No longer satisfied with just two weeks a year, the emerging tourists began taking as much as four-week reprieves from their hectic lives. As people began snatching up automobiles, they wanted leisure time, and plenty of it.

The newspapers of the day agreed that the notion of touring required a great deal of time and planning. There was a lot to see in the way of scenic wonders across America. There was no television in those days and average people only saw the Rocky Mountains, the Grand Canyon, and Yellowstone Park in books and in photographs. They wanted to see those things in person and were desperate to take the highway in order to see them.

As people became more aware of the emerging highways, the Old Trails Road remained the most popular route for traveling from east to west. The reasons were obvious, since this cross-continent path included much of the country's most picturesque scenery, especially in the Southwest. It traveled near the Grand Canyon and along the Colorado River, as well as the Petrified Forest, the Painted Desert, cliff dwellings and Indian pueblos, the Mojave Desert, Raton Pass, Walnut Canyon National Monument, and scores of other points of interest.

The 1930 summer tourist season, in spite of the tumbling stock market and slumping economy, broke all previous records with more than 45 million Americans taking to the highways. In July, a national parks record was established with over 1 million visitors driving into parks during a single week. In fact, traffic at the national parks and monuments was so high that 12 of the 21 operating at the time opted to remain open all year around. This decision paid off for the parks in the Southwest, which began seeing their heaviest traffic in the winter months.

At the same time, roadside entrepreneurs soon discovered that these newly arriving tourists had brought their wallets along on their vacations. Vacationers were spending money, and lots of it. Anyone who thought they had some sort of gimmick discovered they could quickly turn it into cash. Soon, a new racket called the "tourist trap" began to appear across the landscape of America. It was designed for the sole purpose of convincing the tourists to part with their money.

The tourist traps needed a way to get people into their locations as they passed by on the highway, which created work for the advertising men. They unveiled an entirely new twist in advertising and it was simple and very attention-getting – they helped the roadside showmen to employ the services of larger-than-life statues, dinosaur sculptures, bright colors, huge billboards, wild claims, far-fetched slogans, bumper stickers, and oddly-shaped buildings that were guaranteed to catch the eye of the tourist.

With all of the automobiles and all of the advertising hoopla, competition began heating up in all facets of roadside service. Hotels, motels, diners, auto camps, drive-ins, hot dog stands, filling stations, repair garages, and every sort of related business literally battled it out in the streets. All of them competed for – and most received – their slice of the pie.

William Bryant, chairman of the Detroit AAA, was right on target when he announced that roadside vacations were financially profiting the entire country, from the gas stations to the restaurants to the motor lodges. "Competition for the dollar of the traveler has to be one of the keenest struggled on the national arena... perhaps as keen as anything business or industry has witnessed in the history of the world."

And he was right. The new marker shields that sprang up on the highway now known as Route 66 meant freedom and adventure of the tourist and prosperity for the merchants of the road. Suddenly, while the new highway was still being paved, life had become good for those who traveled, lived, and worked along Route 66.

Dust Bowl Days

But the good times couldn't last forever. The Great Depression soon began settling in on the entire country, making it difficult to feed the family, let alone take an automobile vacation across America. There was nowhere in the country, though, that was hit by the hard times as badly as the American Great Plains.

By 1933, the final 12 miles of Route 66 between El Reno, Oklahoma, and the east end of the new Canadian River bridge near Bridgeport was paved and open to traffic. The highway was almost entirely surfaced with only a three-mile stretch between the west end of the bridge and Bridgeport still to be completed. Under different circumstances, this would have been a reason for the people of Oklahoma to celebrate. Yet, the festivities were dampened by the winds that were beginning to blow across the farms and fields of the state. The eerie howling was a predecessor of the dark times that were coming to the Heartland. Within a few short years, the central west would experience the most severe drought of the twentieth century.

It all began with a few rain-starved years that dried up the land, destroying grass, crops, and spawning choking clouds of dust. By 1935, dry regions stretched from New York and Pennsylvania, across the Great Plains, and as far west as California. What came to be called the "Dust Bowl" covered about 50 million acres in the south-central plains.

In Oklahoma, tumbleweeds became a familiar sight as wind whipped across the panhandle, wearing down the crops, trees, and even houses. The land was literally sandblasted with relentless wind storms that stripped the fields bare, churned up the soil, and sent tons of dust into the air. As far as the eye could see, the only thing visible was barren earth, divested of every living thing and coated with thick, cloying dust. There was no point in trying to work the land with the plow for nothing would grow. Entire crops of grain failed, or were lost to the winds. Thousands of jackrabbits, which were doomed to starvation, swarmed like locusts, hoping to find whatever scraps of food remained. They devoured anything that was left growing, devouring the desperate attempts that farmers made to coax anything from the ground.

At the same time that farmers were battling the rabbits, a deadly new disease called "dust pneumonia" was born as a result of the unending winds. The disease struck the very old and very young, and doctors were at a loss to stop it. There were no known remedies for the condition except to advise people to remain indoors as much as possible and to wear masks over their noses and mouths.

One by one, farmers saw their hope of a future decimated. Many of them held on as long as they could, their farms turning into deserts by the dust and wind. On Wednesday, April 11, 1935, the worst dust storm on record blew unabated for two days and dumped tons of dirt over the land. Visibility throughout Oklahoma was cut to one-fifth of a mile and dust blew into homes through every crack, door frame, and window sill. Dismayed housewives were unable to see from the living room to the kitchen and saw footprints left behind on their dust-covered floors. Farmers could only look wistfully at the once fertile lands that were transformed into desert wastelands. What could they do? Where could they go? With nothing left but hope, they gathered together, loaded their furniture into trucks, and formed a ragged caravan of cars. A grim headline appeared in the *Oklahoman*: "Record Barrage of Dirt Sends Families out of Panhandle in Search of Homes Elsewhere."

There was only one chance left to them now – the road.

Many of the Oklahomans heard stories of California, a lush, green place that was rich with crops and where jobs were plentiful. California farmers needed field hands to help pick all of the ripe vegetables, luscious fruits, and white cotton. California became the "promised land." The refugees of the Dust Bowl were willing to work hard and wanted to regain their lives in a place where the dust wasn't blowing and where crops would grow again.

Rusty, broken-down Model T's, overloaded with household belongings and crowded with family members, began moving westward. The vehicles coughed and bounced along the rural roads until they joined up with the new transcontinental highway – the newly dubbed "Mother Road."

Route 66 embraced the "Okies," as they came to be called, and carried them toward California. The highway became more than just a thoroughfare that took tourists on vacations to see America's natural wonders. It became an escape route that guided the dispossessed safely to a new place of hope – a place where dreams could come true. A fresh and better life was just waiting for them around the next bend in the road.

It would be thanks to the Dust Bowl that Route 66 would gain its greatest fame – and earn a place in the American imagination. The saga of the Okies was told by author John Steinbeck in what is perhaps his finest book, *The Grapes of Wrath*. It quickly became an American classic after it was published in 1939. That year, it sold more than a half-million copies and garnered the praise of readers and critics alike. Route 66 literally became a major character in the book. Steinbeck wrote:

Highway 66 is the main migrant road. 66 – the long concrete path across the country, waving gently up and down the map, from Mississippi to Bakersfield – over the red lands and the gray lands, twisting up into the mountains, crossing the Divide and down into the bright and terrible desert, and across the desert to the mountains again, and into the rich California valleys.

66 is the path of the people in flight, refuges from dust and shrinking land, from the thunder of tractors and shrinking ownership, from the desert's slow northward invasion, from the twisting winds that howl up out of Texas, from the floods that bring no richness to the land and steal what richness is there. From all of these, the people are in flight, and they come into 66 from the tributary side roads, from the wagon tracks and the rutted country roads.

66 is the mother road, the road of flight.

The Golden Era Begins to Dim

U.S. 66 – sometimes called the Main Street of America – not only is one of the most important highways between Chicago and the West Coast, but it is also one of the nation's most rewarding vacation routes.
Chicago Tribune, November 24, 1957

Route 66 – the highway memorialized in poetry, gasoline, song and memories of millions of persons who traveled it or watched the television show – will be no more. Beginning January 1, Illinois is dropping the U.S. Highway 66 designation from its maps and road signs on the 290-mile highway between Chicago and St. Louis. It will be known as Interstate 55.
Chicago Tribune, November 28, 1976

The Great Depression came to an end just before the United States entered into World War II, ushering in another legendary era in American history. During the war, Route 66 was used to transport vehicles and supplies from one end of the country to the other. With the end of the war, a new period of prosperity brought even more people to America's greatest highway, which in 1946 actually gained its own theme song.

"(Get Your Kicks on) Route 66" was composed by American songwriter Bobby Troup in 1946. It was first recorded in that same year by Nat King Cole and has been subsequently covered by many artists including Chuck Berry, The Rolling Stones, Depeche Mode, Brian Setzer, Tom Petty, and dozens of others. The song's lyrics followed the path of Route 66, running from Chicago to Los Angeles.

Troup came up with the idea of the song while driving west from Pennsylvania to Los Angeles, and the lyrics – which include references to Route 66 and many of the cities that it passes through – celebrate the romance and freedom of the road during the golden era of the highway. In one interview, he said the tune for the song, as well as the lyric "Get your kicks on Route 66," came to him easily, but the remainder of the lyrics eluded him. More in frustration than anything else he simply filled up the song with the names of towns and cities on the highway.

The lyrics are sort of a travelogue of all of the major stops on the route, listing many cities and towns that Route 66 passes through, including St. Louis, Missouri; Joplin, Missouri; Oklahoma City, Oklahoma; Amarillo, Texas; Gallup, New Mexico; Flagstaff, Arizona; Winona, Arizona; Kingman, Arizona; Barstow, California; and San Bernardino, California. Winona is the only town out of sequence -- it was a very small settlement east of Flagstaff, and might indeed have been forgotten if not for the lyric "Don't forget Winona," written to rhyme with "Flagstaff, Arizona."

21

Depending on the version of the tune that you hear, it's a great song and it probably went further in cementing the idea in people's minds of taking a trip in Route 66 than anything else that had been written about the famous highway. It became the essential booster for getting people out onto the open road during the late 1940s and into the 1950s.

By that time, the highway had become a genuine celebrity. Families could leave their homes in the East and Midwest and drive out to the Grand Canyon or the Painted Desert. They could go all of the way to the Pacific on a highway that passed through towns where Abraham Lincoln once lived, Jesse James robbed banks, and Will Rogers learned to twirl his famous rope. They could cross over Mark Twain's famous river, visit caves where outlaws hid from the law, and pass through small towns where real-life cowboys still punched cattle. They could stop and buy chunks of petrified wood in Arizona, or shot glasses and spoons from the Ozarks. There were snake pits, prairie dog villages, wild critters, and genuine Indians, sitting like wooden statues and selling rings and bracelets made from silver and turquoise. The lure of Route 66 grew even greater in the late 1950s when Walt Disney created Disneyland among the orange groves of Southern California.

But it was also in the 1950s that the bright lights of fame that had shone on Route 66 for so many years began to grow dim. In 1954, President Dwight D. Eisenhower established a President's Advisory Committee on a National Highway Program. The committee marked the start of the decline of the legendary highway. Eisenhower had been intrigued by the efficient German autobahn during his tenure as supreme commander of the Allied Forces during World War II and envisioned such a system in America.

The final report by the committee led to the enactment of the Federal Aid Highway Act in 1956, which spelled out the guidelines for a 42,500-mile national interstate highway system. Despite the fact that the old highway was being maintained, and had been turned into a four-lane road in many locations, it was clear that Route 66 could no longer handle the increasing volume of traffic.

The coming of the interstates was long and laborious. Construction costs tens of billions of dollars, yet the federal government not only persisted, it footed the bill. A piece of Route 66 was replaced here and there, bypasses were constructed around towns and cities, and little by little the old highway was turned into a service road as it was replaced.

By the start of the 1960s, travelers were no longer motoring from one location to the next. They were intent on seeing how quickly they could get to their destination. As interstates replaced the blue ribbons of highways, auto vacations and road trips began to change. With their smooth surfaces, gradual curves, and occasional exits, the new expressways were allowing a scenery-killing speed of 70 and 75 miles per hour.

In Illinois, Route 66 was swallowed by the new Interstate 55, a full-speed expressway where cars could cruise from Chicago to St. Louis in a matter of hours. At the kind of speed the interstate allowed, stopping to get a bite to eat or use the restroom was a major inconvenience. So, instead of forcing motorists to exit the interstate, states built "rest areas" that provided motorists with easy on and off access. Built in pairs, the rest areas were situated on each side of the expressway to meet the needs of travelers moving in both directions and were situated about 50 miles apart.

The new roads were in great demand, and thanks to the flow of money from the government, they were constantly in the works. At the time, most travelers embraced the new roads, although many were frustrated over construction delays and confusing road signs that often carried several names for a single route. It was impossible to ignore the fact, though, that change was coming. It was essential to embrace it, or be left behind by progress.

Amidst all of the changes, the appeal of taking a road trip on Route 66 was beginning to wane. Instead, people began finding it easier to see the sights of America from the comfort of their living room, without the hassle of traffic or the expense of buying a tank of gas, booking hotel rooms, and everything else that went along with a vacation.

But in October 1960, *Route 66* came to American televisions with the premiere of a television show that ran until 1964 on CBS. The show, about two young men traveling across America on Route 66 in their Corvette, captivated audiences from the start. It ran weekly and starred Martin Milner as Tod Stiles and, for two and a half seasons, George Maharis as Buz Murdock. Maharis was ill for much of the third season, during which time Tod was shown traveling on his own. Tod met Lincoln Case, played by Glenn Corbett, late in the third season, and traveled with him until the end of the fourth and final season. The series not only popularized the Corvette convertible used on the show (which was light blue, not red, as many viewers of black and white television believed), but the instrumental theme song (performed by Nelson Riddle), which became a major hit.

Route 66 embraced an American theme that so many loved in its idea of two guys on the road, but it was something different as well. It was a combination of episodic television drama, which had continuing characters and situations, and the anthology format (like *The Twilight Zone*), in which each week's show had a completely different cast and story. *Route 66* had just three continuing characters, no more than two of whom appeared in the same episode. Like Richard Kimble from *The Fugitive*, the characters traveled from place to place and got caught up in the lives of the people they met. Unlike Richard Kimble, nothing forced the guys to stay on the move, except for their own sense of adventure.

Little was known about the main characters. All we are told is that, after the death of his father, Tod Stiles inherited a new Corvette and decided to drive across America with his friend, Buz. Tod, portrayed by clean-cut Martin Milner, was sort of the moral anchor of the series. He was clean-cut and all-American, while Buz (George Maharis) was a looser, hipper member of the Beat Generation of the time. Later on, after being away from many episodes due to illness, Maharis left the show and Tod traveled alone. Later, he gained a new traveling companion named Lincoln Case (Glenn Corbett). Case was a darker character than Buz Murdock, an army veteran haunted by his past. He was quieter than Buz and sometimes had an explosive temper, but he nonetheless turned out to be a reliable friend as the duo continued their travels.

The series concluded in 1964 with an episode where Tod got married and Lincoln announced his intention to return home to his family in Texas after a long period of estrangement. This made the series one of the earlier prime-time television dramas to have a planned series finale resolving the fate of its main characters.

Even though it was called *Route 66,* the show actually had very little real connection with the highway. Most of the locations visited throughout the series were far afield from the territory covered by Route 66, which only wound through a total of eight states. The series, meanwhile, took place throughout the lower 48 American states, and two episodes were actually filmed and took place in Canada. Route 66, the actual highway, was briefly referred to in just three early episodes of the series and was shown only rarely. Even so, *Route 66* remains one of the very few series in television history to be filmed entirely on the road. This was done at a time when the United States was much less homogeneous than it is now. People, their accents, livelihoods, ethnic backgrounds, and attitudes varied widely from one location to the next. Scripted characters reflected a far less mobile, provincial society, in which people were more apt to spend their entire lives in one small part of the country. Whether or not the show really took place along Route 66, it still managed to offer a slice of American life like nothing that is seen on television today.

But no television show was enough to stop the interstates from coming – or to delay the inevitable. Originally, the national interstate plan was supposed to take 12 years to complete. It ended up taking twice that long. Finally the last stretch of U.S. Highway 66 was bypassed in 1984, near Williams, Arizona, when a final stretch of the Mother Road was replaced by a section of Interstate 40.

Bypassing Route 66 had actually taken five different interstates – Interstate 55 from Chicago to St. Louis; Interstate 44 from St. Louis to Oklahoma City; Interstate 40 from Oklahoma City to Barstow, California; Interstate 15 from Barstow to San

Bernardino; and Interstate 10 from San Bernardino to Santa Monica. The opening of the interstates made it possible to drive all the way from Chicago to the Pacific Ocean without stopping, someone commented. The government called this progress, but thankfully, not everyone agreed.

Even as the Route 66 road signs were being auctioned off and the road maps changed, history buffs and activists came forward and began trying to protect the legacy of the legendary road. They remain today and are a wide array of people from all walks of life who believe that the spirit of the Mother Road will never be forgotten. They are people (like me, and probably like you, if you're reading this book) who want to see the highway's history survive. We are the people who get a thrill when we hear about someone reading or watching the *Grapes of Wrath* for the first time, or listening to a cool version of the classic song, or actually getting off the mind-numbing interstate and driving a stretch of the lost highway that remains.

Route 66 lives on in the hearts and minds of thousands of people, and remnants of the road remain in every one of the eight states that Route 66 crosses. In many of those places, the old signs are returning, the name never really surrendered. There are still motor courts, filling stations, curio shops, and tourist attractions that thrive on the nostalgia that is still felt by those of us who refuse to give up on America's past.

Come along now, get behind the wheel, and let's recapture a little of the lost people, places, and ghosts that linger from the America of yesterday.

MOTORING THROUGH THE LAND OF LINCOLN

Route 66 begins in Chicago, America's "Windy City," which was named not for the speed of the air currents off Lake Michigan, but for the hot air expelled by local politicians when the city was trying to obtain the rights for the famed World's Columbian Exposition in 1893.

The start of Route 66 has moved a few times over the years. Originally, it began on Jackson Boulevard at Michigan Ave, but in 1933, it was moved east onto reclaimed land for that year's World's Fair at Jackson and Lake Shore Drive.

It's a fitting start for "America's Main Street," because it begins at a place that didn't even exist when Chicago was founded. This patch of land, along with Lake Shore Drive and everything else east of Michigan Avenue, was part of the lake until city developers needed a place to put all of the refuse from burned-out portions of the city after the Great Chicago Fire.

Chicago, considered an upstart of a city by easterners, was officially incorporated (in the city's first incident of voter fraud) in 1837. It began years earlier as a trading post and the ill-fated site of Fort Dearborn, which was wiped out and burned during the War of 1812. After the railroads reached Chicago in 1848, the city was on its way to becoming one of the largest in the nation. In 1871, though, disaster struck when the Great Chicago Fire reduced a large part of the city to ashes. Believe it or not (aside from the deaths that occurred, of course), the fire was the best thing that could've happened to the city.

Mrs. O'Leary's Cow

In 1871, Chicago was truly a boomtown. It had become one of the fastest growing cities in America and because of this, construction standards had been "loose," to say the least. Beyond the downtown area, the city was miles and miles of rickety wooden structures. Most of the working-class neighborhoods consisted of wooden cottages and tenements, all of which made for dangerous fuel in the event of a fire.

And fire was always a possibility. "The absence of rain for three weeks," reported the *Chicago Tribune* in the fall of 1871, "has left everything in so flammable a condition that a spark might set a fire that would sweep from end to end of the city."

According to the legend, the Great Chicago Fire was started by a cow belonging to an Irishwoman named Catherine O'Leary. She ran a neighborhood milk business from the barn behind her home. She carelessly left a kerosene lantern in the barn after her evening milking and a cow kicked it over and ignited the hay on the floor. Whether fact or fancy, the legend of Mrs. O'Leary's cow became an often-told tale in

Chicago. The truth was, the fire did start in the O'Leary barn, but whether or not the cow was culpable in the blaze remains in question.

Neighborhood gossip told a different story. On the night of October 8, the home of Patrick O'Leary was a lively place. O'Leary, his wife and five children were already in bed, but the two front rooms of the house were rented to Patrick McLaughlin, a fiddler, who, with his family and friends, was entertaining his wife's cousin, who had recently arrived from Ireland. The rooms were filled with music and drinking and at some point, a few of the young men who were present went out to get another half-gallon of beer --- or so Mrs. McLaughlin would later swear. But that's not what actually happened, it was said. At some point in the evening, some of the McLaughlin clan decided to prepare an oyster stew for their party and a couple of the young men were sent to get some milk from the cow that the O'Learys stabled in a barn at the rear of the house. A broken lamp found among the ashes of the stable a few days later gave rise to the legend that the cow had started the fire that destroyed Chicago.

No matter what the cause, the Great Chicago Fire did break out near the O'Leary barn at 137 De Koven Street on the city's West Side and by 10:00 that evening, the fire had spread from the O'Leary's backyard and across the West Side in two swaths that were so wide that all of the engines in town were clanging in the streets and the downtown courthouse bell pealed incessantly. The watchman on the City Hall tower had misjudged the blaze's location and called for a fire company that was located a mile and a half out of the way, causing a terrible delay. In addition, a strong, dry wind from the southwest was blowing. To make matters even worse, most of Chicago's fire companies had been exhausted by a fire on the West Side the day before and had celebrated the defeat of the blaze by getting drunk.

Within half an hour, all of Chicago was on the streets, running for the river. Most could not believe what they were seeing as a wall of flames, miles wide, and hundreds of feet high, devoured the West Side and was carried on the wind toward the very heart of the city. By 10:30 p.m., it was officially out of control and soon the mills and factories along the river were on fire. Buildings, even across the river, were hit by fiery missiles from the main blaze, and began to burn. Owners of downtown buildings began throwing water on roofs and walls as the air filled with sparks and cinders that contemporary accounts described as resembling red rain.

Even then, the crowds were sure that the flames would die out when they struck the blackened, four-block area that had been burned during the previous night's fire. But with the force of hundreds of burning homes and buildings behind it, the blaze passed over the burned-out path, attacked the grain elevators along the river, and fell upon the Union Station.

From the West Side, a mob poured into the downtown section, jamming the bridges and flooding the streets. It was believed that the river would stop the fire in its path, but when a blazing board that was carried on the wind settled on the roof of

The Great Chicago Fire in October 1871

a tenement building at Adams and Franklin -- one-third of a mile from any burning building – the fire had hungrily jumped the river. Fire engines, frantic to save the more valuable property of the business district, pushed back over the bridges from the West Side.

Among the first downtown buildings to be engulfed was the new Parmalee Omnibus & Stage Company at the southeast corner of Jackson and Franklin streets. A flying brand also struck the South Side Gas Works and soon this structure burst into flames, creating a new and larger center for the fire. At this point, even the grease- and oil-covered river caught fire and the surface of the water shimmered with heat and flames.

In moments, the fire also spread to the office buildings along LaSalle Street. Soon, the inferno became impossible to battle with more than a dozen different locations burning at once. The fire swept through Wells, Market, and Franklin streets, igniting more than 500 different buildings. One by one, these great structures fell. The *Tribune* building, long vaunted as "fireproof," was turned into a smoking ruin as was Marshall Field's grand department store, along with hundreds of other businesses.

Many of the great hotels, like the Palmer House and the Sherman, were reduced to blazing ash. The Grand Pacific Hotel, which had just been completed and was not yet open, crashed down in flames. Another new hotel, the Bigelow, with its art gallery, Turkish carpets, and carved wood furniture, was also consumed. The Tremont House burned for the fourth time in its history and the manager, John Drake, left the place in a hurry, carrying the contents of the hotel safe in a pillowcase. Unshaken, though, Drake passed by the Avenue Hotel on Congress Street and noting that it was untouched by fire, entered and approached the distracted owner with a startling offer to buy the place, right then and there with $1,000 from the Tremont's safe as a down payment. The deal was made and a hasty bill of sale was written, witnessed by fleeing guests. Drake then departed and went home with his pillowcase full of silver. He knew that he had an even chance of being a hotel owner the next morning. As it turned out, the Avenue Hotel survived, but Drake had to insist on his ownership rights with a pistol.

In the early morning hours of Monday, the fire reached the courthouse, which stood in a block surrounded by LaSalle, Clark, Randolph, and Washington streets. A burning timber landed on the building's wooden cupola and soon turned into a fire that blazed out of control. The building was ordered evacuated. The prisoners, who had begun to scream and shake the bars of their cells as smoke filled the air, were released. Most of them were allowed to simply go free, but the most dangerous of them were shackled and taken away under guard. Just after 2:00 a.m., the bell of the courthouse tolled for the last time before crashing through the remains of the building to the ground beneath it. The roaring sound made by the building's collapse was reportedly heard more than a mile away.

Around this same time, the State Street Bridge, leading to the North Side, also caught fire and the inferno began to devour the area on the north side of the river. Soon, stables, warehouses, and breweries were also burning. The lumber mills and wood storage yards on the riverbanks were eaten by the fire and many people who were dunking themselves in the water had to flee again to keep from being strangled by the black smoke. Some people threw chairs and sofas into the river and sat with just their heads and shoulders visible. Many of them stayed in the river for up to 14 hours.

Then, the fire swept into the luxurious residential district surrounding Cass, Huron, Ontario, Rush, and Dearborn streets, home to the mansions of some of Chicago's oldest and most prominent families. By daylight, these beautiful homes were nothing but ruins. The servants of the rich desperately buried the contents of the mansions in hidden places on the grounds. Oddly enough, at least a dozen pianos were later unearthed in gardens. Also discovered were family silver collections that, despite being buried, had melted into twisted masses.

The flames were not the only threat that the residents of the city had to worry about. In the early hours of the fire, looting and violence had broken out. Saloonkeepers, hoping that it might prevent their taverns from being destroyed, had foolishly rolled barrels of whiskey out into the streets. Soon, men and women from all classes were staggering in the streets, thoroughly intoxicated. The drunks and the looters did not comprehend the danger they were in and many were trampled in the streets. Plundered goods were also tossed aside and were lost in the fire, abandoned by the looters as the fire drew near.

During the early morning hours, panicked North Side residents ran ahead of the fire, toward the waters of the lake. Women's dresses caught on fire. Sick and injured people, carried on mattresses, stretchers, and chairs, were knocked to the ground and trampled. Some of the fugitives, insane with fear, plunged into blazing alleyways and were burned alive. Many of the elderly were crushed under the feet of the frantic crowds and a number of housewives, rushing into their homes for cherished possessions, perished in the inferno. The Chicago Historical Society was destroyed, losing city records of incalculable value and the original draft of the Emancipation Proclamation, which Abraham Lincoln had written during the Civil War.

On the lakefront, thousands took refuge away from any buildings that might burn, but they were still tortured by the heat and the storm of falling embers. Men buried their wives and children in the sand, with a hole for air, and splashed water over them. Many fled to stand chin-deep in the waters of Lake Michigan, breathing through handkerchiefs.

Throughout the day on Monday, the fire kept to its wind-driven task, finishing the business section and the North Side. The wind blew so hard that firefighters could get water no more than 10 feet past the nozzles of their hoses. Streams of water could not carry above two stories. Fire engines were destroyed in the flames and companies were separated from their officers. The fire department, like the city of Chicago, was destroyed.

Thankfully, the fire began to die on the morning of October 10, when steady and soaking rains began to fall.

The Great Fire, as it was called from then on, was to be the most disastrous event in America until the San Francisco earthquake and fire of 1906. The people of the city were devastated, as was the city itself. Over 300 people were dead and the fate of many more was never reported or

MRS. O'LEARY'S COMET?

Could a comet from space have started the Great Chicago Fire? Aside from the O'Learys' unfortunate cow, there have been other causes suggested for the fire, including one that was first brought up in 1882. The Chicago Fire was not the worst conflagration to sweep through the Midwest; it was not even the worst one to start on October 8, 1871!

On that hot and windy autumn night, three other major fires occurred along the shores of Lake Michigan. About 400 miles to the north, a forest fire consumed the town of Peshtigo, Wisconsin, along with a dozen other villages, killing 1,200 to 2,500 people and charring approximately 1.5 million acres. The Peshtigo Fire remains the deadliest in American history, but the remoteness of the region meant it was little noticed at the time. Across the lake to the east, the town of Holland, Michigan, and other nearby areas burned to the ground. Some 100 miles to the north of Holland, the lumbering community of Manistee, also went up in flames.

Farther east, along the shore of Lake Huron, another tremendous fire swept through Port Huron, and much of Michigan's "thumb."

That four large fires occurred all on the same day, all on the shores of Lake Michigan, suggests a common root cause and some believe that cause was Biela's Comet, which broke up and rained down over the Midwest at that time. It has been theorized that the eyewitness accounts of spontaneous ignitions, a lack of smoke from all of the fires, and flames falling from the sky could have been the result of pieces of the comet falling to earth.

Could one of these sparks have landed on the O'Leary barn, thereby letting the cow off the hook for Chicago's greatest fire?

their bodies were never found. Another 100,000 were without homes or shelter. The fire had cut a swath through the city that was four miles long and about two-thirds of a mile wide. Over $200 million in property had been destroyed. Records, deeds, archives, libraries, and priceless artwork were lost, although a little of it had survived in public and private vaults. In the destruction of the Federal Building, which, among other things, housed the post office, more than $100,000 in currency was burned.

Chicago had become a blasted and charred wasteland.

As terrible as the disaster was, Chicago was not dead but merely shaken and stunned. Within days of the fire, rebuilding began on a grand scale. The vigor of the city's rebirth amazed the rest of the nation and within three years, it once again dominated the western United States. It soared from the ashes like the fabled phoenix and became the home of the nation's first skyscraper in 1885. The city then passed the one million mark in population five years later. The Great Chicago Fire marked the beginning of a new metropolis, much greater than it could have ever become if the horrific fire had never happened.

And it created a whole new section of the city, where Route 66 would someday begin. With gigantic piles of debris that had to be cleared away before new construction could begin, workers moved the burned wood, charred brick, and scorched waste beyond the lakefront beaches and created a new area of land that would become the lakefront that we know today. Michigan Avenue, which was once the edge of Lake Michigan, became one of the city's most famous streets, located west of where the end of the lake had once been.

Motoring Chicago

The city quickly bounced back from the fire and introduced the world to skyscrapers. In 1891, it became home to the elevated railroad system that continues to serve the city today.

Two years later, in 1893, Chicago hosted the World's Columbian Exposition, which brought an entire country to the "White City," as the lakeside fairgrounds were dubbed. Many firsts were introduced to America during the fair, including Cracker Jacks, Cream of Wheat, Juicy Fruit gum, Shredded Wheat, Pabst Blue Ribbon beer, and more. It was here that the concept of a carnival was introduced and the hamburger was born – two pieces of Americana that would find their respective places along Route 66.

By the 1920s, Chicago had become a dangerous place. Feuding gangs battled over liquor sales during the years of Prohibition, earning the city a designation as the most dangerous place in America. The "Beer Wars" raged throughout the decade, leading to the death of many rivals of Al Capone, the man who became known as Chicago's most famous gangster. The violence reached its peak on February 14, 1929, when seven members of George "Bugs" Moran's gang were gunned down in the "St. Valentine's Day Massacre." The city turned on Capone and within two years he was in prison, serving time for tax evasion instead of the bootlegging and murder. Capone would have a lasting influence on Chicago, as well as a number of locations along Illinois' stretch of Route 66.

Chicago offers only a handful of relics from Route 66, but those that remain are worthy of the legend of the road. At 17 West Adams Street is the **Berghoff Restaurant**, which was opened in 1898 by Herman Joseph Berghoff, a German immigrant who started brewing Berghoff's Beer in Fort Wayne, Indiana, in 1887. Looking to expand, he came to Chicago and operated a beer concession at the 1893 World's Fair. The popularity of his brew inspired him to open a café to showcase his beer, which sold for a nickel. Sandwiches were offered for free. The bar remained open during Prohibition by selling legal near-beer, which contained less than 0.5% alcohol, as well as a new line of Bergo sodas, and expanded into a full-service German restaurant. After Prohibition was repealed in 1933, the Berghoff was issued Chicago's Liquor License No. 1, a designation that has been honored by the city every year since.

Herman Berghoff died unexpectedly on December 31, 1934. The restaurant was then run by two of his seven children, Lewis and Clement, who had both joined the business prior to Herman's death. Over the next five years, the Berghoff grew into three restaurants under one roof: the original bar, a large two-room restaurant, and a casual downstairs café, called the Annex, which was opened in 1939.

Lewis and Clement remained active in the restaurant until about 1960. Various family members succeeded them, but bickering and clashes in management style went on for years, leading the Berghoff to close in 2006. But it didn't stay closed for long. A few months later, Carlyn Berghoff, Herman's great-granddaughter, re-opened the basement café and then the original bar. The main restaurant was turned into a banquet room. But the crowning achievement was the return of the Berghoff beers, which had been lost after they were sold to the Falstaff brewery back in 1954.

Nearby is Chicago's **Union Station**, which has been preserved and still serves passengers today. It was once home to one of the many Harvey House Restaurants, which served rail travelers and Route 66 motorists for years.

The Harvey House chain of restaurants, hotels, and other hospitality businesses traced its origins back to 1875 when two railroad eating houses opened in Wallace, Kansas and Hug, Colorado, along the Kanas Pacific Railway. The cafes were opened by Fred Harvey, who was then a freight agent for the Chicago, Burlington & Quincy Railroad. The café operation only lasted a year, but Harvey had been convinced that he could make a lot of money by providing high-quality food and service at railroad restaurants. His longtime employer declined his offer to establish a system-wide diner operation at all railroad meal stops, but the Atchison, Topeka & Santa Fe Railway decided to take a chance and allowed Harvey to open several eateries on a trial basis. The first one opened in Florence, Kansas, in 1878 and others soon followed.

Fred Harvey is credited with creating the first restaurant chain in American history and the Harvey Houses were leading promoters of tourism for the American Southwest in the late nineteenth century. The company and its employees, including the famous waitresses who came to be known as "Harvey Girls," successfully brought fine dining to what was still considered the "Wild West."

Despite the decline in passenger train service in the twentieth century and the advent of the automobile, the company survived and prospered, by marketing its services to the motoring public. After highways like Route 66 faded into history, the company adjusted to the trends, operating the first Illinois Tollway "oasis" stops in the late 1950s. The Fred Harvey Company was eventually bought out in 1968 and closed a unique chapter in roadside history.

Another icon that remains today is **Lou Mitchell's Restaurant** at 565 West Jackson

Boulevard. Founded in 1923, Lou Mitchell's is a frequent starting point for those who plan to travel the length of Route 66. The diner originally gained fame by handing out fresh donut holes to

The Western Electric Company's Hawthorne Works

people in line and for handing out free boxes of Milk Duds instead of after-dinner mints.

After crossing Ashland Avenue, Route 66 turns southwest onto Ogden Avenue and heads toward Cicero. As the road travels along, on the right and just past Keeler Avenue, is the site of the old **Hawthorne Works**, a large factory complex of the **Western Electric Company** that opened in 1905. The factory was named for the town of Hawthorne, Illinois, which later was incorporated as Cicero. The factory consisted of several buildings and contained a private railroad to move shipments through the plant to the nearby Burlington Northern Railroad freight depot. The plant employed more than 45,000 workers and, at one time, produced virtually all of the telephones in the United States.

But that's not how Western Electric earned its notoriety. The company became famous for a company picnic that took place in 1915 – or which would have taken place if disaster hadn't struck.

The Eastland Disaster

The afternoon of July 24, 1915, was a special day for thousands of Chicagoans. It was the afternoon that had been reserved for the annual summer picnic for employees of the Western Electric Company. Officials at the company had encouraged the workers to bring along as many friends and relatives as possible to the event, which was held across the lake at Michigan City, Indiana. Even after this open invitation, managers were surprised to find that more than 7,000 people showed up to be ferried across Lake Michigan on the three excursion boats that had been chartered for the day. The steamers were docked on the Chicago River, between Clark and LaSalle streets, and included *Theodore Roosevelt, Petoskey* and *Eastland.*

Eastland was a rusting Lake Michigan steamer that was owned by the St. Joseph-Chicago Steamship Company. It was supposed to hold a capacity crowd of 2,500 people, but it is believed that on the morning of July 24, more than 3,200 climbed on board. In addition to being overcrowded, the vessel had a reputation for being unstable. Years before, it was realized that design flaws in the ship made it top-heavy. In July 1903, a case of overcrowding had caused *Eastland* to tip and water to flow up one of its gangplanks. The situation was quickly rectified, but it was only the first of many such incidents. To make matters worse, the new federal Seaman's Act had been passed in 1915 because of the *RMS Titanic* disaster. This required the retrofitting of a complete set of lifeboats on *Eastland*, as well as on other passenger vessels. *Eastland* was so top-heavy that it already had special restrictions about how many passengers it could carry. The additional weight of the mandated lifeboats made the ship more unstable than it already was.

The huge crowd, the lifeboats, and the negligence of the crew created a recipe for disaster.

On the unseasonably cool morning of July 24, *Eastland* was moored on the south side of the Chicago River in downtown Chicago. After she was loaded with passengers, the aging vessel would travel out into Lake Michigan, heading for the Indiana shoreline. Excited, happy, and nervous passengers lined the riverside docks, eager to get on board. The morning was damp, but better weather was promised for the picnic in the afternoon.

After the passengers were loaded on board, the dock lines were loosed and the ship prepared to depart. The massive crowd, dressed in their best summer clothes, jammed onto the decks, calling out and waving handkerchiefs to those who were still on shore. Many of the passengers went below decks, hoping to warm up on this cool, cloudy morning. As the steamer eased away from the dock, it started to tilt to the port side. Unknown to the passengers, the crew had emptied the ballast compartments of the ship, which were designed to provide stability, so that more passengers could be loaded on board. They didn't count on a sudden shift in weight that would cause the vessel to lean even farther toward the port side. That sudden shift was caused by a passing fireboat, which fired off its water cannons to the delight of the crowd. The passengers hurried over to the port side for a closer look and moments later, *Eastland* simply rolled over. It came to rest on the river bottom, which was only 18 feet below the surface.

The passengers who had been on the deck were thrown in the river, thrashing about in a moving mass of bodies. Crews on the other steamers, and on passing

The *Eastland* capsized, sending hundreds of passengers to their deaths.

vessels, threw life preservers into the water, while those on shore began tossing lines, boxes, and anything that would float to the panicked and drowning passengers. The overturned ship created a current that pulled many of the floundering swimmers to their doom, while many of the women's long dresses were snagged on the ship, tugging them down to the bottom.

The unluckiest passengers were those who had been inside the ship when it turned over. These ill-fated victims were thrown to one side of the vessel when it capsized and many were crushed by the heavy furniture below decks, which included tables, bookcases, and even a piano. As the river water rushed inside, those who were not immediately killed were drowned a few moments later. A few of them managed to escape to the upturned side of the ship, but most of them didn't. Their bodies were later found trapped in a tangled heap on the lowest side of *Eastland*.

Firefighters, rescue workers, and volunteers soon began to arrive and started cutting holes in the ship's hull that was above the water line. A few who had scrambled to safety inside the ship emerged from the holes, but for most of them, it was simply too late. Those on shore eagerly watched for more survivors, but no one emerged from the wet darkness. The men who had come to rescue the trapped and the injured had to resign themselves to pulling waterlogged corpses from the river instead. The bodies were wrapped in sheets and placed on the nearby *Roosevelt*, or lined up along the docks. The large stores downtown, like Marshall Field's, sent wagons to carry the dead to the hospitals, funeral homes, and the makeshift morgues.

Corpses were fished out of the river using large grappling hooks, but those who had been trapped beneath the ship had to be pulled out by police divers and volunteers. According to newspaper accounts, one of these divers, who had been bringing up bodies from the bottom of the river for hours, went insane. He had to be subdued by friends and police officers. City workers dragged the river where *Eastland* had capsized, using large nets to prevent the bodies from being pulled out into the lake. By the time it was all over, 841 passengers and four crewmembers perished in the disaster. Many of them were women and children and 22 families – husbands, wives, children, even grandparents, cousins, aunts, and uncles -- were completely wiped out.

The hundreds of bodies that were recovered on the morning of the disaster were taken to the nearby Reid–Murdoch Building and to local funeral homes and mortuaries. The only public building that was large enough to be used as a morgue was the Second Regiment National Guard Armory, which was located on Carpenter

The bodies of the dead were laid out in long rows for identification.

Street, between Randolph Street and Washington Boulevard. The dead were laid out on the floor of the armory in rows of 85 and assigned identifying numbers. Any personal possessions that were found with the corpses were placed in envelopes bearing the same number as the body.

Chicagoans with loved ones who had perished in the disaster filed through the rows of bodies, searching for familiar faces, but in the mentioned 22 cases, there was no one left to identify them. The names of these unidentified victims were learned through the efforts of neighbors, who came searching for their friends. The weeping, crying, and moaning of the bereaved echoed off the walls of the armory for days. The American Red Cross treated 30 women for hysteria and exhaustion in the days following the disaster.

The final body was identified on Friday, July 30. A 7-year-old boy named Willie Novotny of Cicero, #396, was the last. His parents and older sister had also died on *Eastland* and his identification came from extended family members, who arrived nearly a week after the disaster took place. After Willie's name was learned, a chapter was closed on one of Chicago's most horrific events.

Officially, the mystery of what happened to *Eastland* that day was never solved. No clear accounting was ever made to explain the capsizing of the vessel. Several hundred lawsuits were filed, but almost all of them were dismissed by the Circuit Court of Appeals, which held the owners of the steamer blameless in the disaster. After the ship was raised from the river, it was sold at auction. The title was later transferred to the government and the vessel was pressed into duty as the gunboat *U.S.S. Wilmette.* The ship never saw action but was used as a training ship during World War II. After the war, it was decommissioned and put up for sale in 1945. Finding no takers, it was scrapped in 1947.

Eastland was gone, but her story has continued to linger for years.

On the morning of the *Eastland* disaster, many of the bodies of the victims were taken to the Second Regiment National Guard Armory. As the years passed, there was no longer a need for a National Guard armory to be located so close to downtown Chicago. It was closed down by the military and the building was sold off. It went through several incarnations over the decades, including uses as a stable and a bowling alley, before being purchased by Harpo Studios, the production company owned by Oprah Winfrey.

Unfortunately, though, the success of the Winfrey's talk show, which was filmed in the former armory, did nothing to put to rest the spirits that lingered from the *Eastland* disaster. A number of staff members, security guards, and maintenance workers claimed that the ghosts of the disaster victims who perished in 1915 restlessly wandered the building. Many employees had encounters with things that could not easily be explained away, including the sighting of a woman in a long, gray dress who walked the corridors and then mysteriously vanished into the wall. There were many occasions when this woman was spotted, but each time she was approached, she always disappeared. Some surmised that she was the spirit of a mourner who came looking for her family and left a bit of herself behind at the spot where she felt her greatest pain.

The woman in gray may not have been alone in her spectral travels throughout the old armory. Staff members also claimed to hear whispers, the sounds of people sobbing, moaning noises, and phantom footsteps. The footsteps, which sounded as though they belonged to a group of several people, were usually heard on a staircase in the lobby. Doors that were located nearby often opened and closed by themselves. Those who experienced these strange events came to believe that the tragedy of yesterday was still replaying itself on the former armory in its later incarnation.

The site of what became the Second Regiment Armory morgue was not the only location in Chicago that resonated with chilling stories of *Eastland* disaster ghosts.

There were reports of the ship itself being haunted that date back to the time just after the disaster and prior to its sale to the Navy. During that period, it was docked near the Halsted Street Bridge and regarded with superstition by passers-by. One lonely caretaker, Captain M.L. Edwards, lived aboard it and said he was awakened by moaning noises nightly, though he attributed them simply to the sound of the ship falling apart. Amused as he claimed to be to see people hurry across the bridge, terrified when they saw a light in his cabin, he was very glad to move off the ship after its sale to the Navy in December 1915.

The site on the river where the disaster occurred has its strange stories to this day. For many years, people who have passed on the Clark Street Bridge have claimed to hear moaning and crying sounds coming from the river, along with bloodcurdling screams, and pleas for help. In addition, some witnesses state that the cries are accompanied by the sounds of someone splashing in the river, and even the apparitions of people helplessly flailing about in the water.

During several incidents, witnesses have called for help from emergency services, believing that someone was actually drowning in the river. At least one man jumped into the water to try and save what he thought was a person who was unable to swim. When he returned to the surface, he discovered that he was in the river alone. He had no explanation for what he had seen, other than to admit that it might have been a ghost.

In the same way that the former armory seems to have replayed an eerie recording of past events, the Chicago River also seems to be haunted. It appears that the horror of the *Eastland* disaster has left a memory behind at this spot and it continues to repeat itself over and over again – ensuring that the luckless victims from the *Eastland* will never truly be forgotten.

Going Out to Cicero

Most of the old highway has been lost in this area, but by driving along Ogden Avenue, the traveler will end up in Cicero. This is the former home of gangster Al Capone, who left Chicago after a reform mayor was briefly voted into office. Capone and his men virtually took over the small working-class town, installing speakeasies, bordellos, and gambling parlors in scores of locations throughout the community. Capone himself set up his headquarters at the Hawthorne Hotel, which was once devastated by tommy-gun fire when rival gangsters tried to assassinate him. The mob released its hold on Cicero after Capone went to prison, but it took decades to rid itself of a reputation for crime and corrupt city officials.

Along Ogden Avenue is the **Cindy Lyn Motel**, which still operates today. Opened in 1960, this classic motor lodge was built along Route 66 to attract travelers on their way to Chicago. It was marketed as the "last motel before the city." When the motel opened, rooms were $6.18 a night, and if a cab dropped off a customer, the cab driver would receive a free Cindy Lyn Motel lighter.

Just down the street is **Henry's Drive In**, with a 1950s-era neon sign that is right at home on Route 66. The classic Chicagoland hot dog stand was started by the Henry family in the 1950s. Their first location was not a location at all, but a hot dog wagon on Austin Avenue, just north of Ogden. With Route 66 still in full swing, Henry opened up the place that still stands today. Luckily for highway buffs, Henry's neon sign is also alive and well. It shows a hot dog with toppings and fries on top (how they're served at Henry's) and a neon arrow pointing toward it and proclaiming the slogan, "It's a Meal in Itself!"

The Bunyon's Hot Dog Man

Nearby was once the site of Route 66 icon, **Bunyon's Drive In**. The hot dog stand was opened in the 1940s by Hamlet A. Stephens, a former self-employed mason and builder. In the 1960s, he decided to augment his fast food business with an eye-catching fiberglass giant, which he customized with a giant hot dog.

During the heyday of both automobile vacations and Route 66, motorists passed by hundreds of signs, murals, and other forms of roadside advertising, each intended to grab its share of attention. Among the most famous were

41

the fiberglass giants – like the Bunyon's Hot Dog Man – that were created in the 1960s by International Fiberglass of Venice, California. Roughly 150 of these giants were produced before the molds were broken and the concept discontinued. There are dozens of them along the length of Route 66, including in Illinois.

Originally, Hamlet Stephens placed his fiberglass giant on the top of the building, but he soon took him down so that kids could touch him and sit on his feet. Guests could actually walk through his legs to get into the restaurant. He became a beloved figure on the highway and very effective advertising for the tasty road food that the drive-in offered. And while he was slightly lumberjack in appearance (many roadside giants had beards and carried an ax to look like the "Paul Bunyan" of legend), Hamlet had him made with a hot dog instead. He also misspelled "Bunyon's" on purpose, he claimed, for trademark differentiation.

In October 2002, Bunyon's Drive In became a part of Route 66's lost history. Hamlet turned 80 that year and finally had to call it quits. He passed away in 2012. The Hot Dog Man was put up for sale, and while several towns vied for the statue, he was eventually moved to Atlanta, Illinois, and put on display as a symbol of Route 66.

Fairyland Park

As travelers continued south and west out of Chicago, they found two separate alignments for Route 66 at Harlem Avenue. The pre-1928 alignment continued down Ogden Avenue, crossed the Des Plaines River, and eventually re-connected at Joliet Road and Lawndale Avenue. By taking the post-1928 alignment, though, they entered the town of Lyons, where they discovered the first sizable tourist attraction on Route 66: **Fairyland Park**. It seems fitting that an amusement park anchored the east end of the highway, just as the Santa Monica Pier anchored the west. Both amusement parks – east and west -- were small and featured the classic rides like carousels, Ferris wheels, chutes and ladders, tilt-a-whirls, and funhouse mirrors. Both parks were located mercifully outside of swelling cities and came at a time before corporate giants had laid claim to nearby entertainment dollars. Neither park claimed to be anything other than a collection of rifle ranges and kiddie rides, but they snagged their customers with little fanfare and sent them on their way with smiles on their faces.

Fairyland Park, located on the west side of Harlem Avenue between 39th and 40th Streets, was not the first to offer amusement at that site. The grounds themselves once served as a gypsy camp of Romany people. Weekends saw Lyons locals visiting the camp to find their fortunes in tea leaves, palms, and crystal balls. After midnight, they could dance to music that was played around roaring campfires. On Sunday afternoon, one of the Romany men appeared at nearby Cermak Park with a muzzled black bear. He'd strap roller skates on the bear and pass the hat as the bear skated in circles near the park's Ogden Avenue entrance.

The first real amusement opened nearby in the late 1920s, stretching along Lawndale Avenue and Route 66, between Lyons and McCook. It was called the "Whoopee" Coaster and it was a one-of-a-kind carnival ride made up of planks and modest hills that wound around an otherwise empty field. The Whoopee Coaster offered a catch, though: riders rode it in their own automobiles! No one really knew who owned it, but there was an old man who took admission and let people onto the property. He allowed entrance to one automobile at a time and they'd motor along the wooden road, up and down the hills, to the end of the ride.

By 1938, the Whoopee Coaster had seen its last rider, likely done in by the weight of newer, heavier cars. The gypsies had left Lyons, too, and so local residents Richard and Helen Miller started raising the steel skeleton of Fairyland Park on the old camp property.

For many years, Richard's brother, Charles, had operated Miller Amusements in La Grange, Illinois. The company managed traveling carnivals and provided entertainment at special events all over downstate Illinois. Fairyland may have been the family's first stationary endeavor, but the attractions that filled the park were the tried and true rides that could be found at county fairs all over the state. Opening day features included miniature gas autos, outdoor bowling, live Shetland pony rides, and a Ferris wheel.

Fairyland Park survived its first decade, and even thrived during World War II. The five-acre park was the perfect fit for post-war Chicagoans, who had started to leave behind the big city parks in favor of smaller, suburban amusement centers. It was truly a family business, as relatives and friends kept the rides and concession stands operating. In 1955, Richard and Helen's son, Allen, and his wife, Georgia, took over the park and they began making improvements. Soon, many of the attractions were enclosed in a large, heated and air-conditioned building so that it could operate in bad weather. The park operated from Palm Sunday to Halloween each season and the prices ranged between 8 and 12 rides for a dollar.

Al Miller found an antique fire engine for sale in Tennessee and brought the truck to Fairyland, where it became a popular attraction. Kids climbed aboard the engine for slow rides through the park, the siren whooping all the way. When the engine was not entertaining the kids at the park, it was ringing its way through small town parades and picnics – with advertising space on the rear for whoever wanted to sponsor its appearance.

Advertising for Fairyland was mostly word of mouth, as well as by the sight of the place as travelers passed by on Route 66. On occasion, courtesy passes appeared on local lunch counters, but they could never afford advertisements in the Chicago newspapers. In spite of this, Fairyland outlasted all of Chicago's larger and more popular parks. Riverview Amusement Park closed in 1967 and the South Side's White City (where Fairyland had purchased its carousel) had shut down in the late 1930s. Fairyland remained in business, even boxed in by motels and drugstores, until 1977.

Today, there is no trace that Fairyland ever existed. The site has been erased by department stores and auto dealerships, but memories of the place remain – as do a few vestiges in other locations. The old carousel was sold to the Barn of Barrington Restaurant in Barrington, Illinois, and was disassembled into the Carousel Bar and Café. Patrons can still have a seat on the wooden backs of the trusty steeds that once circled Fairyland and dream of the old days and the simpler times that used to be.

The Wishing Well Motel

Continuing south along the highway, motorists reached the town of La Grange, which was home to the historic **Wishing Well Motel**. The motor court, which was built by John Blackburn in 1941, operated until the late 2000s, when it was razed to make room for development. It started out with 10 cabins, an office, and a small house out back  that was the owner's residence. In 1958, Blackburn sold the motel to Emil and Zora Vidas, and they later connected the cabins to increase capacity and turned the small house into guest quarters.

Emil Vidas passed away in 1985 and Zora became the sole manager and caretaker. During its years of operation, the Wishing Well treated its guests to a quiet, country-like atmosphere within shouting distance of the city. And yes, there is a stone wishing well located on the property.

During its heyday, the motel was often a home away from home to celebrities like Guy Lombardo, musicians from the Glen Miller Orchestra, the rock band Chicago, and many of the big band musicians who were booked at the nearby Willowbrook Ballroom, which is linked to the famous ghost story of "Resurrection Mary" – a true spirit of the road. Even though the ballroom is slightly off Route 66, it's still a story worthy of mention because, while there are scores of other roadside spirits and vanishing hitchhikers across America, Mary is the most famous highway ghost of all.

Resurrection Mary

The legend of "Resurrection Mary" was born on August 10, 1976.

Around 10:30 p.m., a driver was passing by the front gates of Resurrection Cemetery in Justice, Illinois. As he traveled along Archer Avenue, he happened to glance over and saw a girl standing on the other side of the gates. He said that when he saw her, she was wearing a light-colored dress and was grasping the iron bars of the gate. The driver was considerate enough to stop down the street at the Justice police station and alert them to the fact that someone had been accidentally locked in the cemetery at closing time. A patrolman named Pat Homa responded to the call, but when he arrived at the cemetery gates, he couldn't find anyone there. He called out with his loudspeaker and looked for her with his spotlight, but there was no one to be seen. He finally got out of his patrol car and walked up to the gates for one last look. As far as he could tell, the cemetery was dark and deserted and there was no sign of any girl.

But his inspection of the gates, where the girl had been seen standing, did reveal something unusual. What he saw there chilled him to the bone. He found that two of the bronze bars in the gate had been blackened, burned and --- well, pulverized. It looked as though someone had taken two of the green-colored bars in his or her hands and had somehow squashed and twisted them. Within the marks was what looked to be skin texture and handprints that had been seared into the metal with incredible heat. The temperature, which must have been intense, blackened and burned the bars at just about the spot where a small woman's hands would have been.

The police officer didn't keep the story to himself. In fact, the story of the handprints made the newspapers and curiosity-seekers came from all over the area to see them. In an effort to discourage the crowds, cemetery officials attempted to remove the marks with a blowtorch, making them look even worse. Finally, they cut the bars out of the gate and installed a wire fence until the two bars could be straightened or replaced.

And while the furor over the mysterious handprints eventually died down, the cemetery always emphatically denied the supernatural version of what had happened to the bars. In fact, in 1992, they offered an alternate explanation. Officials claimed

The bars at Resurrection Cemetery with the mysterious handprints burned into the metal

that a truck backed into the gates while doing sewer work at the cemetery and that grounds workers tried to fix the bars by heating them with a blowtorch and bending them. The imprint in the metal, they said, was from a workman trying to push them together again. While this explanation was quite convenient, it did not explain why the marks of small fingers were clearly visible in the metal or why the bronze never reverted back to its green, oxidized state.

As mentioned, the bars were removed to discourage onlookers, but taking them out actually had the opposite effect. Soon, people began asking what the cemetery had to hide. The events allegedly embarrassed local officials, so they demanded that the bars be put back into place. Once they were returned to the gate, they were straightened and left alone so that the blackened area would oxidize to match the other bars. Unfortunately, though, the scorched areas continued to defy nature and the twisted spots where the handprints had been impressed remained obvious until the late 1990s, when the bars were finally removed permanently. At great expense, Resurrection Cemetery replaced the entire front gates and the notorious bars vanished for good.

But by then, it was too late – a legend was on its way to being born.

The incident in 1976 may not have been the first encounter with what the newspapers would soon call "Resurrection Mary," but it would become the first widely reported one. Soon after, the number of "Mary sightings" began to increase. People from many different walks of life, from cab drivers to clergy claimed they picked her up and gave her rides. They encountered her in local nightspots and saw her vanish from the passenger seats of their automobiles. The beautiful blond came and went like a mysterious shadow, sometimes asking for a ride home and then vanishing from the car in front of Resurrection Cemetery.

Other types of accounts began to surface around this same time, and now, Mary was being reported running out into the middle of Archer Avenue in front of the cemetery, where she was struck by passing cars. These reports, although unknown to most of those who submitted them, hearkened back to the middle 1930s -- a fact that would later become apparent.

In these new accounts, though, drivers began to report a young woman with brown hair, wearing a light-colored dress, who ran out in the front of their automobiles. Sometimes, the girl would vanish just before colliding with the car and, at other times, they would feel the impact and see her crumple and fall to the road as if seriously injured. When the motorist stopped and went to help the girl, she would either disappear before their eyes or no sign of her body would be found.

According to the legend, Mary's story began at the Oh Henry Ballroom (later to be re-named the Willowbrook Ballroom), a rambling, Tudor-style building at 8900 Archer Avenue that was a popular place for swing and big-band dancing during the middle 1930s. In those days, the ballroom was located on a secluded stretch of Archer Avenue in unincorporated Willow Springs, a town with a "wide open" reputation for booze, gambling, and prostitution. Young people from all over Chicago's southwest side came to the Oh Henry Ballroom for music and dancing, and owner John Verderbar was known for booking the hottest bands in the area and the biggest acts that traveled around the country.

The story goes that Mary came to the Oh Henry one night with a boyfriend and they spent the evening dancing and drinking. At some point, they got into an argument and Mary stormed out of the place. Even though it was a cold winter's night, she decided that she would rather face a cold walk home than spend another minute with her obnoxious boyfriend. She left the ballroom and started walking up Archer Avenue. She had not gotten very far when she was struck and killed by a passing automobile. The driver fled the scene and Mary was left there to die.

Her grieving parents buried her in Resurrection Cemetery, wearing her favorite party dress and her dancing shoes. Since that time, her spirit has been seen along Archer Avenue, perhaps trying to return to her grave after one last night among the living. Motorists started picking up a young woman on Archer Avenue, who offered them vague directions to take her home, who would then vanish from the automobile at the gates to Resurrection Cemetery.

Or so the story went.

But oddly, many of the people who claimed to pick up "Mary" for a moonlight drive were picking her up within a few blocks of the ballroom. Was this merely a coincidence? Probably not, since strange occurrences connected to Mary had taken place at the Willowbrook Ballroom for many years.

The site of the ballroom in Willow Springs started as a beer hall that was operated by the Verderbar family in 1920. In 1929, the original structure burned down and was replaced by an elaborate ballroom. They called it the Oh Henry, but the name was later changed to the Willowbrook. Starting in the 1930s, the ballroom gained a reputation as one of the best dance clubs in Illinois and attracted customers from all over the area. The ballroom developed a strong following, and today, it is one of the last of the old-time ballrooms in Chicago.

Since the 1930s, Mary has been encountered numerous times on the dance floor by customers and employees alike. Commonly, reports tell of an attractive young woman in a white party dress who is seen from the opposite side of the ballroom. Occasionally, she is dancing, and at other times, she is just standing at the edge of the floor, watching people with a slight smile on her face. At times, she vanishes without warning, and on other occasions, she disappears whenever someone tries to approach her.

But in the early 1980s, few were going to the Willowbrook Ballroom to seek out Mary – that was still to come. There were still a flurry of sightings that had yet to occur. This time period proved to be one of the last truly prolific periods for Mary encounters. Mary was seen on the highway by dozens of people, from lawyers to police officers, housewives, and even a deacon from the nearby Greek Orthodox Church. Many of the witnesses contacted the Justice Police Department about their sightings. Squad cars were dispatched, and although the police could not explain the mass sightings of a young woman who was not present when they arrived, they did find the witnesses themselves. Many of them flagged down the officers to tell them what they had just seen.

The flurry of sightings went on for several years but by the middle 1980s, they began to fade. The stories were suddenly less frequent than they had once been and Mary was no longer being seen in the bars and dance halls along Archer Avenue. She no longer danced by the side of the road or ran out in front of passing cars. Yes, there were still encounters with a mysterious figure into the 1990s, and even today, but authentic encounters with the spirit are now few and far between.

Strangely, this is not the first time that Mary has disappeared from our consciousness. It happened before in the 1940s and she did not return again until the 1970s.

Based on the research that I've done over the years, I believe the first reports of Resurrection Mary came from the late spring of 1934. It was at this time that motorists on Archer Avenue, passing in front of Resurrection Cemetery, began telling of a young woman who would appear on the roadway, as if trying to hitch a ride. On some occasions, she became frantic as cars passed her by. Motorists told of a woman

The gates of Resurrection Cemetery on Archer Avenue

running toward them across the road, trying to climb onto the running boards of their automobiles, and sometimes, even trying to climb into the open back windows. They all described her in the same way, wearing a light-colored dress and having curly, brown hair that reached to her shoulders.

What made matters worse is that many of the people in these automobiles, who were residents of Chicago's Southwest side, actually recognized this young woman. Her name was Mary Bregovy and some of these motorists were her friends. They laughed with her, drank with her, and often danced with her at their favorite spot, the Oh Henry Ballroom. Of course, that had been in the past, because when they began seeing Mary trying to flag them down on Archer Avenue she had been dead for several weeks.

Of course, Mary Bregovy is not the only young woman who has been named as the identity of "Resurrection Mary" over the years. Even though most of the "Mary encounters" that have been collected were believable, they were also confusing and often contradictory. In one case, Mary would be a beautiful blond, and in another, she would be a pretty, curly-haired brunette. Assuming that Mary was not a client at some otherworldly beauty salon, what was going on here? Could some of these people be mistaken? Was it really Mary they were encountering or some other ghost entirely?

The more that I researched the history of the case, the more convinced I became that these motorists and witnesses really were encountering Resurrection Mary. The problem was that "Resurrection Mary" was actually more than one ghost. I have come to believe that the legend of Resurrection Mary has been created from two very different young women.

Over the years, there have been many who have searched for the earthly counterpart of Resurrection Mary and a number of candidates have emerged. Some are more likely than others. One of the options is Mary Duranski, who was killed in an auto accident in 1934. Another is a 12-year-old girl named Anna Norkus, who died in another tragic accident in 1936. That same year marked the date of another

accident that some believe spawned Resurrection Mary. In this case, a farm truck collided with an automobile and three of the four passengers in the sedan were killed. One of the victims, a young woman, may have become Resurrection Mary. Others believe Mary can be traced to an incident near Resurrection Cemetery that occurred in the 1940s. In this case, a young Polish girl had taken her father's car to meet her boyfriend in the early morning hours. She died in an accident and was buried in the nearby cemetery. Most believe this to be little more than a neighborhood cautionary tale told by protective parents, but it certainly adds another element to the legend.

It's possible that any one of these young women could still haunt Archer Avenue and may have contributed to the Resurrection Mary legend. However, I believe that the majority of the sightings that have occurred can be connected to two young women who, ironically, lived only a few blocks away from one another in life.

You could say they have become "sisters" in death…

Mary Bregovy was twenty-one years old in March 1934. She had been born on April 7, 1912, and attended St. Michael's Grammar School, a short distance from her home. She lived in a small house at 4611 South Damen Avenue, which was in the Back of the Yards neighborhood of Bridgeport. She was of Polish descent and was employed at a local factory, where she worked hard to help support her mother, father and two younger brothers, Steve and Joseph, during the early days of the Great Depression.

Friends would later remember her as an extremely fun-loving girl who loved to go to parties and go out dancing, especially to the Oh Henry Ballroom, which was her favorite place. Her best friend was LaVern Rutkowski, or "Vern" as she was commonly known, and she grew up with Mary and lived just two houses away from her. Vern spent Mary's final day with her on March 10, 1934. The two of them spent a lot of time together, and years later, Vern would vividly recall going out with Mary to dance halls all over the Southwest side. Ironically, Mary's parents had forbidden her to go out on the night of March 10, and Mary might have listened to them if she and Vern had not met a couple of young men earlier that day. These two men, who are believed to have been John Reiker and John Thoel, were in the car that night when Mary was killed.

Mary and Vern spent that Saturday afternoon shopping at 47th Street and Ashland Avenue, and it was in one of the stores located at the busy intersection that they met the two boys. After getting into their car to go for a ride, Vern took an instant dislike to them. She was frightened by their reckless driving, turning corners on two wheels, and speeding down narrow streets. Finally, she demanded to be let out of the car a few blocks from home. She asked Mary if she planned to go out with the young men that night and Mary said that she did. Vern urged her to reconsider, not only because she didn't like the boys, but also because Mary's parents had already told her that she needed to stay home. Mary shrugged off her friend's warnings and Vern stood watching on the street corner as Mary and the young men roared away in the car. It was the last time that she would see her friend alive.

No one knows how Mary Bregovy spent the rest of the day, but a few clues have emerged from family members over the years. The wife of Mary's younger brother, Steve, reported in 1985 that she had received a letter from a friend of Mary's years before that stated Mary planned to attend a novena at church before she went out dancing that night. The Bregovys were devout Catholics and this would not have been out of the ordinary for Mary to do. She also said that she believed Mary had been going to the Oh Henry Ballroom that night.

But did she ever arrive there? No one knows for sure, but tradition holds that Mary and her new friends, who now included a young woman named Virginia Rozanski, did go dancing at the Oh Henry that night. After the ballroom closed, they drove into the city, where most of the clubs stayed open much later. In the early morning hours, they were leaving downtown, traveling along Wacker Drive, likely headed for Archer Avenue, which would take Mary home to Bridgeport, when the accident occurred. One has to wonder if alcohol, combined with the reckless driving described by Vern Rutkowski, combined to cause the crash.

The accident occurred along Wacker Drive, just as it curves to the south and away from the Chicago River. At the point where Wacker crosses Lake Street, there is a large, metal support for the elevated tracks overhead. If a driver was coming along Wacker too quickly, it could be easy to not make a complete turn and collide with the support column, which is almost in a straight line around the curve. This is apparently what happened to John Thoel that night.

When the automobile collided with the metal column, Mary was thrown through the windshield and instantly killed. Her body was badly cut up by the glass. Before her funeral, the undertaker had to sew up a gash that extended all of the way across the front of her throat and up to her right ear. Tragically, Mary was not even supposed to be sitting in the front seat when the accident occurred. Her parents would later learn that she had switched places with Virginia Rozanski because Virginia didn't like John Thoel, who she had been sitting next to in the passenger's seat. She had asked Mary to sit in front with Thoel and Mary had agreed. Unfortunately, her good-natured personality would turn out to be fatal for her.

Vern Rutkowski accompanied Mary's mother and her brother, Joseph, to the morgue to identify the body. Mary was taken to the Satala Funeral Home, located just a couple of blocks from the Bregovy home, to be prepared for burial. The owner at the time, John Satala, easily remembered Mary. In 1985, he recalled: "She was a hell of a nice girl. Very pretty. She was buried in an orchid dress. I remember having to sew up the side of her face."

Mary was buried in Resurrection Cemetery and this is where some of the confusion about her story comes along. According to records, Mary was buried in Section MM, Site 9819. There was a Mary Bregovy buried here, but it was not the young woman who was killed in March 1934. A search for this gravesite revealed that the Mary Bregovy laid to rest here was a thirty-four-year-old woman who was born in 1888 and died in 1922. This is a different Mary Bregovy altogether. Family members of Mary Bregovy said that Mary was actually buried in a term grave and never moved. After World War II, when space was needed for more burial sites at Resurrection Cemetery, some of the term graves were moved but others, like Mary's, were simply covered over. For this reason, according to Mrs. Steve Bregovy, the location of Mary's grave is unknown – but she would not rest in peace.

In fact, the stories of Mary Bregovy's ghost began a very short time after her death. In April 1934, a caretaker at Resurrection Cemetery telephoned funeral home director John Satala and told him that he had seen the barefooted ghost of a young girl walking around the cemetery. She was a lovely girl with brown hair and she was wearing a pale, orchid-colored dress. The caretaker was positive that the ghost was the woman that Satala had recently buried. Satala later said that he recognized the description of the girl as Mary Bregovy.

Soon after, other stories began to circulate, claiming that motorists on Archer Avenue in front of Resurrection Cemetery were encountering a frantic woman who tried to hitch a ride with them. These Archer Avenue sightings also included reports from people who actually recognized the ghost as Mary Bregovy.

I'm convinced that these reports were the beginning of the Resurrection Mary legend. These were the first stories of a young woman hitching rides on Archer Avenue, and thanks to the destination of many of these motorists, combined with the fact that the Oh Henry Ballroom was Mary's favorite dance spot, the story began to grow. I believe that many of the reports of a ghostly woman being seen around Resurrection Cemetery can be traced to Mary Bregovy --- the "original Resurrection Mary."

But Mary Bregovy does not haunt this stretch of Archer Avenue alone...

Mary Bregovy may have started the legend of Resurrection Mary, but she was not the only phantom haunting Archer Avenue and the area around it. As readers have likely realized, the stories of a "beautiful blond" don't physically match Miss Bregovy, who was certainly pretty, but definitely not a blond. She had naturally curly, brown hair, which means that she is not the same spirit who was so frequently being picked up by motorists and spotted on the side of the road.

However, thanks to a letter that I received in 2005 (and the interviews that followed it), I believe that I may just have the identity of the second woman who has contributed to the legend of Resurrection Mary, who also may be the same woman encountered by a young man at the Liberty Grove & Hall in 1939.

Aside from the harried motorists who encountered Mary along Archer Avenue in the 1930s, there were those who came face to face with her under other conditions. One of these people was a young man named Jerry Palus. His experience with Mary took place in 1939, but would leave such an impression that he would never forget it until his death in 1992. Palus remained an unshakable witness and appeared on a number of television shows to discuss his night with Resurrection Mary. Regardless, he had little to gain from his story and no reason to lie. He never doubted the fact that he spent an evening with a ghost.

Palus met the young girl, who he described as a very attractive blond, at the Liberty Grove & Hall, a music and dancing venue that was near 47th Street and Mozart in the Brighton Park neighborhood. As it happens, this dance hall, which was a "jumping spot" on the city's Southwest side for many years, was located not far from both of the homes of the women that I believe have created the "Resurrection Mary" legend. However, because of his description of the girl as an "attractive blond," I'm reasonably sure that I now know who Jerry Palus encountered.

That night at the Liberty Grove & Hall, Jerry asked the girl to dance. He had been watching her for some time that evening, although he admitted in later interviews that he never saw her come into the place. She spent a couple of hours sitting by herself, since she didn't seem to know anyone, and Jerry finally gathered the courage to take her out onto the dance floor. The girl accepted his invitation and they spent several hours together. Strangely, though, she seemed a little distant and Palus also noticed that her skin was very cold, almost icy to the touch. When he later kissed her, he found her lips were also cold and clammy.

At the end of the evening, the young woman asked Jerry for a ride home. He readily agreed to give her a lift. When they got to his automobile, she explained that she lived on South Damen Avenue but that she wanted to take a ride down Archer Avenue first. Jerry shrugged and told her that he would be happy to take her wherever she wanted. By this time, he was infatuated with the girl and likely wanted to extend the night for as long as he could. He knew that it would be quite some distance out of the way to drive down Archer Avenue but he didn't mind, so he put his car into gear and drove off.

To reach Archer Avenue from the Liberty Grove & Hall, Jerry only had to travel west on 47th Street. Once he made it to the old roadway, they traveled southwest to Summit and then on to Justice. It was a dark, dimly lit road in those days, but Jerry was somewhat familiar with the area, so he just followed the course of the road, heading eventually, he thought, towards Willow Springs.

But as they approached the gates to Resurrection Cemetery the girl asked him to pull over. She had to get out here, she told him. Jerry was confused, unable to understand why she would want to get out at such a spot, but he pulled the car to the side of the road anyway. He agreed that he would let her out, but only if she allowed him to walk her to wherever she was going. There was a row of houses to Jerry's right, about a block off Archer Avenue, and he assumed that she was going to one of them. He wanted to be sure that she made it there safely.

The beautiful young girl refused to allow this, though. She turned in her seat and faced Palus. She spoke softly: "This is where I have to get out, but where I'm going, you can't follow."

Jerry was bewildered by this statement, but before he could respond, the girl got out of the car and ran not in the direction of the houses but across Archer Avenue and toward the gates of Resurrection Cemetery. She vanished before she reached them -- right before Jerry's eyes. That was the moment when he knew that he had danced with a specter.

Determined to find out what was going on, Palus visited the address the girl had given him on the following day. The woman who answered the door told him that he couldn't possibly have been with her daughter the night before because her daughter had been dead for years. However, Palus was able to correctly identify the girl from a family portrait in the other room.

Needless to say, Jerry was stunned by this revelation, but apparently, the address and identity of the woman were forgotten over the years. Some time later, when Palus was contacted again about his story (when the passage of time had renewed interest in the elusive ghost) he was unable to remember where he had gone on the day after his encounter. Despite this memory lapse, Palus' story remains one of the most credible of all of the Resurrection Mary encounters.

So, who was the blond woman that Jerry Palus danced with that night? I believe that she was a young woman named Mary Miskowski. Little has been previously known about her except for the fact that she was killed in October 1930 by a hit and run driver. She was allegedly crossing the street while on her way to a Halloween costume party.

In July 2005, I received a vague letter from a woman who promised me information about Resurrection Mary, claiming that the real-life counterpart of Mary had once been her mother's babysitter when she was a child. If I was interested, I could call her and get more information. Her mother was still alive and would be happy to speak with me about it. When I called, she gave me a few details of the story and then gave me the telephone number of her mother, who was 85-years-old, and urged me to contact her. The next afternoon, I called the number that she gave me and was soon speaking with Mrs. Martha Litak, who grew up on South Damen Avenue on Chicago's Southwest Side. I told her why I was calling and asked her what she could tell me about the story of Resurrection Mary.

Her answer surprised me. She laughed and said, "Resurrection Mary was my babysitter!"

According to Mrs. Litak, Mary Miskowski had lived down the street from her family when she was a child. Mary's house was located at 4924 South Damen Avenue (interestingly, just three blocks away from Mary Bregovy, so it seems possible these two women could have known one another) and she often watched neighborhood children to earn extra money. Mrs. Litak was not sure if Mary had a regular job or not. She lived with her parents, but she was old enough to be out of school.

Martha did remember Mary very well: "She was a very pretty girl. She had light blond hair with just a little bit of curl to it. It was cut short, just a little below her ears. All of the boys in the neighborhood were in love with her. I do remember that she liked to go on dates but I don't recall that she had any one boyfriend in particular."

Martha remembered that her cousins told her that Mary loved to go out dancing, including to the Oh Henry Ballroom, which had opened in 1921. Her favorite place, though, was the Liberty Grove & Hall, which was located about a dozen blocks from her home. I've since come to believe that Mary Miskowski was the ghost that Jerry Palus encountered at the dance hall that night. Mary certainly matched the description that Palus (and many others have given over the years) later gave of the young woman that he met and who vanished from his car in front of Resurrection Cemetery.

But this was not the only thing that convinced me.

Martha told me that she had spoken with her younger brother, Frank, after her daughter told her that I might get in touch. She had asked him if he could remember anything about their old babysitter, Mary Miskowski. Frank was only seven years old at the time Mary died, but he did recall what she looked like. In fact, he remembered her very well because Frank believed that he saw Mary one night about 10 years after she died! He was a young man at the time, out driving his first car on Archer Avenue. As he was driving north on the road, he saw a woman standing on the side of the road. He slowed down to take a look at her and as he did, the woman turned in his direction. He was stunned when he saw her face – it was his dead babysitter, Mary Miskowski! Frank slammed on his brakes and slid over to the side of the road. He looked frantically backward, but the woman was gone. In a matter of seconds, she had simply vanished. Frank was so shaken by the encounter that he didn't drive that particular stretch of Archer Avenue again for years.

According to newspaper accounts, Martha Litak said, Mary Miskowski had been killed by a hit and run driver in October 1930. A car had struck her as she was crossing 47th Street and had sped away. Whoever the driver was, he was never caught. Martha surmised that perhaps this incident was how the story got started about Resurrection Mary being run over by a car and left for dead on Archer Avenue. With the Oh Henry Ballroom, and later the Willowbrook, being so closely tied to the legend, she was not surprised that the accident had been moved to a location that was closer to the dance hall. Mrs. Litak also confirmed that Mary had been on her way to a costume party that night. She had been dressed as a bride, wearing her mother's old wedding dress. Martha didn't know what Mary had been buried in, but she did believe that perhaps the white dress that so many people reported Resurrection Mary wearing could have been this dress from the early 1900s.

Mrs. Litak further connected Mary Miskowski to the legend by adding that she had been buried in Resurrection Cemetery. I have been unable to confirm this but Martha and Frank were both sure this was the case. They told me that she had been buried in a term grave (just like Mary Bregovy) but she did not know the ultimate location of the site.

If any of this is accurate, it may explain the Resurrection Mary encounters that don't match the description and behavior of Mary Bregovy. Could the presence of Mary Miskowski explain the sightings of a pretty, blond phantom who hangs out in dance halls and vanishes from cars? And could she be the ghost who is seen running across the road in front of the cemetery where she is buried, perhaps re-enacting her final moments over and over again as she is stuck by a passing automobile?

I think it's possible, perhaps even likely. It's a fascinating and compelling story -- compelling enough that it prompted my theory that Resurrection Mary is not just one ghost, but two, or maybe even more.

But why did the stories of Resurrection Mary fade in the 1940s, only to be revived with such intensity in the 1970s? It was three decades after the stories waned that Resurrection Cemetery began undergoing major renovations, including the movement of the term graves that had been in place for so many years. Some of the graves were moved to other locations, while others, according to the relatives of some who had loved ones buried in the cemetery, were reportedly bulldozed under the earth. It's believed that this disturbance may have been what caused the frequency of sightings to increase so drastically in the 1970s. But once the work was finished, the sightings began to peter out again, just as they had done years before.

So, who is Mary and does she really exist?

I believe that she does and I also believe that we know the identities of at least two of the women who have created her enduring legend. But there are many other theories that also exist. Mary Bregovy and Mary Miskowski may be just two of the candidates for Resurrection Mary, and there may be many more.

Does she really exist? Many still remain doubtful about her, but I have found that their skepticism doesn't really seem to matter. Whether these people believe in her or not, people saw (and in some cases are still seeing) Mary walking along Archer Avenue at night. Motorists still stopped to pick up a forlorn young woman who seemed inadequately dressed on cold winter nights, when encounters seemed to be the most prevalent. Even today, curiosity-seekers still come to see the gates where the twisted and burned bars were once located, and some even roam the graveyard, hoping to stumble across the place where Mary's body was laid to rest.

We still don't know for sure who she really was, but that has not stopped the stories and even songs about her. She remains an enigma and her legend lives on, not content to vanish, as Mary does when she reaches the gates to Resurrection Cemetery. You see, our individual belief, or disbelief, does not really matter. Mary lives on anyway --- a mysterious, elusive, and romantic spirit of the open road.

Dell Rhea's Chicken Basket

As the road rolls on along into Willowbrook, hungry travelers will soon discover one of the best fried chicken joints in America. It was near this spot that a man named Irv Kolarik ran a gas station where he also served pie, coffee, and sandwiches at a lunch counter. One day, two local women heard Kolarik say that he dreamed of opening a restaurant and they offered to teach him how to fry chicken if he agreed to buy his chickens from them. A deal was struck and the rest, as they say, was history.

The chicken became so popular that he converted the two service bays of his filling station into a dining room. In June 1946, he bought the adjacent property and opened a real restaurant that became known as the Nationally Famous Chicken Basket, abandoning the earlier names of Club Roundup and the Triangle Inn. The diner quickly began pulling in customers from Route 66, since it was the perfect stopping spot for those going to or coming from Chicago. The perfect location also led to the Chicken Basket becoming a Blue Bird bus stop. People came to the Chicken Basket to purchase bus tickets to travel as far away as Los Angeles or to send packages to loved ones anywhere in between Chicago and L.A. Never one to pass up publicity, Kolarik frequently came up with new schemes to drum up business. One winter, he flooded the roof of the restaurant and hired ice skaters to perform up there under spotlights. Needless to say, they made quite a scene at night.

The restaurant's need for chicken soon outgrew the capability of the two local women, and another local farmer who was just moving into the area, took over. That farmer was none other than Stanley Helma, father and grandfather of today's owners.

The restaurant changed hands two times in the 1950s and 1960s, and when four-lane Route 66 bypassed the Chicken Basket, the place fell on hard times. People who remembered the restaurant couldn't figure out how to get to it and it almost went out of business for lack of customers. In 1963, Dell Rhea and his wife, Grace, bought the restaurant at a bargain price and changed its name to **Dell Rhea's Chicken Basket**. Dell, being very well known in the area, used his reputation to help bring people back to the place.

With a lot of hard work, good food, fair prices, friendly faces, and a nostalgia for the Mother Road, the restaurant continues to thrive today. The restaurant looks much like it did in 1946 and still serves some of the best fried chicken that you'll find between Chicago and Los Angeles.

The 1940 Alignment

In 1940, Route 66 was realigned to pass through Plainfield and bypass the city of Joliet. Multiple additional alignments were done over the subsequent years while building the new interstate – at the time called "freeway" – in accordance with a 1943 bill. The newer route passed through Plainfield, Shorewood, Channahon, Braidwood, Godley, and Braceville, before (today) coming to a dead end.

Travelers looking for Route 66 sites are forced to take the interstate for a few miles before exiting back onto the pre-1940 highway, just past Bolingbrook. The exit is home to an old gas station and café, as well as Montana Charlie's Flea Market.

Romeo & Juliet.... Oops, Romeoville and Joliet

Romeoville, the next stop on Route 66, was first called Romeo when nearby Joliet was still called Juliet. At the time of its founding, the settlement was a twin and rival town of Juliet, unlike the romantic pair in Shakespeare's play. It got its start in the early 1830s and was known for its rich farmland and large number of stone quarries. In 1845, the city of Juliet's name was changed to Joliet to honor the famous explorer, Louis Jolliet. When this happened, Romeo acknowledged the ridiculousness of the two former names by becoming Romeoville.

Located on the western bank of the Des Plains River, Romeoville supplied Chicago with farm products using the Illinois & Michigan Canal, which opened to traffic in 1848. However, its main source of wealth came from the stone quarries that operated in the area. During the heyday of "Stone City," as it came to be called, two trainloads of limestone were shipped to Chicago from Romeoville every morning.

During the early 1900s, Romeoville thrived as a resort town for wealthy Chicagoans. In those days, a streetcar line ran all of the way from Chicago, bringing excited vacationers to Isle La Cache and Romeo Beach.

The two cities drifted further apart as time went on, and eventually, the rivalry – and the unusual names of both towns – was largely forgotten.

"World's Greatest Chicken"

White Fence Farm, which became an iconic dining spot on Route 66, came about because of an idea hatched in the middle 1920s by wealthy Chicago coal magnate Stuyvesant "Jack" Peabody, son of Peabody Coal Company founder Francis Peabody. It was opened on a 12-acre piece of land that Jack Peabody owned across Joliet Road from his 45-acre horse farm. The story was that Jack Peabody often had weekend guests at his horse farm, but there was no restaurant in the area where he could entertain them – so he started one himself. The roadside restaurant, which opened in a converted farmhouse, was known then for its hamburger sandwiches and Guernsey milk products, including ice cream. "White Fence Farm," as he dubbed it, became a true "out in the country experience" for Chicago residents who had never been on a farm. It was just far enough outside of the city to be rural and yet close enough to attract more than scores of customers.

By the time Route 66 opened in 1926, White Fence Farm had already served several thousand customers. It was reviewed several times during the Peabody years by the early restaurant critic Duncan Hines, who had been a fan of the restaurant since the late 1920s. After Prohibition ended, Jack Peabody promoted California wines at the restaurant and helped to revive the California wine industry, as he had earlier helped to revive thoroughbred horse racing in Illinois during the 1910s and 1920s. Peabody operated the restaurant successfully until his death in 1946.

After that, the restaurant was first leased to several different renters, then was purchased by the Hastert family in 1954. Robert Hastert, and his wife, Doris, were the first family owner-managers. Hastert had started as a wholesale poultry dealer at the Aurora Poultry Market during World War II and later owned the Harmony House restaurant, which he had opened four years before he bought White Fence Farm. It was during this time that the restaurant's famous fried chicken recipe was added to the menu after an industrial-sized hospital autoclave was converted into an outsized pressure cooker for their unique method of cooking the chicken.

It was the chicken that stirred up competition with its nearby rival, Dell Rhea's Chicken Basket. White Fence Farm bills itself as having "the world's greatest fried chicken," a claim that the Chicken Basket has issues with. But once a matter of dueling billboards on Route 66, the competition is now limited to a contest between menu items. Whereas Dell Rhea's can claim that it began serving its famous fried chicken years before its competitor did, White Fence Farm prides itself in serving an alcoholic brandy ice dessert, made strictly for adults.

White Fence Farm's 12 dining rooms can serve an astounding 1,000 people at a time so there's no question that it's a must-stop location on old Route 66 for hungry tourists. While there, you can also visit the classic car museum and send the kids out to the petting zoo, where sheep, llamas, and goats can entertain them while waiting to dig into a platter of hot fried chicken.

"Behind These Walls" at Joliet Penitentiary

Although far from a tourist attraction on Route 66, motorists who passed through Joliet couldn't help but notice the ominous walls of the nearby prison as they passed through town. The Joliet Penitentiary was meant to be the last stop for many of the thieves, killers, and desperate criminals who found themselves locked behind the prison's fortress-like walls. It was not designed to be a place of hope or rehabilitation, but a place of punishment for the men who chose to ignore the laws of society. The Joliet Penitentiary broke the bodies and minds of scores of criminals over the years of its operation, and for many of those who perished there, the prison became their permanent home. There was no escape, these luckless souls discovered, sometimes even after death.

For more than forty years, from Illinois' statehood in 1818 to around 1858, there was only one state penitentiary in Illinois, located in the Mississippi River town of Alton. The prison was completed in 1833, but soon it deteriorated beyond repair, which was a major concern since the state's population was growing rapidly and along with it, the crime rate. During his inaugural speech in 1853, newly elected Governor Joel Mattson, a Joliet native, spoke out for the need of a prison in northern Illinois. By the middle 1800s, the population center of the state had shifted from southwestern Illinois toward the expanding city of Chicago. In 1857, spurred by scandals involving the horrific conditions of the Alton prison, the Illinois legislature finally approved a commission to scout for locations for the new penitentiary.

Governor Mattson's friend, Nelson Elwood, a former mayor of Joliet, was appointed to the Board of Penitentiary Commissioners, and it was Elwood who convinced the members of the board to build a prison at a site that was then two miles north of the city of Joliet. The location boasted a fresh water spring, proximity to railroads and the Illinois & Michigan Canal, and the city of Chicago. But the greatest argument in favor of the fifteen-acre site was the limestone deposits that lay beneath it. The deposits were so deep that no inmate could escape by tunneling out through them.

Construction on the penitentiary began in 1858. The workforce consisted of 53 prisoners that had been transferred in from Alton. They lived in makeshift barracks while they mined the Joliet-Lemont limestone quarry just across the road from the building site. Local private contractors supervised the construction and the prisoners. Quarry drilling was done entirely by hand and the huge blocks were hauled by mule cart to the road. A conveyor belt was later built to transport rocks to the surface. As work progressed, more prisoners were transferred to Joliet and assigned to work on the construction. There was no shortage of stone or labor and, in 1859, the first building was completed. It took just 12 years for the prisoners to construct their own place of confinement. By then, the Alton prison had been completely shut down and all of the state prisoners had been sent to Joliet.

The Joliet Penitentiary contained 1,100 cells – 900 for the general population, 100 for solitary confinement, and 100 to house female inmates. At the time it was finished, it was the largest prison in the United States and was adopted as an

architectural model for penitentiaries around the world, including Leavenworth and the Isle of Pines in Cuba.

Prisoners were housed in two-man cells that were six by nine feet, with no electricity, plumbing, or running water. Each cell had a pitcher for fresh water and a bucket for waste. The stone walls of the cells were eight inches thick with only a door and a small ventilation hole for openings. The cellblocks were built running the length of the middle of each building, away from any natural light. The cells were grim, confined, dimly lighted chambers that offered little hope for the men incarcerated in them.

Life in the new penitentiary was harsh and sometimes brutal. The inmates at Joliet passed their days under a strict regime of silence, but were allowed to speak to their cellmates during the evening hours in quiet voices. Contact with the outside world was severely limited, and no recreational activities were offered.

Prisoners moved from place to place within the prison using a "lock step" formation, which was a sort of side-step shuffle with one hand on the shoulder of the man in front of him. Inmates' heads had to be turned in the direction of the guards, who watched for any lip movement that signaled when someone was talking. The lock step formation also made it easier for one guard to watch over a larger number of prisoners. Floggings, being placed in the stocks, and extensive time in solitary confinement were common punishments for those who broke the rules. The inmates wore striped uniforms. Men who were deemed to be escape risks were shackled.

Convict labor, under constant discipline, allowed the Joliet Penitentiary to initiate factory-style working conditions at a profit. Lucrative contracts were sold to the highest private bidder, who then sold the products manufactured in the prison on the open market. Under the constant scrutiny of the guards, the prisoners were put to work producing an array of goods: rattan furniture, shoes, brooms, chairs, wheelbarrows, horse collars, and dressed limestone. The prison was also self-sufficient in most aspects of daily life. It had a thriving bakery, a tailor shop, a hospital, and a library, which was administered by the prison chaplain.

The prison buildings were impossible to keep warm in the winter and very hard to keep clean, which made it a breeding ground for lice, rats, and various diseases. Tuberculosis, pneumonia, and typhoid were the main causes of death among inmates. Unclaimed bodies were buried in a pauper's graveyard, called Monkey Hill, near the prison on Woodruff Street.

The strict silence, unsanitary conditions, forced labor, and harsh punishments gave the Joliet Penitentiary a reputation as the last possible place that a man wanted to end up.

Prison reform was first introduced at Joliet in 1913 with the appointment of Edmund Allen as the warden. By 1915, the striped uniforms and the lock step formation were gone, and the rule of silence ended. Prisoners were allowed recreation privileges and a baseball diamond was built. Warden Allen also started an honor farm on 2,200 acres four miles north of the prison. Prisoners were allowed to work in the fields, and on the farm, as a reward for good conduct.

Ironically, Warden Allen, who lived in an apartment on the prison grounds with his wife, Odette, experienced personal tragedy, possibly at the hands of one of the trusted inmates. On June 19, 1915, Allen and his wife planned to leave on a trip to West Baden, Indiana. Mrs. Allen's dressmaker had not quite finished two of her dresses, and Odette persuaded her husband to go ahead and leave without her. Early the next morning, a fire broke out in the warden's apartment. When the prison fire department responded, they discovered Mrs. Allen was dead, and her bed engulfed in flames. The fire was ruled as arson and a trustee, "Chicken Joe" Campbell, who had been Mrs. Allen's servant, was charged with the crime. Campbell was tried, convicted, and sentenced to death, despite the fact that the evidence against him was purely circumstantial. At Warden Allen's request, Illinois' Governor Dunne commuted his sentenced to life imprisonment.

Construction on a new prison, called Stateville, began in 1916 on the land where the honor farm was located. It was originally intended to replace the older prison, but the national crime sprees of the 1920s and 1930s kept the old Joliet Penitentiary open for another 80 years.

During its time in operation, the prison housed some of the most infamous and deadly criminals in Illinois history. Some of them were already well-known when they walked through the front gates while others gained their infamy inside the walls.

Famous Chicago gangster George "Bugs" Moran served three terms for robbery at Joliet between 1910 and 1923. After the murder of his crime mentor Dion O'Banion in 1926, Moran became the leader of Chicago's North Side bootleggers. His time in power lasted until 1929, when seven of his men were slaughtered by the Capone gang in the St. Valentine's Day Massacre. Moran turned to a life of petty crime and died in Leavenworth in 1957.

Frank McErlane was considered one of the most vicious gunmen in Chicago, and before being sent to Joliet, was credited with killing nine men, two women, and a dog. Arrested for his part in the murder of an Oak Park police officer in 1916, he served one year at Joliet before trying to escape. He was caught and served another two years for the attempt. Shortly after the start of Prohibition, McErlane began running a gang with his partner, Joseph "Polack Joe" Saltis, on Chicago's south side. Later, they allied with the Capone gang against the south side O'Donnell Brothers. During the war with the O'Donnells, McErlane introduced the Thompson machine gun to Chicago and with it, killed at least 15 men during the Beer Wars. McErlane was suspected to have taken part in the St. Valentine's Day Massacre, and he suffered serious wounds during a gun battle with George Moran in 1930. While recovering, Moran sent two gunmen to kill him, but McErlane pulled a revolver from underneath his pillow and began firing, driving off the surprised gangsters. McErlane was wounded in the gunfight, suffering two wounds in his injured leg and one in his arm, but he recovered. In 1932, he became ill with pneumonia and died within days.

Nathan Leopold and Richard Loeb, two college students from wealthy families, were sentenced to life imprisonment at Joliet in 1924 after kidnapping and murdering 14-year-old Bobby Franks. They had been attempting to pull off the "perfect crime." Warden John L. Whitman was firm in his assertion that the young men received the same treatment as the other prisoners, but this was never the case. Leopold and Loeb lived in luxury compared to the rest of the inmates. Each enjoyed a private cell, books, a desk, a filing cabinet, and even pet birds. They also showered away from the other prisoners and took their meals, which were prepared to order, in the officers' lounge. Leopold was allowed to keep a flower garden. They were also permitted any number of unsupervised visitors and were allowed to keep their own gardens. The doors to their cells were usually left open and they had passes to visit one another at any time. Loeb was stabbed to death by another inmate in 1936. Leopold was eventually released in 1958, after pleas to the prison board by poet Carl Sandburg. He moved to Puerto Rico and died in 1971.

George "Baby Face" Nelson also served time at Joliet. In July 1931, he was convicted of robbing the Itasca State Bank and sentenced to one year to life at Joliet

Penitentiary. He served two months before being sent to stand trial for another bank robbery. He was under armed guard and on his way back to Joliet when he escaped and went back to robbing banks with the Dillinger gang.

One of the more recent inmates at Joliet was serial killer John Wayne Gacy, one of Chicago's most notorious murderers. Between 1972 and 1978, Gacy tortured and killed 33 young men, burying 28 of them under his home. He was sentenced to death in 1980 and spent some of his time on death row in a cell at the Joliet Penitentiary.

In 2001, the Joliet State Penitentiary was closed down. The crumbling old prison had finally been deemed unfit for habitation and all of the prisoners were moved out. But, as many who came to tour the penitentiary were soon to discover – the prison may have been abandoned, but it was certainly not empty.

The first mention of ghosts connected to the old penitentiary was not so much a story about the prison being haunted, but rather one of the inmates. That man's name was Adolph Luetgert, Chicago's "Sausage King." Luetgert was a German meatpacker who was charged with killing his wife, Louisa, in May of 1897. The two of them had a stormy marriage and when Louisa disappeared, detectives feared the worst and searched the sausage factory that was located next door to the Luetgert home. In one of the vats in the basement, human bone fragments and a ring bearing Louisa's initials were found and Luetgert was arrested.

His first trial ended with a hung jury on October 21, after the jurors failed to agree on a suitable punishment. Some argued for the death penalty, while others voted for life in prison. Only one of the jurors thought that Luetgert might be innocent. A second trial was held, and on February 9, 1898, Luetgert was convicted and sentenced to a life term at Joliet. He was taken away, still maintaining his innocence and claiming that he would receive another trial. He was placed in charge of meats in the prison's cold-storage warehouse and officials described him as a model inmate.

By 1899, though, Luetgert began to speak less and less and often quarreled with the other convicts. He soon became a shadow of his former self, fighting with other inmates for no reason, and often babbling incoherently in his cell at night. But was he talking to himself or to someone else?

According to legend, Luetgert began to claim that he was talking to Louisa in his cell at night. His dead wife had returned to haunt him, intent on having revenge for her murder. Was she really haunting him or was the "ghost" just the figment of a rapidly deteriorating mind? Based on the fact that residents of his former neighborhood also began to report seeing Louisa's ghost, one has to wonder if Luetgert was mentally ill – or if the ghost had driven him insane.

Luetgert died in 1900, likely from heart trouble. The coroner who conducted the autopsy also reported that his liver was greatly enlarged and in such a condition of degeneration that "mental strain would have caused his death at any time."

Perhaps Louisa really did visit him after all....

In 1932, the Joliet Penitentiary gained statewide attention, and great notoriety, for a strange ghostly phenomenon that was allegedly occurring at Monkey Hill, the old pauper's burial ground on the property.

In the 1930s, the prison maintained a large field behind the compound for grazing cattle and a limestone quarry that served to provide the prisoners with hard labor. Nearby was the pauper's graveyard where the unclaimed dead were buried. The graveyard was a desolate place that was largely ignored by those who lived nearby. It probably would have never been talked about at all, if not for the fact that an unexplained voice began to be heard in the cemetery in July 1932.

On July 16, the night of a full moon, a woman named Mrs. Dudek was standing in her backyard, which adjoined the potter's field. As she was enjoying the cool night air on that summer evening, she began to hear a beautiful baritone voice singing what sounded like Latin hymns from a Catholic Mass. She called to her daughter, Genevieve, and the two of them took a flashlight and pointed it in the direction the voice was coming from. They saw nothing there.

The next evening, Mrs. Dudek's son, Stanley, and her husband, George, both of whom had been away the night before, also heard the singing. They searched the cemetery but found no one. They were unable to determine where the sound was coming from. News of the voice spread through the neighborhood and those who came to listen to what the Dudek's claimed to hear went away stunned. They quickly realized that the voice was not coming from someone's radio. It was a ghost, they said – a ghost in the old prison cemetery!

News of what was assumed to be a specter in the potter's field spread throughout Joliet and soon people from all over town were coming to hear the mysterious singing. Lines of cars filled Woodruff Road and then turned into the prison field, where neighborhood boys directed them to parking places. The procession began early in the evening each night since the voice began to sing around midnight.

After about ten days of this, word of the enigmatic voice had spread all over the Chicago area. Curiosity-seekers came from the city, from Indiana, and from the nearby cities of Plainfield, Lockport, Aurora, and Rockdale. The story was picked up in the local newspapers, and then in Chicago and Indiana, and, finally, across the country. The people of Joliet had a genuine mystery on their hands.

People soon began to come from as far away as Missouri, Wisconsin, and Kentucky to hear the singing. The prison field became a frequent stop for travelers on Route 66. According to the local newspaper, a man named Joshua Jones from Sickles Center, Missouri, was sent by a local contingent from his town. "Folks in my town read about this in the newspapers but they won't believe it until they hear it from me," Jones told a reporter.

The visitors to the old cemetery started off numbering in the hundreds and the groups of thrill-seekers soon began to grow into the thousands. From the beginning, the tourists attempted to uncover the source of the "ghostly" sounds, or at least the whereabouts of the person pretending to be a ghost. Whenever the singing began, the searchers rushed into the field, looking behind bushes, in trees, and even below ground for any hidden caverns. They looked for wires, loud speakers, and concealed microphones, but found nothing. In spite of this, the singing persisted night after night, and each night it was the same: a low, mournful calling of Latin hymns.

The skeptics who came in search of a reasonable answer went away confused. People soon began to accept the genuineness of the phenomenon, as all attempts to prove it was a hoax had failed. Each night, thousands of people drove to the field and climbed the hill to what had once been a lonely graveyard. They sat on the flat gravestones, spread their blankets in the grass, and brought along picnic baskets and thermoses of coffee. The crowds waited expectantly for the eerie voice and, for a time, were never disappointed.

Eventually, though, the voice began to miss its nightly performance. And when it did come, it was sometimes as late as 4:00 a.m., several hours after it had originally started. The faithful stayed and waited for it, though, huddled in blankets and sleeping in the chilly air of the early morning hours. They claimed the voice was offended by those who came only for thrills. It waited for the quiet, attentive listeners, who received a performance of prayerful hymns.

However, even the most devoted still searched for an explanation for the voice. Was it some sort of heavenly visitor? The ghost of a deceased prisoner? No one knew, but in late July, officials at the prison announced that they had an explanation for the singer. They claimed that it was merely an Irish-German prisoner, a trusty named William Lalon Chrysler, who was singing in joy about his upcoming parole. Chrysler had been convicted of larceny and had served four years of his term before becoming eligible for parole. Toward the end of his sentence, he had been placed in charge of late-night inspection of water pumps at the nearby quarry. It was said that the mysterious singing was Chrysler intoning Lithuanian folk songs in English to relieve the monotony down in the depths of the quarry. The prison officials reported that the bare stone walls of the quarry were a perfect sounding board for enhancing and throwing Chrysler's voice to the hilltop more than a quarter mile away. They added that if there were a wind from the north, it would sound as though the voice was right inside the cemetery, where the crowds had gathered. The case was closed – there was nothing supernatural about the voice, they said, it was merely a trick of sound and the wind.

Many people went away convinced that this "official" story was the final word on the subject, but others were not so sure. Many believed that the prison officials were more concerned about getting rid of the crowds than with solving the mystery of the voice. For the entire month of July, thousands of people had encroached on the prison's property. The barbed wire fence that had surrounded the prison field was broken down and the cow pasture had been turned into a parking lot.

To make matters worse, Joliet police officers were unable to deal with the massive numbers of people who came to hear the voice. Local criminals began preying on the tourists, picking pockets and breaking into cars, while some of the less savory neighborhood youths began a car parking racket that extorted money from those who parked in the field. They began threatening motorists with broken windshields if they didn't pay protection money to keep their autos safe. The situation had become a far cry from the first days of the phenomenon, when neighborhood children were helping to direct traffic.

Since the prison officials were unable to stop the voice from being heard, they discredited it instead. William Chrysler provided the perfect solution. He was assigned to the sump pumps at the quarry, so he was outside, and he was due for parole at any time, which meant that he wouldn't chance offending prison officials by denying that his voice was the one heard singing. The officials named Chrysler as the source of the unexplained voice and they closed off the fields to trespassers for good.

The Joliet Singer had been given an official solution, but did the explanation really measure up to the facts in the case? Not everyone thought so in 1932 and not everyone does today. In the official version of the "facts," Chrysler was at the bottom of a quarry when he sang and his voice was transported to a hilltop about a quarter mile away. He had to have had a light with him in the bottom of the quarry, because it was otherwise pitch dark, and yet no one who searched the area reported seeing a light.

Another problem with the story is how Chrysler's voice could have been heard over such a distance. The "quarry as a sounding board" theory does make sense, but it is unlikely that the sound could carry anywhere other than inside the quarry and to a short distance around it. No one who searched the area ever reported hearing the singing coming from the quarry, which means that Chrysler would have had to have been purposely hoaxing the crowds by using ventriloquism. However, magicians and ventriloquists who were interviewed in 1932 stated that this would have been a very difficult, if not impossible, trick, especially for someone with none of the necessary skills. Chrysler readily admitted that he had never been trained in magic or in the art of throwing his voice.

And finally, strangest of all, why did no one ever report hearing the sump pumps at the quarry? According to the official story, Chrysler was out in the field because he was manning these pumps while singing to himself. If this was the case, then how could spectators hear his voice, but not the much louder sounds of the mechanical pumps?

Even with these lingering questions, it must be admitted that the singing voice was never heard again after Chrysler's "confession" and the closing of the field. Was the whole thing really a hoax? Or was it simply that the voice was no longer heard singing because people stopped coming to listen for it? One has to wonder what a visitor might hear today if he happened to be on that field some summer night near midnight.....

After the Joliet Penitentiary closed in 2001, questions remained as to what would become of the old building. It sat empty for the next several years and then, interestingly, became the setting for the Fox television series *Prison Break*. Standing in as the fictional "Fox River Penitentiary," the Joliet Prison became the setting for the first season of this innovative television show. In the series, actor Wentworth Miller played Michael Scofield, a structural engineer who gets himself thrown into prison to try and save his brother, Lincoln Burrowes (played by Dominic Purcell), who was framed for murder and is scheduled for execution. Scofield has the blueprints for the prison cleverly disguised in the tattoos on his body and has created an elaborate plan to help his brother escape – which, of course, goes awry along the way. The highly rated series continued for additional several seasons, eventually leaving "Fox River Penitentiary" behind.

Shortly after the large cast arrived for filming at Joliet, they began to realize there was something not quite right about the old prison.

Lane Garrison, the actor who played "Tweener," a young convict, on the show, stated that standing in the shadow of the prison walls made it easier for him to get into his character. He recalled, "My first day here, I walked through those gates and a change happened. You see the walls and the razor wire, and you feel the history here. It's not a positive place. We do some stuff in Gacy's cell, which is really scary."

Rockmund Dunbar, who played the inmate called "C-Note," was usually the most creeped out of the cast and referred to the prison as "stagnant." He often refused to walk around in the cell blocks by himself. "You're expecting something to come around the corner and grab you. I don't go into the cells. I just don't want to get locked in there."

He was also the first cast member to admit that he believed the prison was haunted. "There were stories of neighbors who called, saying 'stop the prisoners from singing over there' – and the prison was closed!" he said.

Perhaps the one cast member to talk most openly about his strange experiences and haunted happenings at Joliet was Dominic Purcell, who played the ill-fated Lincoln Burrowes. Purcell's office on the set was John Wayne Gacy's former cell, which Purcell said was not a nice place, and "a little creepy." He added, "If I let my imagination run away with me, I can start to pick up on some stuff. I don't like to spend too much time in there, knowing that one of the world's most notorious serial killers was lying on the same bunk that I'm lying on. It ain't a comfortable feeling."

Purcell confessed that many members of the cast and crew believed that the spirits of former prisoners still lingered at Joliet. He described one weird incident that he personally experienced. "I had something touch me on the neck. I looked around and thought, 'It's weird', and blew it off and didn't think about it too much. Then, in the afternoon, one of the other actors came to me and said 'Did you just touch me on the shoulder?' No…. Then I went back to my little thing and said 'Hmmm', and the crew was starting to talk about the weird stuff that's going on. Some said the prison's known to have been haunted for a long time," he said.

Purcell, like Lane Garrison, admitted that it was easy to get into character after setting foot inside the prison's walls, but when the time came to wrap up filming for the day, he was always ready to leave. "I am always relieved to leave, always. You never want to hang out there by yourself. The corridors are long, so far, and you get creeped out exploring. There's a section in the yard where they used to do hangings, and you can see the foundations of what they used to use.

That place left a brutal impression on me. It ain't a place for the faint-hearted," he concluded.

Today, the Joliet Penitentiary still stands, slowly crumbling as the years pass by. What will become of this old place? Many locals consider it an eyesore and embarrassment, but still others see it as an important place in Illinois history. It's been a target for the wrecking ball, and been named as a possible historic site, but, for now, its future remains a mystery.

Do the ghosts of the past still linger in this place, trapped here in time as they were trapped in the cells that once held them? Many believe this to be the case, leading them to wonder what will happen to these mournful spirits if the prison that holds them is lost. Only time will tell….

Motoring through Joliet

Located at 102 North Chicago in Joliet is the **Rialto Square Theatre**, which premiered as a vaudeville theater and movie house in 1926. Opened by the six Rubens brothers, who formed the Royal Theatre Company, it was designed by the Rapp and Rapp Architect firm of Chicago, the theater boasted a dizzying mix of Italian Renaissance, Greek, Roman, Byzantine, Venetian, and Baroque architecture. It cost nearly $2 million to build – a staggering amount at the time – and opened on May 24, 1926.

The Rubens brothers, who built the place as a "palace for the people," leased the operation of the theater to Great States Theatres, Inc., and on its opening night, patrons paid 50-cents to see the film "Mademoiselle Modiste." They must have been amazed to enter the lobby, styled after the Hall of Mirrors at the Palace of Versailles in France, and to see the dome in the rotunda, which was designed after the Pantheon in Rome and contained one of the largest, hand-cut crystal chandeliers in the country. The theater was filled with sculptures, original art, elaborate drapes and furnishings, and for its patron's comfort, was fully air-conditioned.

The Rialto Square served the community for decades, entertaining the public with vaudeville and stage productions, ballet and opera, and served as a movie house during the classic years of early film. Over the years, it hosted performers like Andy Williams, Mitzi Gaynor, Red Skelton, Victor Borge, Liberace, and hundreds of others. It was also rumored to be one of Al Capone's favorite places to take in a show.

But the good times didn't last. Time took its toll on the magnificent theater and by the 1970s, it was faced with possible demolition. Before the wrecking ball was called in, though, the theater was rescued by the Rialto Square Arts Association, now called the Cultural Arts Council of the Joliet Area. With help from local businesses, funds were obtained from city, state, and federal officials and soon the theater was undergoing restoration. Actual work began in April 1980, and it re-opened the following year, restored to its former glory.

The Rialto Square Theatre continues to host plays, concerts, local shows, events, and meetings today and, according to the stories, is also home to a couple of resident ghosts. The most often encountered is a spectral woman who is thought to have once been an actress at the theater. She is described as being in her early twenties and very pretty. She has been seen around the theater by staff, customers, and workmen, especially after-hours when the building is not open to the public. Two other spirits, a man and a woman, are sometimes seen in the theater's balcony. Legend has it that they fell to their deaths in a tragic accident, and they simply won't move on. Most of the eerie happenings are accompanied by feelings of icy coldness, strange sounds, objects that move around by themselves, and an assortment of unexplained noises and footsteps.

The "Wilmington Spaceman"

Winding past Joliet on the pre-1940 alignment, Route 66 curves into Wilmington, a small town that is split in half by the Kankakee River. Founded in 1834 as a sawmill town on the river, an industrious businessman named Thomas Cox purchased 400 acres of land from the government and built a sawmill. He later added a corn cracker, a gristmill, a wool carding machine, and began calling the place "Cox's Mills." He soon saw his businesses being patronized from settlers from as far as 50 miles away.

In the spring of 1836, Cox laid out the town of "Winchester" and began to sell lots. One home, built from stone by Daniel McIntosh, still stands today, just south of Route 66. Another building constructed that same year also stands: the **Eagle Hotel**, which became a stagecoach stop. It was later used as a station on the "Underground Railroad" in the years before the Civil War. The hitching yard for the stage stop was located on Main Street, between Baltimore and Jackson. An early stage line connected Chicago with Pontiac.

In 1837, a post office was established and a year later, the name of the town was changed to Wilmington. Before long, new businesses arrived in town. A man named Elias Brown opened a second hotel, and Henry Brown opened a store. A public school was established in 1839.

When the Chicago and Alton Railroad arrived in town on July 4, 1854, it brought new prosperity with it. Land prices tripled and Wilmington was incorporated as a village. In the 1870s, several manufacturing companies started a flour mill, a butter and cheese factory, and a paper mill in town.

By the time Route 66 pushed through, Wilmington responded with services for the many travelers of the Mother Road. The Eagle Hotel, which had suffered greatly when the more luxurious Exchange Hotel was opened by Elias Brown in 1844, began to see an increase in business after Route 66 came along, but it didn't last for long. After the 1940 alignment, the Eagle was forced to convert to a boarding house to stay in business. Later in the 1940s, it converted to apartments, retaining small business in the storefront until 1982. The Wilmington Area Historical Society purchased the building that year and converted it into a museum. But a fire badly damaged the structure in 1990 and the building was abandoned.

By then, the city of Wilmington was considering demolition until it was purchased by Bill Scales, a man with a real estate and building background. He made plans to restore the hotel and re-open it as a restaurant, but soon ran into trouble. Counting on grants that never materialized to finish the project, it eventually fell apart and left the future of the historic structure in danger.

Another Route 66 icon in Wilmington, the **Mar Theatre**, opened in 1937 and is still in business, showing first-run films.

But the most famous landmark in town is undoubtedly the **Launching Pad Restaurant**, or perhaps more accurately, the "Gemini Giant" who stands outside.

Fiberglass giants, like the Wilmington Spaceman or the Bunyon's Hot Dog Man, are often referred to as "Muffler Men," because most of them were designed to hold automobile mufflers and were originally placed in front of service stations as retail attention-getters. As many of these businesses closed, though, or the giants were sold off, they soon became everything from lumberjacks to cowboys, spacemen, and more. The Gemini Giant is one of the "muffler men" who became much more in his second life.

It's an easy joke to say that the food at the Launching Pad is "out of this world" but in this case, it's true. Travelers will find some of the best burgers and fries on the Illinois stretch of the highway at this fun little spot. And watching over the roadside diner is the 28-foot-tall spaceman with a silver space helmet and shiny green body suit. He holds a rocket ship in his hands as he looks out over Route 66. The giant was erected in 1965 after original diner owners John and Bernice Korelc saw the fiberglass statue at a restaurant trade show in Chicago. The United States was heavily into the space program at the time and the Korelcs came up with the idea of the Launching Pad to go along with it.

John and Bernice had opened the "Dari Delite" in Wilmington in 1960, specializing in hot dogs and ice cream. With the arrival of the giant, they changed the name and added hamburgers, chili, and fries to the menu. They have since become famous for their tasty meals – and, of course, for their giant spaceman.

Rossi's Ballroom

Along the next stretch of road were once many of the first great landmarks of highway, including classic filling stations, motels, and diners. One of them is the **Polk-A-Dot Drive In**, which opened in 1956. It still serves burgers, fries, ice cream, and fried chicken to travelers in a Route 66 theme setting.

As the road eases into Braidwood, it reaches the site of what was once one of the great ballrooms of Route 66, **Rossi's Ballroom.**

Peter Rossi, Sr. was born in Busano, Italy in 1851. He spent his early life as a government employee, specializing in grain milling and macaroni manufacturing. In

The Rossi family outside of "Eagle Park"

1876, he opened his own noodle factory, but then two years later, decided to come to America. He settled in the small town of Braidwood, where he took work as a weight checker for the Crumby Mine before opening the town's first hardware store. In 1886, he returned to his first love and started the Peter Rossi Macaroni Factory on 4th Street. He later moved it to the old Broadbent Hotel on 1st Street, which would be adjacent to Route 66.

Peter's son, Stephen, was an industrious boy and earned money selling pocket knives door to door. When he grew up, he opened the Stephen Rossi Saloon on the south side of Main Street, west of the railroad tracks. "Spaghetti" Rossi – as he became known to his friends and customers – sold beer for a nickel a bucket and offered a free spaghetti lunch in the back room. In 1920, after Prohibition closed the bar, he opened a grocery store and filling station.

An odd occurrence happened outside the store one day that would permanently alter the fortunes of the Rossi family. Stephen's son, Peter, was playing in front of the shop when an eagle fell out of the sky. The bird was crippled and would never fly again. Peter decided to care for the bird, placed it in an iron cage, and displayed it in an empty lot next door to the store. The bird became a novelty, not only to locals, but to travelers who passed through town. Later, Peter moved the bird to the grounds where he would build his dance hall, which earned it the name "Eagle Park."

Peter christened Eagle Park in the middle 1920s, hanging his hopes on a clearing southwest of town. His younger brother, John, became his partner, and in 1927, Rossi's Ballroom at Eagle Park opened its dance floor.

The Rossi family built the ballroom in the midst of Prohibition, a time that has come to be considered the height of the dance hall era. Taverns and beer gardens were empty in those days and people wanted to get out and enjoy some music and do something fun. Although Peter installed a baseball diamond at the back of the property, Eagle Park was an elegant place. The stone façade of the hall was speckled with a colorful leaf motif, opening up with wide arches, and decorated with marble statues. Stone planters erupted with bright flowers and the grounds were filled with trees, giving the place an almost otherworldly quality after dark.

The hall was equipped with a huge stage and from the beginning, Rossi's ballroom booked the finest bands that Chicago had to offer. Peter, John, and Stephen routinely traveled to the city and engaged acts from the Music Corporation of America. Groups that were on their way from Chicago to St. Louis routinely stopped at Rossi's for a gig and traveling money. Among the performers were Danny Russo, Art Kassel's Radio Band, Clyde McCoy, the Jimmy Raschel Orchestra, Earl Gray and his Orchestra, and scores of others. On other evenings, bands from nearby Joliet filled the bill or "Amateur Night" provided locals the chance to entertain. Farmer's Dances offered free cider and doughnuts to those who attended in barnyard clothes and Maggie Rossi opened a lunchroom on the premises, attracting even more people to the park.

A large sphere with colored lights, taken from a building at the Chicago World's Fair, was placed over the dance floor and, on one occasion, sparkled over the most exhaustive exhibition of dancing that Will County had ever seen. In 1931, marathon dancers came to Rossi's Ballroom to plod their way through 10 days of footwork. The contest lasted an agonizing 252 ½ hours.

The ballroom was a booming place in the late 1920s and early 1930s. Peter and John built a service station on the property and then added cabins for overnight guests. After Peter's eagle died, they renamed the grounds Rossi's Park. Prohibition ended in 1933 and ballroom attendance began to dwindle. With people returning to taverns once more, the Rossi family turned to movies to keep things going. They began screening Open-Air Vitaphone movies, sometimes silent, and sometimes talking shows that were billed as the perfect way to beat the summer heat. Unwilling to lose customers to a dancehall, the nearby theater in Morris began billing itself as "70 degrees cool" and the Blackstone Theatre in Dwight upped the ante by booking "Simplicio and Lucio, the Siamese Twins and their Beautiful Dancing Brides!"

On Thanksgiving evening of 1933, Rossi's Ballroom took, what can be seen in hindsight as, one last shot to stay alive. That night, the park became the site of one of the biggest boxing matches to ever be put on in the area. Ladies were even invited. A dance after the bout started at 10:00 p.m. The program itself featured seven bouts of boxing, including a finale that pitted Russell Kamp (Kankakee's 135 lb. Wonder) against Otto Geisholt (Dwight's 135 lb. Fighting Dutchman). A warm-up bout featuring midget boxers kicked off the evening.

By the time that a fire broke out at Rossi's Ballroom in 1935, Peter had lowered the dancehall admission price to 10-cents. The fire started when a worker left a can of paint too close to a stove, burning the place to the ground.

But the blaze did not put Peter Rossi out of business. In 1939, Braidwood's alignment of Route 66 was re-routed and Peter opened a new service station that managed to get three-quarters of the local gas business. Next to it, the Rossi family opened a restaurant. Then, in 1950, they built the Rossi Motel. Not long after, Peter raised his last building, this time in Joliet. It was a restaurant, motel, and banquet room with an indoor pool that he called Autumn Acres. Today, it serves as the Joliet Elks Club.

After all of these years, everything that Peter built – aside from Eagle Park – still stands. Rossi's service station, café, and motel still exist in Braidwood along the old section of road at Route 66 and Highway 113, although they are now a tire store, a Laundromat, and the Braidwood Motel. They no longer resemble the buildings that they once were, but their mere existence shows the indelible mark that the Rossi family left on the small town they called home.

"Al Capone Drank Here"

After leaving Braidwood, Route 66 travels through Godley and Braceville before easing into Gardner. But just two miles before a traveler gets to town, they'll pass a site that became a place of legend.

Anyone with an interest in gangster lore can easily turn up literally dozens of places in Illinois, Indiana, Wisconsin, Iowa, and beyond that lay claim to being a former hideout of gangster Al Capone. In truth, though, Al would have never had time to take care of his business if he was spending his time driving to all of the places that claim he used to drink there. In some cases, though, the story is true and really was a spot where Al (or at least one of the Capone brothers) used to wet his whistle. The old **Riviera** roadhouse outside of Gardner was just one of those places.

The Riviera got its start in 1928, at the height of Prohibition, but that never stopped them from serving liquor. In those days, the establishment offered a restaurant upstairs and a tavern below, fully equipped with a peephole admittance policy and protected by local law enforcement officials who never let the law stand in the way of a cold brew.

The roadhouse was opened by James Girot, a businessman from nearby South Wilmington. He constructed the place by dragging an old payroll office from a defunct South Wilmington coal mine and an empty Gardner church to a wooded spot along Route 66. Girot hired some men to help him dig, called the resulting hole a cellar, and then nailed the two buildings together on top of it. During its heyday, it would offer food, drink, a zoo, picnic grounds, and a swimming hole, all with the picturesque Mazon River just a short distance away. At the height of its popularity, the restaurant served homemade Italian food, chicken, steak, and seafood.

The Riviera was a lucky place from the start. Jimmy Girot had traded away all of the stocks that he owned for the property – just months before the stock market crash. He skated through Prohibition, always at least one step ahead of the law. Even during

The old Riviera Road House – if Al didn't drink here, then he knew a lot of the guys that did!

the Depression, business never faltered and the family came through relatively unscathed.

The building itself (thanks to its rather odd construction) frequently changed. Dining rooms were moved around and changed so often that regular diners rarely sat in the same place twice. The old coal office safe became a walk–in cooler and Girot's chance meeting with a traveling artist resulted in a bunch of papier-mâché cave stalactites that decorated the ceiling above the bar for years. The building upstairs (which later became the kitchen) was originally the restaurant's eating area and those who walked in were treated to the best counter service in the county, courtesy of Mrs. Girot. Cowboy star Tom Mix had dinner there one evening, after parking his Rolls Royce in the parking lot, and on another occasion, Gene Kelly stopped in for a bite. At that time, the Riviera had installed some gas pumps out front, and Kelly pulled in to fill up his yellow and white convertible with gas. He told the attendant, "I'm on my way to Hollywood and I'm going to be famous. You'll see my name in lights some day!" He gave the attendant a dollar tip and danced across the parking lot to the restaurant. Years later, the attendant would admit that he thought the guy was nuts.

After Prohibition was repealed, the Riviera hit full stride. Orchestras drew crowds, the bar was packed every night, and frog legs became the place's most popular dish. Dinners began being served downstairs and meals were sent from kitchen to table on a dumbwaiter that Girot had installed between floors.

Organized crime reared its ugly head in the 1930s with territorial disputes over slot machines. Girot originally installed his own devices at the Riviera, but found them quickly replaced by slot machines owned by local political bigwigs. Those machines were in turn replaced by machines owned by area gangsters and so on – to the point that Girot had no idea who was running what. The Riviera was raided several times at night and all of the machines were busted into pieces. On other nights, mysterious men came in, hauled out the old machines and replaced them with new ones. Girot wisely chose to just stay out of the business altogether.

In 1950, Jimmy Girot died of smoke inhalation after battling a blaze that began as a kitchen grease fire. The place was temporarily closed but Girot had managed to save the place – at the expense of his life. His wife, Rose, remarried and the Riviera continued on. In 1972, Rose sold the place to longtime Chicago saloon owners, Bob and Peggy Kraft.

They carried on the Riviera tradition of good food and drinks and it survived for many more years as a sort of time capsule of yesterday – a weird conglomeration of architecture, light-up monkeys, stalactites, jazz music, toilets on stairs, and more.

But time finally caught up with the Riviera in June 2010 when a fatal fire burned the place to the ground. Another piece of Route 66 history was lost in a matter of moments.

Motoring to Dwight

As Route 66 travels along today next to the present-day interstate, it travels toward Dwight. When Route 66 was built in 1926, the town was actually bypassed, so most roadside businesses started on the highway a bit out of town. One of them, the **Ambler-Becker Texaco** station, was restored by the community in 2003. Another well-maintained local relic is the **Marathon Oil Station**, which was built in 1932. The **Carefree Motel**, once a Route 66 landmark in town, is now a private residence.

One of the oddities in town, pre-dating Route 66, is the former **Keeley Institute**, which was founded under the dubious auspices of Dr. Leslie Enright Keeley to treat alcoholics and drug addicts. The institute also had a connection to one of the most infamous killers in Illinois history, H.H. Holmes.

When the Keeley Institute was founded, Dr. Keeley owed the great success of his popular health regimen more to his self-promotion than to the proven virtues of his program. There is no evidence that his famous "Keeley Cure for Alcoholism" was based on any research or experimentation, but this didn't stop nearly a half-million Americans from subjecting themselves to his questionable methods.

Keeley was born in Ireland in 1834 and grew up in New York. He graduated from the Rush Medical School in Chicago and settled in Illinois after serving in the Union Army's medical corps during the Civil War. In 1880, he widely advertised that he had discovered a cure for alcoholism, which he found was caused by the alcoholic poisoning of the nerve cells. His "cure" consisted of a strict dietary regimen accompanied by regular injections of "bichloride of gold." Keeley never revealed the

The Keeley Institute "Lodge" at Dwight, Illinois

contents of this suspicious medicine, but historians believe that it was a concoction of gold salts and vegetable compounds. It was harmless, but certainly wouldn't have any effect on anyone's cravings for alcohol.

Shortly after making his announcement, he founded the first Keeley Institute, his sanitarium in Dwight. The institute was first introduced to Chicagoans in 1891, when the *Chicago Tribune* published a series of stories about his "Gold Cure." Before long, thousands of alcoholics who wanted to dry out were flocking to Dwight, eager to break the hold that liquor had on their lives. Keeley, of course, capitalized on the publicity, sending "graduates" of the Institute on lecture tours around the country. He also formed a Keeley League, whose dry members met in annual conventions, and he even organized the wives of former members into a women's auxiliary group. The Keeley Institute eventually had over 200 branches in the United States and Europe.

After Dr. Keeley died in 1900, interest faded and the organization, which had always drawn criticism, faded into national oblivion. By the late 1930s, most physicians believed that "drunkards are neurotics and cannot be cured by injections," and while the Institute hung on for a time, it was eventually shut down.

In 1892, though, the Keeley Institute was at the height of its popularity and the original sanitarium in Dwight was still attracting alcoholics by the thousands. Among the patients at that time was a man named Benjamin Pitezel, the accomplice of H.H. Holmes, a swindler and killer who was then in the process of constructing a "Murder Castle" in Chicago that would lead to the disappearance of an unknown number of people during the World's Columbian Exposition. Pitezel was an invaluable accomplice to Holmes' schemes, but a problem drinker. He shared many of his employer's darkest secrets and Holmes had begun to fear what stories Pitezel might

Benjamin Pitezel

tell if his alcoholism got the better of him. With this concern in mind, Holmes checked Pitezel into the Keeley Institute in the spring of 1892.

New patients who arrived at the Dwight institute were introduced into an open, informal environment where they were first offered as much alcohol as they could drink. The institute operated out of homes and hotels, using a spa-like atmosphere of peace and comfort. All patients received injections of "bichloride of gold" four times each day. They were also given other secret "tonics" to assist in their cure. To this day, no one knows for sure what made up the mysterious ingredients in the injections and tonics, but they were believed to include strychnine, alcohol, apomorphine, willow bark, ammonia, and atropine.

The patients received individually prescribed tonics every two hours throughout the day. When not being treated, the patients were free to stroll the grounds of the institute, as well as the streets of Dwight, which was then described as a "therapeutic community."

Ben Pitezel completed his four weeks at the Keeley Institute and returned to Chicago in early April 1892. He was a changed man, a walking testimonial to the truth of Dr. Keeley's elaborate claims. He was sober, happy, and healthier than he had been in years. But like the other "cured" alcoholics that eventually ruined Keeley's

Serial Killer H.H. Holmes

reputation, Ben found it impossible to stay sober. Within a few months of his stay in Dwight, Pitezel starting drinking again.

In spite of this, Holmes was not completely dismayed with the amount of money that he had spent on Ben's stay at the sanitarium. His friend had been sober for a time and, in addition, he brought back tales of a young woman who worked at the Institute whose name was Emeline Cigrand. According to Pitezel, she was a tall, beautifully-shaped blond, 24-years-old, and "as pure as the driven snow."

A native of Lafayette, Indiana, Emeline had worked for one year as a stenographer in the Tippecanoe County Recorder's office before going to work at the Keeley Institute in July 1891. She had been there for less than a year when Ben began his treatment at the facility. Amazed by her beauty, he struck up an acquaintance with her and, likely in an attempt to seduce her, did his best to impress her with his importance. He represented himself as a partner of Dr. H.H. Holmes, one of the most prominent businessmen in Chicago. Emeline, who had never been to Chicago or any other city larger than Lafayette, was suitably impressed with her new friend. Their relationship never went beyond the acquaintance stage, but when Ben returned to Chicago, he talked constantly about Emeline, and intrigued, Holmes decided to try and lure her to his city.

Holmes wrote to Emeline and offered her a job as his private secretary for $18 per week – more than double what she was being paid at the Keeley Institute. In May 1892, she left Dwight, and moved into a boarding house that was located about one block away from the Holmes' Castle.

Holmes immediately began trying to seduce her. He bought her flowers, took her on sight-seeing excursions around the city, and treated her to small gifts. Soon, he began taking her to the theater and treating her to expensive dinners at downtown restaurants. They spent Sunday afternoons bicycling in the park and strolling around the neighborhood. Holmes was the perfect gentleman, and Emeline could hardly believe that such a wonderful, charming man was so interested in her. Holmes' secret was knowing that a beautiful woman is easy to charm when she does not realize just how beautiful she is.

By the middle of summer, she was his new mistress, but little is known about their relationship. However, it is believed that by the fall of 1892, she expected him to marry her. In fact, it appears that Holmes allowed her to pass this happy news on to her relatives and friends, but he never allowed her to use his name. He insisted, because of legal complications, that she only give his name as "Robert E. Phelps."

That fall, Emeline wrote a number of letters to her old friends in Dwight that gushed about Phelps, her husband-to-be. She described him as wealthy, kind, generous, and the perfect gentleman. For their honeymoon, she told them, he was going to take her to Europe.

The plans for the wedding of Emeline and Holmes continued and a date for the private, civil ceremony was finally set for the first week in December. In November, Holmes came to Emeline with a dozen white envelopes and asked her to address them to her family and closest friends. He explained that he wanted to have formal marriage announcements printed and would mail them out immediately after their wedding. Emeline did what he asked and penned all of the addresses that same afternoon.

Emeline, of course, had no way of knowing the true purpose of Holmes' request and his reason for the envelopes would not become clear until later. By the time he asked her to address the envelopes, Holmes had already decided to kill her.

The "Murder Castle," where Emmeline Cigrand from the Keeley Institute in Dwight met her tragic end

Why Holmes wanted to kill the young woman remains a mystery. Aside from simple blood lust, it's possible that she knew too many of his secrets. She had been his private secretary for more than six months and there is much that she might have seen. There is also the possibility that Emeline had pressured Holmes into marrying her, threatening to leave him if he did not.

Not only did Holmes respond poorly to threats, he may have been afraid to let her out of his control with the things that she knew about him and his business dealings.

One afternoon in early December, Holmes was working in his office and he asked Emeline to get a document for him that was kept in the large walk-in vault next to his office. While she was looking for the paper that he needed, Holmes slammed shut the heavy door of the vault and carefully locked it. It's likely that he could hear her terrified screams, even through the thick steel of the vault's door, as they first raised in pitch and then slowly died away as the air inside of the chamber slowly ran out.

On December 17, 1892, Emeline's family and friends received her handwritten envelopes in the mail. Inside of each of them was a simple, plainly printed announcement that stated that Mr. Robert Phelps and Miss Emeline Cigrand had been married on December 17, 1892 in Chicago.

The newspaper in Lafayette, Indiana, had already announced Emeline's good news. Ten days earlier, the newspaper had printed the following item, under a headline that read, "Miss Cigrand Weds Robert E. Phelps:"

The bride, after completing her education, was employed as a stenographer in the County Recorder's office. From there she went to Dwight, and from there to Chicago, where she met her fate. She is a lady of great intelligence and has a charming manner and handsome appearance. She is a lady of refinement and possesses a character that is strong and pure. Her many friends see that she has exercised good judgment in selecting a husband and will heartily congratulate her.

Emeline Cigrand had certainly "met her fate" in Chicago, but not in the way that the writer of the newspaper article had in mind.

It is impossible to say that Emeline was already dead by the time the newspaper story was printed, but most likely she was. The air in the vault had to have run out days before. In any event, Emeline Cigrand was never seen again – not alive anyway.

A few weeks after her disappearance, though, the LaSalle Medical School became the owner of a new articulated female skeleton, which had been acquired from Dr. H.H. Holmes.

Odell and the Cayuga "Meramec Caverns" Barn

Leaving Dwight, travelers turned left onto Route 66 and continued to the southwest toward Odell. On West Street, across from St. Paul's Church, is the entrance to a 1937 pedestrian tunnel that ran beneath the highway and was known locally as the **"Odell Subway."** In the 1930s, traffic was so heavy on Route 66 that it was nearly impossible to cross the road. The situation was particularly hazardous since St. Paul's Church and School were on one corner and

children needed to get from one side to the other – so the town built a tunnel that went under the highway. Of course, these days, one can stand in the middle of the street for quite some time before a car comes along. It's an unpleasant reminder of how important Route 66 was as a highway and the effect that its loss has had on the small towns that it passed through.

The entrance to the tunnel was filled up during the 1950s, but the first three steps and the railing were replaced in the spring of 2006 by the Illinois Route 66 Association.

Another location of note is the **Odell Station**, an old restored Sinclair gas station on West Street. The award-winning station is an information center today, but it was built in 1932 and served highway travelers until it closed in 1975.

A short distance from Pontiac is the small, forgettable town of Cayuga, which is surrounded by fields, barns, fields, and more fields. But there is a small hidden treasure here of Route 66's glory days – a restored **Meramec Caverns barn**.

Meramec Caverns, a tourist trap located just off Route 66 in Missouri, was owned by Lester Dill, a consummate showman who was always on the lookout for new ways to promote his cave. Besides the millions of bumper stickers attached to cars and the brochures handed out to tourists, Lester promoted the cave by posting signs, mostly painted on barns, along highways in as many as 40 states. Lester and his crew scoured the countryside, especially along Route 66, searching for just the right barns for their eye-catching signs. To entice the farmers who owned the barns, Lester handed out watches, pints of whiskey, and free passes to the cave.

Today, Cayuga and Hamel are the only two Illinois towns along Route 66 with Meramec barns.

The Talking Crow of the Log Cabin Inn

"Nevermore," said the raven in Edgar All Poe's famous poem, but, of course, crows can't actually talk – or can they? According to the lore of Route 66, there really was a talking crow that lived at the famous Old Cabin Inn in Pontiac.

Traveling on south, the forgotten highway passes a number of fading locations that have become a part of Route 66 lore. One of them is the **Log Cabin Inn**, a restaurant that was originally constructed from cedar telephone poles in 1926. But the story of the Inn – as well as the Talking Crow – began years before when Victor Seloti and his wife, Rosa, came to America from Italy. Victor went to work in the coal mines and raised a flock of five boys and three girls. Two of them, Joe and his younger brother, Victor, Jr. or "Babe", turned to the highway to make their living. In 1926, they opened a service station on a patch of road that became Route 66. Next to the station, they built their café from telephone poles and called it the Log Cabin Inn.

While Babe took care of the filling station, Joe cooked at the café. Barbeque became the house specialty and Joe personally manned the barbeque pit, an

enormous container of charcoal and flame that was enclosed in a small shed. Smokehouse windows offered a view of the spitted ham and beef hunks as they slowly turned inside. And on the back of the smokehouse, Joe fashioned a cage for his pet talking crow.

Throughout his life, Joe had been fascinated with anything that flew. He loved speed just as much, and as a teenager had worked with the Ed A. Evans Shows as a motorcycle stuntman. He spent World War I scootering through Germany, and when he came home, he bought a French taxi cab that had transported troops to the first battle of Marne in 1914. In the age of aviation, he bought a Waco 10 bi-plane, christened it *Miss Pontiac,* and parked it on an area farm while be built Pontiac's first airport. The new airport was on Route 66, about a mile north of the Log Cabin Inn. The hangar cost him $2,000 and he covered its 4,200-foot runway with shale and oiled and compacted cinders.

In 1931, when the Forrest Bank was robbed, the sheriff of Livingston County paid Joe $20 to chase down the robber by air. On Sundays, he offered airplane rides for $1 each -- $2 for a sightseeing tour of Pontiac. Airport classes were offered in navigation and meteorology and pilots were on hand to teach students to fly. Periodically, Joe organized the Pontiac Air Circus, which was held in and over a tourist park that was located next to the Log Cabin Inn. The circus included parachute stunts, balloon burstings, bomb drops, a 25-mile race, and daredevils of the air, who defied death at 5,000 feet.

Joe and his friends flew over Pontiac and other Illinois towns for years. In spite of their early equipment, aerial mishaps were few. On one occasion, Art Carnahan, a pilot from Bloomington, dove to save jumper Florence Palmer Davis after her chute caught on the tail of his plane and tore in two. Carnahan hoped to wrap the cords of her chute in his wing struts, but Miss Davis landed in an oat field and sank more than a foot into the ground.

The Pontiac Air Circus continued into the 1930s and only came to an end when the Pontiac airport burned down. The fire destroyed Joe's *Miss Pontiac* and a Curtiss J1 Robin that was owned by his brother, Babe.

Joe made up for his loss with his talking pet crow.

No one ever remembered who discovered the Talking Crow of Pontiac but it was given to Joe as a gift by an elderly judge. Joe then went to great pains to teach the bird to talk – and not just too mimic, people remembered, the crow had an actual working vocabulary. It could carry on a conversation, they insisted, and was most verbal when Joe was cooking because it wanted something to eat. The Talking Crow was most verbal during the summer months, when he had a bigger audience. When the weather was nice, beer drinkers sat outside at tables behind the Log Cabin Inn and were happy to offer the bird a drink when he asked for one. He developed a taste for malt liquor and would entertain – and sometimes frighten – some drinkers when he talked to them and occasionally called them names.

The Talking Crow became a popular roadside personality. Customers, who stopped for a bite to eat or to fill up with gas, often heard him squawking and lingered to see what was going on. Word spread up and down Route 66 and new people stopped by on a regular basis. We'll never know just how much business the Talking Crow brought to the Log Cabin Inn over the years, but it was undoubtedly a lot. He continued talking until old age finally stilled his beak.

The Log Cabin Inn marched on after the loss of its major tourist attraction. The path of Route 66 once ran on the eastern side of the restaurant next to the railroad tracks but when it was re-aligned to the western side, the building was jacked up and rotated with horses so that the front door once again faced the road. The rotation was such a major event that half the town showed up to watch. This has been the only major addition to the building, aside from a new front entry that was added in 1990, since the 1930s.

Today, the place (known now as the Old Log Cabin) still boasts good food and it has an old-time feel to it that can make you forget that time has passed and that Route 66 is no longer the main highway through Illinois.

Route 66 in Pontiac

Like many other small towns, Pontiac has embraced its connection to Route 66. A **Route 66 Museum** opened in an old firehouse in town in 2004 and draws a daily stream of travelers. Next to the museum is the old sign from the former **Wishing Well Motel**, a Route 66 icon.

On the back side of the museum is a massive Route 66 shield that was left behind in Pontiac in 2009 by an international group of muralists and sign painters known as the "Walldogs." Over four days, the more than 150 artists adorned the downtown Pontiac area with 18 new murals. The city's collection of wall art includes images honoring the old *Weekly Sentinel* newspaper, the Pontiac Fire Department, the defunct Bloomington, Pontiac & Joliet Interurban Railroad, and Route 66. The group took their name from sign painters who moved from town to town painting outdoor advertising and "working like dogs." The famed **Pontiac Murals** are a must-see for anyone passing through Pontiac.

Lost in Chenoa

The town of Chenoa had a quiet beginning in 1854, when Matthew T. Scott bought thousands of acres of empty prairie land in the area. He proceeded to lay out lots and streets for this then-unnamed town because he knew it would be prime property at the intersection of the Toledo, Peoria & Western and the Chicago & Alton Railroads. The town's first building was the Farmer's Store, built in 1855 by J.B. Lenney, who is often referred to as the "Father of Chenoa." In time, the settlement became Chenoa, a Native American word meaning "white dove."

Chenoa saw several routings of Route 66 over the years, including a four-lane version with a railroad crossing that caused long delays for travelers going both directions. The town also catered to travelers. During the highway's heyday, gas stations, motels, and cafes lined the streets.

Land for a tourist park, at first simply known as "Tourist Park," and then **Red Bird Park**, was donated by Scott. The park was indicative of Chenoa's early desire to attract travelers. When Route 66 opened, tourists were allowed to camp free of charge in the park until the land was leased and a tourist court was built on the property.

Many vintage structures remain in Chenoa, including a building that has housed a pharmacy since 1889. One building that remains once housed a highway icon called **Steve's Café**, which closed down in 1997. But Steve's was not the first business to call it home. Built in 1918, it was first called Wahls Café, but the name was changed a few years later. Steve's Café, reputedly known for "the finest steaks between Chicago and St. Louis," opened in 1924 as a garage, gas station, and lunchroom built by Tom and Charles Elliott. Paul and Ada Lanterman bought it

Steve's Café, offering the "Finest Steaks Between Chicago and St. Louis."

87

a year later. Elmer and Orville Wahls purchased it in the 1930s, and later owners expanded the restaurant.

The Café was one of the first to have air conditioning outside the Chicago area. The first air conditioning equipment, made by Williams Oil-O-Matic Ice Cold Air, was installed in the restaurant and a large sign was put up on the roof. Every time a new model was introduced by Williams, it was brought to Chenoa to replace the older model and to test it as new equipment. On hot days it was not unusual to see people lined up between the front door and the counter, trying to keep cool.

It had a juke box, which made it popular for teenagers from Chenoa and surrounding towns who, for the price of a 10-cent coke, could spend the evening dancing to Glen Miller, Harry James, and other Big Bands. There were white linen tablecloths and napkins, the waiters and waitresses had a dress code, and Steve Wilcox was the day chef.

In 1942, Steve took took over the restaurant. Never closing – it was said there was no key for the door – Steve's became known for its steaks and homemade pies. Politicians called ahead to order pies to take with them on their way to and from Springfield. Steve catered to nighttime truck drivers, but it was not uncommon to see the Governor, Senators, and Representatives eating there.

The Texaco station that was attached to the café closed down in 1975 and that part of the building was turned into a bar called the Red Bird Lounge, named for the Chenoa high school sports teams. Later that same year, Ken and Peg Sipe took over the building and continued to serve home-cooked meals and "World Famous Pies." During the summer, Steve's sponsored Friday-night fish fries at the local park.

Peg desperately tried to keep the café open after Ken was killed in an auto accident, but eventually had to close the doors in 1997. Since the restaurant closed down, it has been used as an antique store and used-car lot, but for many locals and long-time travelers, memories remain of the "finest steaks between Chicago and St. Louis" and "World Famous Pies."

Lexington's "Memory Lane"

About 10 miles down the road from Chenoa, travelers find Lexington, one of Illinois' oldest towns. Named for the Massachusetts town where an early battle in the Revolutionary War took place, it was founded in 1828. During the heyday of Route 66, the town was bustling with nine service stations and numerous diners and motels. Unfortunately, a June 1970 fire destroyed or damaged many of its businesses and buildings.

Although it's a quite small town these days, it continues to celebrate its Route 66 heritage with an old Art Deco sign pointing the way into Lexington. The neon dates back to 1949, but has been restored to greet Route 66 travelers again. In addition,

Lexington has also taken a one-mile stretch of old Route 66 and turned it into an interpretive walking trail called "Memory Lane." The walking trail uses the original pavement and features road signs, billboards, and even old Burma-Shave signs.

Although few people today have heard of Burma-Shave, during the golden years of Route 66, it was one of the most famous products in the county – and it owed its popularity to its clever brand of advertising.

Burma-Shave was a brand of shaving cream that sold from 1925 to 1966. The company became notable for its clever advertising campaigns, which included rhymes that were posted along America's highways. Typically, they erected six signs in a row, with each of the first five containing a line of verse and the sixth displaying the brand's name.

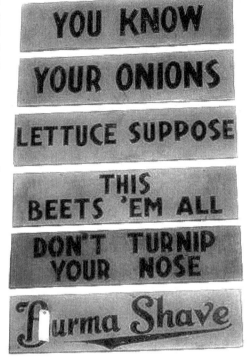

Burma-Shave was the second brushless shaving cream to be manufactured and the first one to become a success. It was sold by Clinton Odell, and his sons, Leonard and Allan. They started off making a liniment, but were not making enough money. They wanted a product that people would use every day. A wholesale drug company told Odell about Lloyd's Euxesis, a British product that was the first brushless shaving cream. It was of poor quality and didn't sell well. So, Odell hired a chemist to produce a quality shaving cream, and after 43 attempts, Burma-Shave was born.

To market the new product, Odell came up with the idea of multiple signs. Allan Odell recalled taking a trip when he saw signs that read Gas, Oil, Restrooms, and finally a sign pointing to a roadside service station. The signs compelled people to read the entire series and kept a driver's attention longer than a traditional billboard. Although Clinton Odell wasn't crazy about the idea, he gave Allan $200 to give it a try.

In the fall of 1925, the first sets of Burma-Shave signs were erected on two highways leading out of Minneapolis. Sales rose dramatically in the area, and soon the signs were appearing across the country. The next year, Allan and Leonard spent $25,000 on signs alone. Orders poured in, and sales for the year hit $68,000.

The signs began appearing all over the country and became one of advertising history's greatest gimmicks. They drew attention from travelers, who were curious to discover the punchline. Within a decade, Burma-Shave was the second-most popular brand of shaving cream in the United States.

The first set of slogans was written by the Odell brothers; however, they soon started an annual contest for people to submit their own rhymes. With winners receiving a $100 prize, thousands of entries flooded the Burma-Shave offices.

At the height of their popularity, there were about 7,000 Burma-Shave signs stretching across America. They became such an icon to early travelers that families eagerly waited for the next set to come along.

Burma-Shave sales rose to about $6 million by 1947, but sales were stagnant after that and, finally, began to fall. Various reasons caused the drop, the main one being urban growth. Typically Burma-Shave signs were posted on rural highways, and higher speed limits caused the signs to be ignored. Subsequently, the company was sold to Gillette in 1963, and the bigger company decided that the signs were a silly idea and they vanished from history.

By 1966, the signs had all disappeared from America's highways. A few ended up in museums, including a couple of sets that are on display at the Smithsonian Institution, one of which reads:

Within this vale
Of toil and sin
Your head grows bald
But not your chin
Burma-Shave

Towanda Meadows

Every one of us who has traveled along old Route 66 north of Bloomington, Illinois, has seen the house, nestled eerily in the cornfields just off in the distance, and every one of us has wondered about it, just as travelers on the Mother Road likely did decades ago. The brick Italianate mansion seems out of place on the Illinois prairie, looking mournfully toward a highway and a railroad line that seems to have passed it by, leaving it stranded in the distant past. It has been crumbling there for many years – lost, abandoned, seemingly forgotten, and some say, haunted by tragedies of yesterday. It is a house of unrealized dreams, great fortune and premature death, strangely suited to the shadowy corners of Illinois.

Although it's been seen by generations of Route 66 travelers, north of Bloomington, few know the heartbreaking history of Towanda Meadows

The grand house, which came to be known as Towanda Meadows, was built in 1874–1875 by William R. Duncan, a pioneer farmer and stock-raiser who came to Illinois in 1863. When he erected the mansion, it was said that he purposely set out to make it so impressive that it would be noticed by travelers between St. Louis and Chicago. He attained his objective, building an Italianate mansion with six fireplaces, a winding staircase with hard-carved walnut spindles, and walls that were more than a foot thick. But he was destined to only enjoy the house for a short time. Not long after it was completed, death and tragedy came calling.

Duncan had been born in December 1818 in Clark County, Kentucky. Raised by wealthy parents in the slave state of Kentucky, William became rich himself after his father's death in 1836. Under the terms of his father's will, the family's slaves were set free, which convinced William to remain loyal to the Union when the Civil War began to rage years later. Eventually, the political division in his home state over slavery caused him to move north to Illinois.

William had a brother, Thomas, and two sisters, Elizabeth and Sally. In their father's will, Sally was described as being unable to care for herself, suggesting that she was mentally ill. If so, it was a condition that would return to haunt the family in

1882, when William's second son, James, was declared insane by a McLean County, Illinois court and sent to the Jacksonville State Hospital.

William married his first wife, Nancy Redmon, in 1835 when both of them were only 17-years-old. She died young in 1848, and William married a second time in 1849. His second wife was a widow, Mary Chorn Quisenberry, and they would have four children, Nannie, Henry, James, and Mary Elizabeth.

In late October 1863, William sold off a large portion of his short-horn cattle herd and moved his family to Illinois. They traveled by train and ended up in Towanda, likely renting a home owned by Nathan Sunderland on property that Duncan eventually purchased in December 1865. But the start of the family's happy life in Illinois was shattered by the death of Mary Duncan on February 23, 1864. William was devastated by the loss of another beloved wife and the children were heartbroken, especially Mary Elizabeth, who was only three-years-old at the time.

Late in 1864, William, now only 45 and widowed twice, traveled back to Kentucky and married his third wife, Sarah Ann Bean, age 29. Sarah was wealthy in her own right and the two of them signed a pre-nuptial agreement of sorts, giving her control over her own money, which was unusual at the time.

The newlyweds returned to Illinois and William began building his cattle business and amassing a fortune. He brought a number of experienced cattlemen with him from Kentucky, including a number of free black men, who had worked for his family for years. In 1866, he became a member of the Advisory Committee of the McLean County Agricultural Society and was appointed to audit the treasurer's books. In some of the minutes of the society meetings, Duncan is referred to as introducing and cultivating some of the finest breeds of foreign cattle to the area. He had formed an alliance with a number of other forward-thinking farmers in the region, who advocated the improvement of crops and livestock through selective breeding and other "scientific means."

Tragedy visited the Duncan family again on June 16, 1868, when Henry, age 12, drowned in a pond on the family's property. He was buried next to his mother in a small home plot, although the bodies were later moved to Evergreen Cemetery in Bloomington. During his son's funeral, a grieving William had the grave of his second wife, Mary, opened up so that he could say goodbye to her one last time.

A few years later, construction was started on Duncan's three-story mansion, Towanda Meadows. The house was unlike anything that had been seen in the area before, and locals came from far and wide to watch the construction take place and to marvel at the unusual elements of the house. William welcomed them with open arms, which bolstered his reputation as a kind and generous man. Most regarded him as one of the esteemed residents of the county, and he was in great demand as a speaker for the State Agricultural Society and at the meeting of the National Agricultural Society, which was held in Cincinnati in September 1875.

Towanda Meadows was completed in 1875 but, sadly, William lived in the house for less than a year before he died in October 1876 at the age of only 57. At the time of his death, he was returning home from the State Fair, which was held in Ottawa, Illinois, that fall. He had been depressed for some time, following the death of his last remaining sister, Elizabeth, who had died in Clinton a short time before. Many blamed his melancholy for the fact that he was unable to shake off a severe cold that he contracted at the fair. After becoming ill in Ottawa, he was put to bed at the home of his friend Abner Strawn and remained there for several days. Feeling better, he departed for Towanda, but only made it as far as Normal before he collapsed. He was taken to the home of relatives and died with his third wife, Sarah, by his side.

Duncan never saw his beloved Towanda Meadows again, but he was buried on the property next to Mary and Henry until Sarah had their remains exhumed and moved to Evergreen Cemetery.

Sarah remained at the farm for a time with eight children, five of her own and three of William and Mary's. They had little time to mourn as drama, tragedy, and death continued to plague the family. Soon after the death of her father, Nannie, William's oldest daughter with wife Mary, filed a lawsuit on behalf of herself and her siblings against Sarah and her children. She was seeking a portion of her father's substantial estate and the courts divided the land into parcels. Nannie later became a schoolteacher and married Franklin Barnes, a successful farmer, in 1878. They had a daughter, Lucy, who was born in 1880.

Like other members of her family, Nannie was doomed to an early grave. In 1884, her health began to fail (although it's not listed in the records, she likely suffered from tuberculosis) and Franklin, very concerned about his wife, sold his farm and moved his wife and daughter to Pomona, California. He hoped that the mild climate might make her better. Unfortunately, California didn't turn out to be beneficial for Nannie. She continued to decline and as she neared death, she told her husband that she wanted to return to Illinois to live out her final days. She passed away while they were on their way home and she was buried in Evergreen Cemetery.

Tragedy struck the family again in 1896 when Nannie's daughter, Lucy, also died from consumption in her father's Bloomington home. Lucy died on the day before her 16th birthday. Her father, Franklin, later moved to Towanda and served as the town's postmaster for a number of years. He remarried and died in November 1905.

William and Mary's third child, James, was only 18 when his father died in 1876. Nelson Jones was appointed by the court as his guardian and James lived each winter in Texas, where he raised horses and brought them back to Illinois for sale. In September 1878, James, age 21, married Flora Dillon of Bloomington and his guardianship by his father's friend, Nelson Jones, was settled. In February 1880, James and Flora had a son, Levi William, and moved into a home next door to his sister Nannie and her husband, Franklin. James worked hard to improve the farm and was soon worth quite a bit of money. He began importing horses from overseas and establishing himself as a successful dealer. A second son, Floyd, was born in November 1882.

But tragedy touched James and his family, as well. In 1883, James, Flora, Flora's sister, Ida Dillon Harding, and other members of the Dillon family, traveled to France for both business and pleasure. James planned to arrange the purchase of a number of horses and to see the sights with his family. As they were preparing to make their way back across the Atlantic, Ida became seriously ill and was unable to depart for the return trip. James and Flora and another couple made the trip so they could care for the horses, but three others remained behind with Ida, who died a few days later.

This was the start of a terrible time for James and his family. In three years, James went from a prominent businessman to a severely depressed and mentally-ill young man. His malady struck in his late 20s and was likely an onset of bipolar disorder, for which no diagnosis existed at the time. On July 7, 1886, Flora's father, Levi Dillon, filed a petition with the court indicating that James, then age 28, was insane and asked the authorities to investigate the allegation. A warrant was issued for his arrest and James was taken to the Illinois State Hospital for the Insane in Jacksonville. He was judged unfit to manage his personal estate of more than $20,000, and while Levi was first appointed to be his conservator, he was later removed and a new one was appointed. There was a lot of controversy about what happened to James' money while he was in and out of the insane asylum, but accusations were made against Levi Dillon, and when James was eventually released from the hospital, his remaining property was restored. James and Flora divorced in December 1891. Their older son was raised by James, and Floyd was cared for by Flora. What happened to James after his release from the hospital and subsequent divorce is largely unknown. In 1891, he appeared in public records working at a livery stable in Bloomington and soon after, vanished from history.

Mary Elizabeth was William and Mary's youngest child and she was in Kentucky when her father died. She had been living there with her uncle, James Chorn, and his family. In 1881, she was in Illinois visiting friends and family when she met Ellis Dillon, Flora's brother. The two fell in love and despite being two years older than Ellis, Mary Elizabeth married him in December 1883.

The couple later moved to Wisconsin and Ellis enrolled at the University of Madison for training to become an electrical engineer. They had four children, Carl, Lula, Helen, and Dorotha and, apparently, lived a happy life for many years. Then, in September 1918, Mary was granted a divorce from her husband on the grounds of cruel and inhuman treatment. According to her testimony, she and Ellis had lived together in the same house for five years but never ate together or slept together and Ellis refused to speak to her. She was unable to cite a cause for this treatment. Ellis was ordered to pay her $50 per month in alimony while she remained unmarried. Ellis later moved to Montana, but what became of Mary Elizabeth is a mystery.

After William's death, Sarah and her five children with William, Asa, William, Eli, Harrison, and John, remained at Towanda Meadows for a short time before returning to Kentucky. Sarah eventually died of pneumonia in February 1922 at the age of 86. She never remarried.

In 1882, Sarah sold Towanda Meadows and her remaining 100 acres to F.M. Jones, who later sold it to D.W. Kraft of Normal. At the time of his death, it was inherited by his daughter, Helen. Over the years, the old mansion had gone through a succession of owners, and during the twentieth century, tenants occupied the grand old home. The fireplaces were bricked up, the second and third story windows shuttered, and it was left to decline in the wind and weather of the Illinois prairie.

It was the tenants who lived in the house who told strange tales of ghosts and lingering memories. Many of them spoke of footsteps on the stairs and in the hallways, whispers, sounds of a woman weeping, and knocking at the front door during the wee hours of the night. Every one of these weird happenings can be directly tied to the mansion's tragic past with a woman crying for a lost child and the fateful knock that summoned Sarah to the bedside of her dying husband. History has left an impression on this creaking old place and seems to be replaying itself over and over again.

One former resident of the house once related his own encounter with a spectral woman on the second floor. He was only a boy at the time but clearly remembered exploring the upper floors of the house when he was living there with his family. In one of the closed-off bedrooms, he clearly saw a woman standing and gazing out of the window. When he sharply inhaled at the sight, the woman quickly turned around and then vanished in front of his eyes. He never forgot the incident, but who the woman might have been in unknown. Despite the efforts of local researchers, no Duncan family photographs have ever turned up.

Do phantoms still linger at Towanda Meadows? No one can say for sure. For years, it has been in the hands of absentee landlords and the unforgiving elements, but efforts to restore it may someday succeed and life may be breathed back into the glorious home of William Duncan once again. Will restoration work manage to bring the spirits "back to life"? Only time will tell.

Motoring into Normal and Bloomington

The next stop down the line on Route 66 is the town of Normal, but travelers always had to watch very closely to be able to tell where Normal ended and Bloomington began.

In 1854, the town of North Bloomington was laid out in an area that was commonly known as "the Junction," the intersection of the Illinois Central and Chicago and Alton Railroads. Although it was platted, the town was not developed until three years later, when Jesse Fell began to build in an area that was northeast of the original plat. Fell is referred to as the founding father of Normal and he soon became a leader in the community's development.

In 1857, Governor William Bissell signed a bill to create a "normal" school, a term that was then used for schools that were established as teacher's colleges. Jesse Fell took up the campaign for Bloomington and managed to obtain financial backing for the school. Abraham Lincoln, who was still an attorney at that time, drew up the bond guaranteeing that Bloomington citizens would fulfill their financial commitments. The college was named Normal University and it held its first classes in Bloomington while the campus was being constructed north of town. Old Main, the original university building, was completed in 1861. Four years later, the town was officially incorporated as Normal.

In the 1920s, buses began to replace the streetcar lines in Normal and Bloomington, and when Route 66 was designated, numerous businesses began springing up to accommodate the many travelers on the new road.

Gus and Edith Belt attached a dining room to the side of their Shell gas station and called it "Shell's Chicken." However, they quickly realized that Central Illinois already had an abundance of chicken restaurants and wanted to do something different. With a little help from friends, Gus began to sell a unique product to the many travelers of Route 66: the steak burger. In February 1934, the very first **Steak-n-Shake** was opened in Normal, Illinois.

Normal continued to grow, and in 1950, Normal University became Illinois State University, no longer serving just as a teacher's college. Along Route 66 in Normal,

the highway passes by other landmarks of the road, including a number of one-time service stations that have today been turned into private homes. The historic **Normal Theater** is located at 209 North Street and is an Art Deco theater that was built in 1937. After showing films for more than 50 years, it closed down in 1990 and then re-opened in 1993 after being purchased by the city. Fully restored, it's now a showcase of 1930s cinema.

Route 66 seamlessly enters Bloomington, a town that was founded decades before Normal was started. In its early years, the settlement was formed near a large grove of trees used by the Kickapoo Indians before white settlers arrived. When they began to build on the land, they called the trees "Blooming Grove," due to the many flowers in the area. The name was later changed to Bloomington.

When Route 66 came through town in 1926, along the Chicago and Alton Railroad corridor, scores of businesses appeared along the highway and in Bloomington's downtown district. Unfortunately, when Interstate 55 replaced the highway, bypassing Bloomington and skirting the west side of town, many of the historic businesses vanished. But memories remain…

Two of Bloomington's most famous eateries are phantoms from the past: **Streid's Motel and Restaurant** and the **Cotton's Village Inn**. There are few records that speak about Streid's, but the once-famous spot offered gas, lodging, and its "renowned charcoal broiler and rotisserie." Postcards that still exist from the spot called the rooms "ultra-modern."

There is a lot of confusion about Cotton's Village Inn, or at least about its location. It was not in the 400 block of North Main Street, it was actually a unique restaurant that was in the basement of a building at the northeast corner of Main and Monroe. The covered outside steps that led down to the restaurant are still there and they took diners into a small eatery with white-washed walls that were decorated with hand-painted ivy and Bavarian scenes. The menu had simple daily specials crammed onto a single typewritten sheet with humorous thoughts and sayings added along the edges. Owner Cotton McNabey himself might show guests to a table in one of the semi-private alcoves (former coal bins) under the sidewalk. It closed down in 1976, and while it re-opened as Halfpenny's Village Inn, it didn't last long.

Another eatery from the Route 66 era has survived, though. Located at 116 East Market Street is **Lucca Grill**, which was established in 1936 by brothers Fred and John Baldini, who named it after their hometown in Italy. It's known today as the "oldest continuously operating pizzeria in the Midwest."

Bloomington is also home to **Beer Nuts**, which had their origins in 1937, when Edward Shirk became the manager of Caramel Crisp, a confectionary on North Robinson Street. The store specialized in "redskins," or glazed peanuts. He changed the name to Beer Nuts in 1953 and began selling packaged nuts through the National

Liquor Store in Bloomington. The current factory opened in 1973 and includes a popular store that sells the trademark nuts as well as souvenirs of all kinds.

A Service Station Like No Other

One of Bloomington's greatest Route 66 icons was the **Sprague Super Service Station** at 305 East Pine Street. It opened in 1931 and served travelers for more than four decades, finally closing in 1976. At the time the station was built, most of the country's gas stations were affiliated with major oil companies like Phillips, or Texaco. Architects for these companies provided functional but standard station designs.   Drivers could glance at a white building with three green stripes, for example, and know at once that because of the recognizable icon it was a Texaco station.

When William Sprague built his station in 1931, there certainly wasn't another one like it in Illinois

But when William Sprague built his station, he took a different approach. A building contractor, he constructed his large, unique, brick, Tudor Revival gas station using high-quality materials and craftsmanship. The result, Sprague's Super Service, appeared to be part manor house and part gas station, and sold City Service gas. Steep gables made up the broad, red roofline and substantial brick columns supported the canopy. It caught the attention of travelers on Route 66 who, after filling their tanks, stepped inside to eat at Sprague's restaurant. There was also a garage for auto repairs. Upstairs, a spacious apartment, complete with a sun room over the gas pump canopy, housed Sprague and his family.   A second upstairs apartment housed the station attendant.

Throughout the 1930s, most people passing through Bloomington–Normal from north or south traveled Pine Street. There was plenty of business to support both Sprague's and, just across the street, **Snedaker's Station and Bill's Cabins**, another 1930s service station jointly administered with a lodging operation. But the heyday of two lanes of traffic on Pine Street was short-lived. In 1940, the new four-lane Route 66 opened around the east side of Bloomington, pulling traffic away from Pine Street. Some traffic still took the Business Route 66 into Normal, so the station remained open, but the property changed hands many times as each new owner sought business opportunities with more appeal for local clientele.

The station was vacant for part of World War II when gasoline and repair parts were scarce. Beginning in 1946, immediately after the war, the owners still sold gas and food, but they added other enterprises as well. Over the years, Joe's Welding and Boiler Company, Corn Belt Manufacturing, Yellow Cab, and Avis Rent-a-Car occupied space at Sprague's. And so did a bridal store, cake gallery, and catering operation. The gas pumps were finally removed in 1979.

The present owner purchased the place in 2006 and two years later, it was listed in the National Register of Historic Places. As of this writing, plans are underway to rehabilitate the lower level of the station for use as a visitor center, restaurant, soda fountain, and meeting and performance space. If it all works out, a little Route 66 history – and the only Tudor Revival canopy gas station in Illinois – will be saved for the future.

Dorothy's Grave

Somewhere over the rainbow -- or at least off of Route 66 in Bloomington -- is the Evergreen Memorial Cemetery. In the depths of the aging graveyard rests the worn and weather-beaten grave of a little girl named Dorothy Louise Gage. She was born on June 11, 1898 to Sophie Jewel and Thomas Clarkson Gage, the brother of Maud Gage Baum, who was the wife of a novelist named L. Frank Baum. He is remembered today as the creator of a wonderful series of books about a magical place named Oz.

The grave of little Dorothy Gage, the namesake of L. Frank Baum's heroine in "The Wizard of Oz"

Maud and her husband had four sons but had always longed for a little girl. For this reason, she was thrilled when Dorothy was born and spent as much time as a doting aunt as she possibly could.

She often traveled back and forth to Bloomington from Chicago, where she and her family were living, especially after Dorothy became ill later that same year. Then tragically, on November 11, five months to the day from when she was born, Dorothy died. The cemetery records state that the cause of her death was "congestion of the brain." When Maud received the news, she traveled back to Bloomington to attend the baby's funeral. She was overcome with grief and when she returned home, she required medical attention. "Dorothy was a beautiful baby," Maud wrote to her sister. "I could have taken her for my very own and loved her devotely."

At the time of the little girl's death, L. Frank Baum was putting the finishing touches on the story that his wife had been urging him to put to paper for so long, a tale called *The Wonderful Wizard of Oz*. The story, as legend has it, evolved as Baum wove it together for his children and their friends. It was a fantasy story about a magical land and a little girl who found herself there and wanted to go home. Seeing his wife so distraught after the funeral of her niece, and not knowing how to comfort her, he decided to name the heroine of his story after little Dorothy, forever immortalizing the child as "Dorothy Gale," rather than "Gage."

For more than a century now, the story of the little girl has been handed down through generations of the Baum family. They tell about a niece named Dorothy who died and was preserved forever in L. Frank Baum's book. It was simply a story that had been passed down until the fall of 1996, when Dr. Sally Roesch Wagner, doing research on Maud's mother, Matilda Joslyn Gage (a suffragist who worked closely with Susan B. Anthony), located Dorothy's grave. The stone was so faded with age that it was nearly illegible, but newspaper stories about her discovery brought great attention to the site. Sadly, though, it looked as though the gravestone here would be lost.

After hearing of this, Mickey Carroll, who had been an original cast member in the MGM film adaption of Baum's book, decided to help out. Carroll, who had played one of the munchkins in the movie, had operated his family business, the Standard Monument Co., in St. Louis for nearly 60 years. He immediately contacted Evergreen Memorial Cemetery and made plans to go to Bloomington and visit the grave. Carroll, an expert stone craftsman, wanted to fashion and donate a new marker for Dorothy and he received permission from the cemetery caretakers to do so. The new stone was installed next to the original, which was also restored as much as possible. In addition, the cemetery board added a children's section to the graveyard and named it the Dorothy Gage Memorial Garden. The new section and the stone were both dedicated in October 1997.

Since that time, the grave of Dorothy –– namesake for one of the most beloved characters in literature and film ––– has been easy to find in Section 7 of the cemetery.

Home of Maple "Sirup"

Motoring past Bloomington, and back into the rural wilds of Illinois, Route 66 travels on to the small community of **Funks Grove**, one of the region's first settlements. About 15 miles south of the twin cities, an old sign stands in the grass on the side of the road that reads simply "Maple Sirup." Nearby, among the prairie grass, sits a natural maple grove that is filled with sugar and black maples of record size.

In 1824, a man named Isaac Funk became the founder of a small community that was dubbed "Funks Grove." It was a natural site for a home with a good water supply, rich land, and plenty of timber. The fact that the timber was mostly made up of maple was a bonus for Funk. He and his family later began making "sirup" and maple sugar for their personal use.

During this era, maple "sirup" was the only kind of sweetener available to the people in the area and Arthur Funk, Isaac's grandson, took advantage of this when he opened the first commercial "sirup" camp at Funks Grove in 1891. Five years later, his brother, Lawrence, took over the operation and passed it on to Hazel Funk Holmes in the 1920s. When Route 66 came through, the maple "sirup" business boomed and the season's stock was sold out almost as soon as it was made.

In 1947, when Hazel was ready to retire, she asked her nephew, Stephen Funk, and his wife, Glaida, to take over the grove and the surrounding farm. However, before she transferred things on, she arranged for a trust that would insure that Funks Grove Maple Sirup would be around for many years to come. Although the trees are worth a huge amount of money, the trust stipulated that they could never be used for anything but the production of maple "sirup." And it added that the word "sirup" always be spelled in its original way.

According to history, "sirup" was the preferred spelling when referring to a product made from boiling sap. "Syrup," with a "y," however, was defined as the end product of adding sugar to fruit juice. Although the "I" spelling is no longer commonly used, the U.S. Department of Agriculture still uses it when referring to pure maple "sirup."

Hazel always insisted on using the "I" spelling during her lifetime, and thanks to the trust, it continues on after her death.

Stephen Funk retired in 1988 and his son, Michael, and his wife, Debby, took over the business. Today, a seventh generation of Funks continues to make "sirup" at this historic place, where it still feels like it's a century ago.

The Blue Phantom of Route 66

At this point in our Illinois route, it seems a good spot to recount a very weird story from the highway when Route 66 was still in its heyday. We usually think of the Mother Road with nostalgia about good times gone by, but in the early 1950s, Route 66 in Illinois became a "highway of terror" for many travelers. Someone, who was driving a blue automobile, was attacking drivers and automobiles along this road, and then strangest of all, was eluding capture and somehow vanishing without a trace. Who the person behind the wheel of what became known as the "Blue Phantom" actually was remains a mystery to this day.

The "Blue Phantom," as the mysterious driver's automobile was dubbed, first appeared on Route 66 near Joliet in May 1952. Two different drivers independently reported that someone had fired a shot at them from a moving, blue automobile. Neither of the drivers was able to get a close look at the car or driver, because it flashed by so quickly, but each of the drivers agreed that a lone man had been behind the wheel. Whoever this man had been, he had fired shots at the other cars and one of the drivers had been wounded, although not seriously. The police investigated and could find no connection between the two drivers and no enemies who would have wanted to kill them. Later on that same day, another driver reported an identical incident --- and an identical blue car. This attack took place three miles south of Lincoln, also on Route 66, and state police officers realized that they had a random shooter on their hands, prowling up and down the busiest highway in the state.

On June 2, the Blue Phantom driver changed tactics and ambushed a passing car from outside of the infamous vehicle. Edward Smith of St. Louis was driving south on Route 66, just past the Sangamon River, when something struck his car with a loud bang. He slowed down and looking into his rearview mirror, saw a man run out of some bushes next to the road. He appeared to be carrying a rifle in his hand. The man quickly climbed into a large blue car, which had been hidden out of sight, and roared back north on the highway. Smith guessed that it was either a Ford or Buick sedan. He reported the incident to the police, who believed that a .38 caliber bullet had struck Smith's rear window.

On June 8 alone, there were 10 shootings reported on Central Illinois highways. One of the shootings even shattered the windshield of a car and all of them were linked to blue automobiles that disappeared without a trace. Miraculously, none of

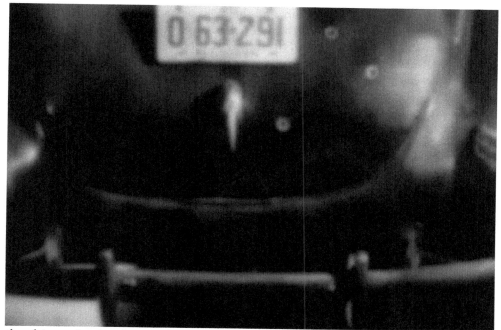

the drivers in the damaged cars were injured. The state police, along with local officers, set up roadblocks along a 75-mile stretch of Route 66. They also hired a small airplane to follow the course of the highway and search for a blue sedan. Owners of ordinary blue automobiles were stopped, and often harassed, but no suspects turned up in the search.

On June 9, another Blue Phantom attack occurred, but this time, it was not on Route 66, but rather near Clinton on Highway 54, which connected to the original highway where attacks had taken place. The driver of the truck that was damaged could not get an idea of the make or model of the car, only that it was blue. He did, however, have two bullet holes in his windshield.

On June 10, the Blue Phantom's driver chose his 15th target, still defying all of the police efforts to stop him. This time, he attacked just before dawn, and then led a police officer on a wild chase that approached speeds of more than 90 miles per hour. The officer eventually lost the elusive vehicle and stated that he was simply unable to overtake the other car at the speed that it was traveling.

A week later, on June 17, the Blue Phantom was off Route 66 again and back onto Highway 54. A witness named D.L. Weatherford observed a man standing on a bridge near Mt. Pulaski. The man wore a khaki shirt and trousers and was holding a revolver. He was standing next to a blue Chrysler sedan and quickly turned away when Weatherford drove past. He wisely did not stop to ask questions, but he did report the sighting of the armed man, and the blue car, to the police. They searched the area, but found nothing. Two nights later, though, along this same stretch of road, a blue automobile reportedly opened fire on a Decatur couple and then pursued them south of Mt. Pulaski toward Route 66.

Another week passed and on June 24, the Blue Phantom, or at least a vanishing gunman in a blue car, made its last appearance near Champaign, about an hour to the east and some distance from Route 66. On this day, a blue sedan pulled up alongside another car and four shots were fired from the sedan. One of the bullets crashed into the passenger side window of the other car. The blue sedan quickly sped away and vanished.

After that, the Blue Phantom was lost to history. The incident in Champaign was apparently the last time the driver struck, and he was never heard from again. Was the curious car merely a figment of the imagination or some lone nutcase looking for kicks by shooting out people's windows? Either of those options is surely possible -- - or perhaps the Blue Phantom was something far stranger, something that exists just on the other side of the unknown.

Dixie Trucker's Home

Continuing south on Route 66 brought travelers to the small town of McLean. Located there today is the **Dixie Trucker's Home**, which was built in 1928 by J.P. Walters and his son-in-law, John Geske. Housed in a rented garage, the first version of the now-classic café had only a counter and six stools.

But throughout its history, the Dixie Trucker's Home has been constantly improved and remodeled. In the late 1930s, six tourist cabins were added and, eventually, the café was enlarged to serve 60 people. In 1965, a grease fire in the kitchen, aided by wooden exhaust ducts, destroyed the restaurant, leaving the tourist cabins and the gas pumps untouched. In fact, that same evening, the gas pumps were back in business and one of the cabins was put into service as a temporary home for the diner. The new Dixie Trucker's Home opened up two years later with the capacity to serve 250 highway travelers.

Over the years, the restaurant has been consistently ranked as one of America's top 10 truck stops, serving guests with all of the southern hospitality that the name implies.

Atlanta

Continuing south, the highway bends into the small, friendly town of Atlanta. Like the famous city that bears the same name in Georgia, the Illinois community also suffered a devastating fire in 1865 that destroyed most of the town. Its rebuilt structures were mostly brick and are remarkably preserved today.

The town's most notable roadside attraction was the **Palms Grill Café**, which opened in 1934. The owner, James Robert Adams, opened the café with one idea

The Palms Grill Café around 1940 – it doesn't look much different these days. Still great food and great service!

in mind – "home cooking, quick service and courteous treatment." Adams had been born in Atlanta but moved to Los Angeles after serving in World War I. He frequently returned home, but spent most of his time in California. When he opened his café, the name came from his love for the palm trees out west and the interior was decorated as homage to his favorite restaurant in L.A.

From the beginning, the "Grill" as it was locally known, seated about 30 people and was more than just a source for good food. It soon became an important part of Atlanta's social scene. Many of the town's teenagers had their first jobs waiting tables or working the grill. Behind the kitchen at the rear of the building was a dance hall, where locals gathered on Wednesday nights to have fun and socialize. The dance hall also hosted large parties and private gatherings. In January 1940, the Palms Grill Café became a designated Greyhound Bus stop. A small light at the bottom of the neon sign out front signaled the drivers if there were passengers waiting to board. The "Grill" thrived as long as cars still traveled along Route 66, but in the 1960s, when highway traffic began to die, the place served up its final meal.

After the restaurant closed, the final owner of the building remodeled the Palms Grill into living and work space and upon his passing in 2002, his family donated the building to the Atlanta Public Library and Museum. But that was not the end of the Palms Grill Café. The interior of the classic diner was remodeled and opened back up for business. It's now a thriving business, serving great meals to travelers in search of good food on Route 66.

And the Palms Grill Café is not the only part of old Route 66 that Atlanta is breathing life back into. The community also boasts the famous **Hot Dog Man** that once stood outside of Bunyon's Drive-in in Berwyn. In 1965, Hamlet Arthur Stephens purchased the giant fiberglass statue and placed it in front of his restaurant. Stephens purposely misspelled the name of his hot dog stand as "Bunyon's" in order to avoid a "Paul Bunyan" trademark infringement. A legend was born and for the next 38 years, the statue stood as a Route 66 landmark. Stephens, with the help of his family and longtime manager Agnes Abruzzo, operated Bunyon's until January 2003. At that time, he retired and closed his business, but was faced with disposing of the giant. The owner solicited

The Bunyon's Hot Dog Man got a facelift and restoration before being moved to Atlanta.

buyers, and received cash offers for as much as $10,000, but in the end, he and his family decided to place the statue on permanent loan to the town of Atlanta as part of a Route 66 heritage exhibit. "Tall Paul," as he's been dubbed, was then refurbished and placed in a central location in downtown Atlanta, welcoming Route 66 visitors to town.

Motoring into Lincoln

As Route 66 continues to the southwest, it soon arrives in the town of Lincoln. The town was settled in the 1830s, but was not officially named on August 29, 1853 in a ceremony that was, well, rather weird. Connected to the ceremony is perhaps the weirdest monument ever built in honor of Abraham Lincoln. It is not a statue of the president, but rather a statue of a watermelon. It should be noted that Lincoln is the only city ever named for Abraham Lincoln with his personal consent and the only

city ever named for him when he was alive. In fact, it was named "Lincoln" when Abe was just a well-known Illinois lawyer and long before he was ever elected to national office. The statue is in the shape of a life-sized watermelon slice, and its subject allegedly played an important role in the founding of the city.

In 1853, Abe Lincoln was just a young lawyer who was called upon to draft the town's incorporation papers. The founders decided to name the place in his honor and Lincoln responded to the suggestion with his usual humility: "I think you are making a mistake," he said. "I never knew of anything named Lincoln that ever amounted to much."

Lincoln then presided over the town's dedication and the official story says that he poured out the juice from a watermelon to christen the ground, but other stories say that he actually spit out a mouthful of watermelon seeds as a christening instead. In 1964, a statue of the watermelon was erected near the train station where it all took place, making this one of the strangest Lincoln sites in the state.

There's also another Abraham Lincoln site in town – the World's Largest Covered Wagon. The **Railsplitter Wagon,** recognized by the Guinness Book of World Records for its size, is piloted by a giant Lincoln lawyer. Created in 2001 by artist David Bentley, the wagon began as a project to kill time while he recovered from surgery. The wagon is built from steel and oak and stands an impressive 25-feet-tall and is 40-feet long. It is designed like a classic prairie schooner, with a deep bed, and a bench in front where the driver would command, in this case, some frighteningly large oxen. Sitting on the bench is, of course, Abraham Lincoln. He is 12-feet-tall and is reading a book simply titled, "Law," while he steers the wagon across the plains.

The wagon was finished to commemorate the 75th anniversary of Route 66, along which the Railsplitter now sits. It was originally placed outside of Bentley's house in Divernon, but was moved to its current home in Lincoln in 2007. A large storm damaged the wagon in 2014, but with the rugged perseverance of the American frontier spirit, local volunteers had it repaired in a matter of days.

The "Killer Curve" and "Bloody 66"

Route 66 was a great place to "get your kicks," but not everyone had a great time motoring on the old highway. When traffic was heavy on the road, its many twists and turns could be deadly. There were tales of wrecks and victims so badly mangled that they begged state troopers to shoot them and put them out of their misery. Many travelers claimed that near Lincoln, car crashes occurred every few hours. On that part of the highway, the route earned the nickname "Bloody 66" or sometimes was simply known as "the Killer."

It seems the deadliest spot in Lincoln was an area known as the Blu Inn Curve," or, as some called it, the "Killer Curve." The **Blu Inn Restaurant** (which went on to be known as the Heritage Inn and Courtyard before it vanished) was just south of the curve, as was the Tropics restaurant, and scores of fatal accidents occurred almost at its front door.

Law enforcement officers, when speaking about Route 66 in Lincoln, all noted that speed and heavy traffic were the contributing factors to the deadly accidents that plagued the curve. Former State Policeman Roy Acup noted that the speed limit on Illinois Route 66 was 70 mph, but that the speed limit posted on the Blu Inn Curve was 45, "but nobody paid attention to it." The highway's design may have also contributed to the deaths. Former Illinois State Policeman Mike Leake described the medians on Route 66 as "real deep. . . . If you ran down into one of the medians on Route 66 it would take off your front bumper and you'd do a flip flop."

Local lore told another story. According to those tales, the beginning of the curve from the north was very gradual, but then suddenly "tightened," causing many speeding vehicles to run off the road. It was said that there were so many fatalities on that stretch of roadway that the civil engineer who designed that section committed suicide because he couldn't live with his mistake.

Truth or fiction? No one knows, but many police officers recalled it as a dangerous spot and handled accidents at the curve on an almost daily basis during the heyday of Route 66.

Down to the Tropics in Lincoln

The **Tropics Dining Room and Cocktail Lounge** opened its doors in 1950 at an intersection known locally as the "Four Corners." It was a prime spot, and the owner, Vince Schwenoha, knew it. Vince was the son of the legendary John Schwenoha, a.k.a. "Coonhound Johnny." John got the nickname for his fondness for hunting raccoons with his four raucous coon dogs. John also ran a Prohibition-era roadhouse just north of Lincoln on Route 66, aptly named Coonhound Johnny's Roadhouse.

After a tour of duty in the military in the late 1940s, Vince came home to Lincoln and opened the Tropics. He gave it the unusual name (for the middle of Illinois anyway) because of his love for the Hawaiian Islands, where he lived during his military service.

One of the most popular items on the restaurant's menu was the "Tropicburger," a combination on one bun and two hamburger patties that Vince first came across in California. The double burgers were selling fast on the West Coast, so he brought the idea back to Lincoln and gave it a familiar name.

In the 1950s, Vince sold the Tropics to Lewis Johnson. Under the new management, the place became more than just a restaurant – it embraced the "tiki lounge" craze that swept America and became a favorite hangout for locals. Scores of community events were held at the Tropics, including a series of beauty pageants. A local radio station was often on hand for live remote broadcasts.

In 1997, Johnson leased the business to James Letsos, who also owned a restaurant on Route 66 in Pontiac. The arrangement only lasted for two years after a lack of business forced Letsos to close. The Tropics opened again for a brief time in 2001, but four years later, it was closed again.

During its heyday, the Tropics was open from 7:00 a.m. to 1:00 a.m. daily and offered a coffee shop, dining room, and the Bamboo Lounge, but today, it stands empty and silent along the once bustling highway. The iconic Tropics sign, with its jaw-dropping neon and glowing green palm tree, was taken down on May 14, 2014, and is now in the possession of the City of Lincoln.

"Save the Mill"

Another of Lincoln's classic Route 66 icons was the **Mill**, a tavern and restaurant that opened in 1929 as the "Blue Mill." Paul Coddington opened the white Dutch building, trimmed in blue, which featured a lighted revolving windmill, a blue interior, waitresses in white dresses and blue aprons, and enameled furniture with Dutch pictures. Travelers on Route 4, which became Route 66, could purchase toasted sandwiches any hour of the day and night. When Albert and Blossom Huffman bought the place in 1945, it still had two serving windows on the front of the building.

Albert and Blossom changed and expanded the business, building a barroom of knotty pine and adding an Army barracks from Camp Ellis to the rear as a dance hall. He abandoned the blue and white theme and painted the building barn red. For a time, they also offered a delicatessen with curb service, but that didn't last. The Mill became best known as the "Home of the Schnitzel," a huge breaded tenderloin sandwich that was first made by Louise "Mom" Rofschansky, an Austrian immigrant who brought the recipe from the old country. The Schnitzel was originally made from veal, and Louise often stayed at the restaurants until 3:00 or 4:00 a.m., pounding it to make sure that it was just right. Later, the sandwich was made from pork.

By the 1980s, the old windmill had come down, but it was replaced by a new one with more lights that also revolved. It was later damaged in a storm. By that time, the interior of the Mill had lost its Dutch motif and had become a museum of oddities: a mechanical leg protruded from the ceiling, an antique beer can collection was behind the bar, a 20-pound stuffed catfish, a suit of armor, four life-sized figures, and more.

In 1996, the Mill finally closed down. It remained there, slowly decaying on the side of a defunct Route 66 until 2007, when a drive began to try and save the place. Just two years earlier, it seemed that demolition might be the only option for the building. The city battled with the property, clearing up several liens against it so that it could be sold at tax auction. But the auction failed to provide a solution. The winning bidder didn't have the resources to tear down the structure because of an asbestos problem. Eventually, he was fined and ended up with legal problems. But luckily, by donating the property to the Route 66 Heritage Foundation of Logan County, the city voted to drop all of the fines and charges against him.

But what about the building itself? Since 2007, volunteers and donors have been hard at work raising money and doing construction on the Mill in hopes of saving it from a cruel fate. The task is an ongoing one, but at least this icon of Route 66 has a chance of being enjoyed by future generations.

Lincoln's Motor Lodges

The original path of Route 66 through Lincoln took travelers through quiet residential neighborhoods that were adjacent to the downtown business district. But around 1940, a bypass of the highway was constructed along the northern and western sides of the city. It was on this "beltline" that the **Buckles Motel** was located.

Located on a small piece of land on the north side of Lincoln, the Buckles Motel was built by Paul and Ruth Buckles around 1949. The motel's design was modeled after a Spanish adobe style, an architectural type that was common in the American southwest, but pretty unusual for Central Illinois at the time.

In the 1950s, it was completely remodeled and updated to a contemporary design. The unique Spanish-style office and home was also remodeled, getting rid of any resemblance to the original architecture.

The motel boasted of having "strictly modern units, central heating, and tub-shower combinations," which were all pretty important things to note at the time. The advertising also promised that there was a restaurant nearby. In time, the motel closed and became a memory of the past.

When Interstate 55 was completed, the Route 66 bypass became Business 55, which is now known as the Lincoln Parkway. The motel's office and home serve as a private residence today and the motel units have been converted to monthly apartments. The buildings that once made up the Buckles Motel have blended into the neighborhood so well, that only a very discerning eye will spot this relic of Route 66's past.

Located a short distance away from the Buckles Motel on Route 66 was the **Redwood Motel**. The motel, operated by Wilfred and Dorothy Werth, opened in 1956 and sat conveniently at the junctions of Routes 66, 10, and 21, with 15 rooms and living quarters attached to the main building. The exterior of the motel was originally constructed of stone and redwood, but by 1960, so many stones were falling off the walls that Wilfred decided to brick the entire exterior. The cost to stay at the Redwood in 1956 was $5 for a single and $8 for a double. When television was installed, the rates were raised to $6 and $10.

In 1934, just over two decades before opening the motor lodge, Wilfred had built a Standard Oil station on the same corner. He often claimed that he had the "first gasoline pumps in the state that showed the dollars and cents through the small windows on the pumps." He loved owning the motel, but sold it in 1963 when Ruth Buckles made him a great offer on the place.

Today, the Redwood Motel still operates in Lincoln. The original motel sign was torn down in a storm, but it was replaced in November 2002. Plans are in the works to remodel the place and make it a "must stop" for modern travelers on Route 66.

"Give Me a Slice of that Pig Hip!"

Motoring on, south of Lincoln, the town of Broadwell once drew large crowds of travelers who came to Ernie Edwards' **Pig-Hip Restaurant**, which was known up and down the highway for its barbeque. Edwards opened the place in 1937, when pork sandwiches could be bought for just 15 cents, with just three tables, a bar, and $150 of borrowed money. He first called the place the Harbor Inn because of a great deal that he got on wallpaper and restaurant glasses with a nautical theme. The name was short-lived. One day, a hungry farmer came into the diner and spotted a freshly baked ham on the stove. He pointed to the ham and said, "Give me a slice of that pig hip" and the rest, as they say, is history. Ernie applied for a patent on his sandwich (a generous helping of thinly sliced ham smothered with Pig Hip Barbeque sauce) and he copyrighted the name of "Pig Hip." The sandwich became incredibly popular and no trip on Route 66 was complete without a stop in Broadwell.

Ernie finally hung up his carving knife in 1991 after being a local legend for 54 years. Ernie's Pig Hip Restaurant was transformed into a small museum in the spring of 2003 and stands today as a tribute to Ernie Edwards and his famous sandwich.

Mysteries of Elkhart Hill

As motorists continued on past Broadwell on Route 66, they soon began to see a rugged hill rising up from the flat prairie. Rising up nearly 800 feet above the surrounding landscape, **Elkhart Hill** looms above the highway and the small village that is nestled below it. It was on the wooded slopes of the hill that an early settler stood in front of the house that he'd built and dreamed about the town that now rests in the shadow of the hill.

According to local lore, John Shockey came west from Pennsylvania to Central Illinois in 1848 to buy cattle – and never left. He loved Elkhart Hill so much that he relocated his wife and his 15 children (two more would be born in Illinois) to the western prairie in 1850. He eventually bought 5,000 acres of land, which included Elkhart Hill. He had the land surveyed and platted, and on April 11, 1855, the "Elkhart City," which later became simply **Elkhart**, was founded. The attorney that drew up most of his papers was a Springfield man named Abraham Lincoln.

But John Shockey's story ended soon after his dream was realized. A devastating crop failure in 1856 wiped out most of his fortune, and he died three years later at the age of only 53. Even though he was financially ruined by the lands he loved so much,

he left property in his will that was to be used to build schools, churches, businesses, and homes.

Unlike the town, Elkhart Hill is an ancient place. It dates back hundreds of thousands of years to when glaciers moved, and then retreated, again and again, burrowing across what would someday be Illinois. During one of these massive upheavals, a great chunk of earth was left behind. As the largest natural formation between St. Louis and Chicago, Elkhart Hill covers almost 700 acres of land. For travelers on old Route 66, it certainly stood out.

Elkhart Hill was first home to the Kickapoo Indians around 1763, and to the white settlers who came after them. Although the Native Americans have been gone for more than two centuries, they left behind the remains of a village, with artifacts, burial mounds, and the name of the hill itself. Tradition has it that during a hunting trip, a chief's daughter, White Blossom, was forced to choose between two suitors. She decided that the warrior whose arrow could pierce the heart of an elk that was passing by would be the man she would marry. The two men, one from White Blossom's own tribe, the Illinois, and another, from the Ohio Shawnee, both took aim at the elk, but the Illinois warrior's arrow hit the mark. From that day on, the warrior and his wife took the elk heart as their totem and the hill became known as Elkhart Hill.

Today, Elkhart Hill rises above the churches, grain elevators, homes, and businesses of the small farming community at its base. It looks much the same as it did when Route 66 passed through the area, although eclectic gift shops, bakeries, and unusual eateries have replaced the services of the past.

The town continues to thrive, still using the same roads that connected it to the rest of the world in the early 1800s. Route 66 was built over a very old path, or trace, that was used for thousands of years by herds of migrating bison and other animals. From Kaskaskia in the south, the trace travels through Cahokia and the Edwardsville area, to Springfield, and then to Elkhart Hill and north to the Illinois River. Native Americans used the trace for hunting, seasonal migrations, trading, and war. Eventually, the path would be named "Edwards Trace" in honor of future Illinois governor Ninian Edwards, who, during the War of 1812, led a group of nearly 400 rangers up the trail to Peoria to fight the Illinois Indians. It later became the main pioneer and stagecoach route through the region, and today, parts of hard roads and highways follow Edwards Trace, including sections of Route 66.

The first white man to settle on Elkhart Hill came to the region on the Edwards Trace in 1819. His name was James Latham and he and his son, Richard, built a double cabin to accommodate their large families. They also built a four-horse mill.

James Latham did not stay long in the area. He was named a judge and, within five years, was appointed by President John Quincy Adams to be the first Indian Agent for the state of Illinois. Latham moved to the Peoria area, but unfortunately, contracted an illness and died in 1826. His body was brought back to Elkhart Hill and he was buried there.

Richard Latham stayed in the area and built a stagecoach stop along the trace called the Kentucky House, a two-story frame building with a two-story porch on the front. Kentucky House was a busy place, attracting circuit-riding lawyers like Abraham Lincoln and Stephen Douglas. In 1853, around the time the railroad came to Elkhart, Latham sold the hotel and land to John Shockey.

The youngest Latham, Robert – along with Lincoln – became one of the key individuals to convince the railroad to come through Elkhart. The railroad would be a key factor in the success of another important man from Elkhart's history, John Dean Gillett.

Gillett originally settled in another part of Central Illinois, where he began raising cattle. In need of a good attorney, he sought out Abraham Lincoln and the two men became business associates and later, close friends. At one time, they even courted the same women, Lemira Parke, who would later marry Gillett. Eventually moving to Elkhart, the couple built a house and barns on Elkhart Hill. A fire destroyed their home in 1870, but they rebuilt three years later.

Gillett became well-known for importing Durham cattle from Scotland and developing the Shorthorn breed. He shipped more than 2,000 head of cattle and 1,000 hogs to Europe every year. The *London Gazette* dubbed him "Cattle King of the World." Thanks to Gillett's success, Elkhart was one of the largest shipping points on the Chicago and Alton Railroad for many years.

Today, Gillett's home and outbuildings are part of the Old Gillett Farm, a historic family farm that is owned by his descendants. The farm is made up of 700 acres of lawns, gardens, woods, and open fields. In addition to the main house, there is a three-bedroom guesthouse and chapel that are available for private bookings, weddings, and events.

Another of Elkhart's famous residents was Richard J. Oglesby, a Civil War hero from Illinois, renowned speaker, three-time Illinois governor, and close friend of Abraham Lincoln. It was Oglesby who suggested the "rail splitter" nickname for the 1860 presidential campaign, and he had the last appointment with the president on the day that he was killed. He was present at his friend's deathbed and was the first to begin raising funds to build Lincoln's monument and tomb in Springfield. Later in life, Oglesby married the Gilletts' oldest daughter, Emma. He built a home on Elkhart Hill that he called "Oglehurst." The 50-room mansion served as their family home for eight years. Oglesby died in the house on April 4, 1889 – and soon gave rise to one of the great ghostly legends connected to the Elkhart Cemetery.

The cemetery on top of the hill is an isolated, seemingly peaceful place that dates back to the 1870s. It was at that time that a town meeting was held and a request made for more cemetery land for the growing village. John Gillett came forward in

May 1874 and offered a parcel of land known as Gillett Grove. In 1890, his wife had a chapel built in Gillett Grove in honor of her husband. The small building, known as the Chapel of St. John Baptist, became the center of Elkhart Cemetery.

After the death of Governor Oglesby, a funeral service was held in the chapel and his body was placed in the chapel's vault until his mausoleum could be finished. It took nine years and he was finally laid to rest on May 8, 1899. The mausoleum was a grand structure, made from solid concrete and with antique bronze doors with glass inserts, but time has not been kind to it. In 1986, the doors were taken from their hinges by thieves, who also took a $5,000 vase. The doors were estimated to be worth at least $20,000. One door was found three weeks later in a field between Elkhart and Broadwell. The entrance was later covered with amber glass and iron bars, but vandals have since broken the glass.

Could this senseless damage be the reason that the cemetery is rumored to be haunted? Supernatural activity has been reported at Elkhart Cemetery for decades, much of it involving the Oglesby Mausoleum. In the days after her husband's death, the former governor's wife, Emma, regularly visited his tomb, sometimes returning several times in one day. Legend has it that she continued these daily visits in death and the figure of a woman in mourning black was often spotted walking to and from, or kneeling outside of the crypt.

Or could the governor himself be restless? Perhaps his spirit is disturbed by the vandalism that has been visiting upon his final resting place. Or perhaps he refuses to rest as he contemplates the life he once led, and the things that he was never able to accomplish.

We may never know, but for those with an interest in ghosts, Elkhart Cemetery is well worth a short side trip off Route 66.

Greetings from Springfield!

The pioneer settlement of Springfield began in 1817 when Henry Funderburk arrived in the area. He had come north through the Cumberland Gap in 1808 and purchased land holdings belonging to Andrew Jackson in Tennessee. In 1815, he continued on north and west to Illinois, settling in St. Clair County, just east of St. Louis. Two years later, he moved his family north to the Sangamon River region and built a home in the Cotton Hill Township. Soon, other settlers followed, including William Nelson and a frontiersman from Alton named Robert Pulliam. Several other families followed them and a small settlement was started. The first church, which doubled as a school, was built in 1821. The first blacksmith shop was built that same year and a grain mill soon followed, turning the small settlement into a thriving community.

The small town, although growing, was still rough in those years and consisted mostly of log cabins with dirt floors. In spite of that, it was chosen to be the county seat for the new county of "Sangamon" in 1821. The exact site of the town was chosen when a wooden stake was driven into a field belonging to a John Kelly. It lay close to Spring Creek, so they chose the name of "Springfield." It was later re-named "Calhoun" in honor of Senator John C. Calhoun, but when he fell out of public favor, the name reverted back to the original.

In 1837, due in some small part to the political maneuverings of a young politician named Abraham Lincoln, Illinois' state capital was moved from Vandalia to Springfield. In April of that year, Lincoln moved to Springfield from the nearby village of New Salem and began practicing law. He had previously tried his hand at a number of endeavors including store clerk, postmaster, surveyor, and riverboat pilot before running for the state legislature in a losing campaign. In 1834, he was elected on his second try.

In 1840, Lincoln met a Kentucky girl named Mary Todd and after a stormy, on-again, off-again romance, they married. Their first son, Robert, was born in 1843 and the following spring, they moved into a house at the corner of Eighth and Jackson Streets – the only house that Lincoln would ever own.

Lincoln practiced law but continued to be active in politics and in November 1860, he was elected president. He left Springfield a few months later, bound for the White House, and never saw Springfield again.

The Civil War took many men from Springfield, but it also boosted the city's economy with many new industries and businesses and the town continued to grow.

When Route 66 came through Springfield, the town responded with even more businesses, all targeted to travelers on the highway. Gas stations, diners, and motels sprang up, seemingly overnight, all hoping to get their share of the customers who were now streaming into the city. When the Route 66 signs came down in January 1977, many of the old businesses inevitably closed down as they were bypassed by the new interstate. However, there are still a number of Route 66 icons that remain in Springfield.

When a motorist first enters Springfield on the north side of town, they'll quickly spot the old **Pioneer Motel**, which was built back in the 1940s. Highly rated back then by AAA, it initially consisted of 12 units arranged in the classic L-shape style, with parking in front of each room. At some point after the original construction, an archway was built over the driveway at the front office and a living room was added to the office space. At one time, another small motel existed adjacent to the Pioneer, but it was eventually absorbed into the larger motel, increasing the Pioneer's total guest rooms to 21. The Pioneer is still open today, and while most of the units are rented out by the month, a few are kept open for those overnight guests who are looking to spend the night at a vintage Route 66 motor lodge.

Not far away, also on the city's north side, was the **Lazy A Motel**, a Route 66 icon that was designed for those who couldn't wait to see the Wild West – long before the highway took them there. The 16-unit motor lodge would have looked right at home in Arizona or New Mexico with its stucco walls and southwestern look. In Springfield, Illinois, though, it was more than a little unusual. The motel came highly recommended by AAA, which noted it for its tiled baths and for the individual, locked garages that came with each unit.

After the interstate came through, the Lazy A faded like the western sunset, and soon, a lack of business forced the owner to close the doors. Eventually, the motel was renovated into an apartment complex, and then later, underwent a conversion to a small business park. The Lazy A still stands today, even though the old fencing, wagon wheels, and western ranch decorations are all distant memories.

Springfield also featured a couple of places to find classic Route 66 road fare. **Coney Island Restaurant** originally opened in 1919 and spent most of its years on North Sixth Street. But construction woes (as recently as making room for the Abraham Lincoln Presidential Library) sent the owners packing on four separate occasions. In 2012, current owners moved into the former home of **Sonrise Donuts**, which had opened along Route 66 in 1947. After the death of the owner in 1998, the donut shop was closed and abandoned until Coney Island moved in, combining two Springfield spots with long ties to the Mother Road.

Home of the "Crusty Cur"

As Route 66 winds its way out of Springfield, it passes by an important location to all fans of drive-in food – the true birthplace of the Cozy Dog. Ed Waldmire Jr. and his friend, Don Strand, developed the Cozy Dog while stationed in Amarillo, Texas, during World War II. To earn extra money, Ed sold the treat, a hot dog on a stick that was dipped in a special batter and deep-fried, at the USO club and the base PX. First called the "G.I. Hot Dog" by appreciative serviceman, it was officially dubbed the "Crusty Cur" by Waldmire.

Upon his return to Illinois, Ed introduced the dogs to the public at the 1946 Illinois State Fair and they were such a hit that he decided to sell his fast food in Springfield.

The first Cozy Dog stand was opened at the Lake Springfield beach house on June 16 to great success. At the insistence of Ed's wife, Virginia, who wondered who would eat anything called a "Crusty Cur," he began kicking around ideas for a new name. After great thought, the name "Cozy Dog" was settled upon and Ed opened a second eatery across town. By the start of the 1950s, car customers were scarfing down so many of his dogs that he was inspired to open the **Cozy Dog Drive-in** on Route 66. Although the secret formula for Waldmire's batter crust was patented, clever cooks across the country began developing their own version of the dog. News of the popular food spread, and soon the "corn dog" had gone nationwide in restaurants, diners, and especially at county and state fairs. Ed operated the drive-in until 1976, when Ed's son, Buz, and daughter-in-law, Sue, leased the place from him. After they split up, Buz sold his half to Sue, who has

Top: The original Cozy Dog stand and (right) the current sign on Route 66.

operated the place ever since. The Cozy Dog moved to its current location in 1996 and sits partially on property that was once part of the former Lincoln Motel, another Route 66 landmark. You can still get the best Cozy Dogs in Illinois at the drive-in, but when you order one -- be sure not to call it a corn dog!

Abraham Lincoln's Haunted House

There is no question that the most famous former resident of Springfield was Abraham Lincoln, our nation's 16th president and one of the most revered figures in American history. Lincoln was a man who believed wholeheartedly in the supernatural, and his connections with the unknown were maintained throughout his life -- some say, beyond it. He believed in prophetic dreams, dabbled in Spiritualism, and was admittedly haunted by the spirit of his dead son. Is it any wonder that he is one of America's favorite ghosts?

But is it the ghost of Abraham Lincoln that reportedly still lingers in his former home in Springfield? Is it Mary Lincoln, returning to one of the few places in life that she knew happiness? Or is it, as I believe, the ghost of another occupant of the house entirely?

Abraham Lincoln was a frontier lawyer who had come to the city of Springfield to earn a living. His new wife, Mary, insisted that they have a good home in which to raise their children, and by 1844, Lincoln was able to afford to purchase a one-and-a-half story cottage at the corner of Eighth and Jackson Streets, not far from Lincoln's law office in the downtown district. The Lincoln's lived in the house from a period shortly after Robert was born until they moved to Washington in 1861.

The house was originally built in 1839 by a Reverend Dresser and was designed in the Greek Revival Style. Lincoln purchased the home in 1844, while it was still a small cottage. It had been constructed with pine exterior boards, walnut interiors, oak flooring, and wooden pegs and hand-made nails held everything together. In 1850, Lincoln improved the exterior of the property by having a brick wall constructed and by adding a fence along Jackson Street but nothing major was done to the house until 1856. At this time, the house was enlarged to a full two stories, adding new rooms, and much needed space.

Today, the house is presented in much the same way as it looked during the Lincoln years. It is now owned and operated by the National Park Service and they are not publicly thrilled that the house has gained notoriety as a "haunted" site. They have always maintained that no ghosts walk here, although many of the witnesses to the strange events have been former employees and tour guides of the house.

There is no question that the house has clear connections to supernatural history, dating back to November 1860, when Abraham Lincoln won the election for President of the United States. After a long day spent with his friends, and a midnight celebration at the telegraph office when the final election results came in, Lincoln returned home during the early morning hours. He went into his bedroom for some much-needed rest and collapsed onto a settee. Near the couch was a large bureau with a mirror on it and Lincoln started for a moment at his reflection in the glass. His face appeared angular, thin and tired. Several of his friends suggested that he grow a

Abraham Lincoln's home in Springfield, Illinois

beard, which would hide the narrowness of his face and give him a more "presidential" appearance. Lincoln pondered this for a moment and then experienced what many would term a "vision" --- an odd incident that Lincoln would later believe had prophetic meaning.

He saw that in the mirror, his face appeared to have two separate, yet distinct, images. The tip of one nose was about three inches away from the other one. The vision vanished, but appeared again a few moments later. It was clearer this time and Lincoln realized that one of the faces was actually much paler than the other was, almost with the coloring of death. The vision disappeared again and Lincoln dismissed the whole thing to the excitement of the hour and his lack of sleep.

The next day, he told Mary of the strange vision and he talked about it to friends for many years to come. Mary believed she knew the significance of the vision. The healthy face was her husband's "real" face and indicated that he would serve his first term as president. The pale, ghostly image of the second face, however, was a sign that he would be elected to a second term --- but would not live to see its conclusion.

Long after the Lincolns left the house, stories began to circulate about the apparition of a woman that had been seen there. Many passed this off to wishful thinking, but in more than one circumstance, the image was spotted by multiple witnesses. Staff members at the Lincoln Home also told their personal stories about toys and furniture that moved about the house, unlit candles that would mysterious burn down, rocking chairs that rocked on their own, being tapped on the shoulder by invisible hands, hearing voices in empty rooms, hearing the rustle of what sounded like a dress passing by them in the hallway, unexplainable cold spots, and , of course, the apparition of a woman in period dress moving about the house and then disappearing in front of their eyes. One tourist, an attorney from Virginia, wrote the staff after he returned home to tell them of his own strange sighting at the Lincoln house. He claimed to see a woman standing in the parlor of the house who abruptly vanished. He had enough time to recognize the woman and he thought it was Mary Lincoln.

But was the ghost really Mary? For those who believe the house is actually haunted, they believe the ghost is not actually one of the Lincoln family, but rather a later occupant of the house, Mrs. Lucian A. Tilton. Mrs. Tilton and her husband, the president of the Great Western Railway, had rented the home from the Lincoln family when they left for Washington in 1861. However, after the president's assassination, his body was placed on display in the house when he was returned to Springfield. Mrs. Tilton had been constantly plagued by visitors during the four years that she lived in the house, prior to 1865. They estimated that at least 65,000 people had visited the home and asked to take a tour of it, ringing the bell, and knocking on the door day and night.

Needless to say, Mrs. Tilton was worried about what might happen to the house during the Lincoln funeral, but she was a kind-hearted person and had already resolved herself to the fact that she was going to allow people to take grass from the yard, flowers from her garden, or leaves from the trees. She had no idea what was coming. By the end of the funeral services, her lawn and gardens had been stripped, paint had been scraped from her house, and bricks had been carried away from her retaining wall as souvenirs.

The Tiltons moved out of the Lincoln home in 1869, but some believe that Mrs. Tilton has never left it. There are those that believe that the ghost who lingers here, and who has been seen on many occasions cleaning and straightening the house, is the beleaguered Mrs. Tilton, still worried over the disruptions that continually marked her brief tenancy in this famous home.

Last Dance at the Lake Club

As Route 66 leaves the city, it passes over Lake Springfield, a man-made lake that was built in the 1930s. It now covers parts of the original two-lane alignment of Route 66 and when the water level is low, glimpses of the old road can still be seen. They

The Lake Club in Springfield during the 1950s

are just a memory now, much like the fabled Lake Club, one of the most haunted locations that ever graced the Mother Road – in any state, not just Illinois.

The Lake Club in Springfield had opened as a nightclub in 1940, but the building on Fox Bridge Road had seen many incarnations in the years prior to that, including as several restaurants and even a skating rink called the Joy Inn. In 1940, two dance promoters named Harold Henderson and Hugo Giovagnoli renovated the place and opened it for business.

The club soon became one of the hottest night spots in Central Illinois, drawing customers from all over the area. It boasted a raised dance floor, which was surrounded by a railing, curved walls, and a swanky atmosphere that made patrons feel as though a New York club had been transported to the shores of Lake Springfield. The owners concentrated on bringing big name entertainment to the club and they succeeded. Among the many top performers were Bob Hope, Ella Fitzgerald, Guy Lombardo, Pearl Bailey, Spike Jones, Nelson Eddy, Woody Herman, Mickey Rooney, and many others. The constant stream of entertainers and big bands brought capacity crowds to the club every night.

The Lake Club thrived for nearly two decades, becoming known not only for its swinging entertainment, but for its first-rate gambling, as well. Wealthy customers and the society elite of Springfield and Central Illinois frequented the club for the musical guests and for the billiard tables, craps and gaming tables, slot machines, and high-stakes card games. This part of the club operated in secret in a back part of the building, known only to high-rollers and special customers. However, in December 1958, the golden days of the Lake Club came to an end. The partners had survived many setbacks over the years, from lawsuits to foreclosures, but the club would not survive the two undercover detectives who gained access to the gambling rooms that Christmas season.

The club was immediately shut down, although the restaurant and dance hall were allowed to operate. This was not enough to save the business. Things began to falter in the wake of the raid and the club finally closed down in the 1960s. Hugo Giovagnoli refused to give up on the Lake Club and opened it up again in the 1970s with other parties managing different projects in the building. During this time in the club's history, it was managed by Bill Carmean and Tom Blasko as a rock club. In 1980, it was leased by Pat Tavine, who also operated it as a rock club until 1988, when it closed down for good. Sadly, the Lake Club was destroyed by fire in 1992.

It was in August 1979 that the Lake Club, known in 1980 as the Sober Duck Rock and Disco Club, gained national notoriety. It was at this time when the ghost of Albert "Rudy" Cranor was finally put to rest.

According to the many patrons and staff members who had experiences there, the haunting of the Lake Club first began in 1974. At the time, the club was in the midst of a revival in interest and the business was under the ownership of Tom Blasko and Bill Carmean, two Springfield men who were booking rock acts into the club. Odd sounds began to be heard in the building, as well as a feeling of being watched in some of the rooms. A piano played by itself. Lights turned on and off, doors opened and closed, and things moved about by themselves. By 1976, the haunting had intensified and things began happening more often, and in front of more witnesses.

Bill Carmean was the first of the club's staff to guess the identity of the ghost who was plaguing the establishment. He recalled that a former employee had committed suicide in the building several years before. On a lark, he started calling the ghost by this man's name --- "Rudy."

Albert "Rudy" Cranor had worked at the Lake Club during its heyday of the 1950s. He was always described as being well-liked and popular with the entertainers and the customers. He was also a very large man, well over 250 pounds, and he had snow-white hair. He was remembered as one of the club's most memorable characters.

After the club fell on hard times following the gambling raid, Rudy also started experiencing some personal difficulties. He was a very private person, so no one really knew what was going on, but they did notice that he began to drink heavily while on the job. He also seemed to be more tired than usual and dark circles had begun to appear under his eyes. One night, he got so sick that he had to be rushed to the hospital. He returned to the club after a two-week stay in the hospital, but he was never the same again.

On June 27, 1968, Rudy committed suicide with a high-powered rifle in one of the back rooms at the club. No one was ever sure why Rudy had killed himself, but regardless, he wouldn't stay gone for long. In a few short years, he would return to haunt his beloved club.

The strange events at the club continued in the form of weird antics and pranks, apparently carried out by the ghost of Rudy Cranor. A frightening event took place in the summer of 1979 when a waitress at the club claimed to see the floating head of a man with white hair who warned that one of the owners of the club was going to die. The waitress fled the room in hysterics and Tom Blasko stated that when he went to investigate, he found that the room was ice cold. Blasko and Carmean were unnerved by the ghost's warning. The two men waited for something terrible to happen and then, two weeks after the incident, Harold Henderson, one of the original owners of the club, died at the age of 69. He was still the owner of the building itself and was an owner that Rudy would have known during his lifetime.

Blasko was shaken by the incident and after two weeks of living in fear, decided to try and get rid of the ghost. He contacted his parish priest, but the man declined to get involved. He suggested that Blasko pray for Rudy on his own and Tom spent the next six months carrying a rosary around the club with him. But it didn't help --- Rudy was still there.

Finally, in August 1979, Blasko attended a high school class reunion and ran into one of his former classmates, Reverend Gary Dilley, a priest who now lived in Texas. Tom mentioned the problems at the club to Father Dilley and the priest was intrigued. After some discussion, he agreed to come out to the club and take a look around. After arriving at the club, Father Dilley also sensed something out of the ordinary there. He was convinced that something was going on, but he declined to do an "exorcism" of the club. To do that, the case would require a thorough investigation and permission from the local bishop, which he doubted he would get. Instead, he decided to bless the place and pray there, hoping this would perhaps put Rudy to rest. He contacted two other priests and they blessed the building with holy water and prayed for the soul of Rudy Cranor. Eventually, they entered the room in which he had committed suicide and prayed that his spirit be at rest.

So, was that the end of the haunting? Apparently, it was. The same people who considered the club to be haunted became sure that Rudy had departed. The day of the religious ceremony was the last day when anyone was aware of Rudy's presence in the building. It seemed that the prayers and blessings had helped the bartender find his way to the other side. It certainly seems possible that Rudy may have chosen to stay behind in a place where he had many attachments in life. Perhaps the intervention of the priests was all that he needed to be convinced to move on.

Rudy had finally found some peace.

Motoring Through Illinois

As the highway continues on southwest of Springfield, it splits into two alignments that are still intact today. The first alignment (1930–1977) begins as a four-lane road that closely follows Interstate 55 and takes travelers to Glenarm, Divernon, Farmersville and Litchfield. Things become pretty confusing when trying to record the history of Route 66 through this section of Illinois, so our narrative is going to have to jump back and forth between the two alignments in the pages to come.

The original Route 66 (1926–1930) alignment – a two-lane road-- is full of twists and turns. You can follow Route 4, the first alignment of Route 66, past Jerome, and then through Chatham. Along this alignment, you'll find an unusual and little-known site near Chatham that has been dubbed "Snake Bridge." To get there, take Chatham Road south as far as it will go and turn right at the stoplight on Woodside. Travel to the first road on the left, which is the old original Route 66 alignment. It will eventually come to a dead end, but if you follow it as far as it will go, you will reach the bridge. Although few people know of the site, it's easy to find and very accessible. The bridge can be found in an area that is now a wildlife preserve and a protected location for the Kirtland Snake, a rare and non-poisonous reptile that is an endangered species. The road comes to an end at the north end of the bridge and be warned – do not try to drive across it. It's in a bad state of repair, but it's safe to walk upon. Just be sure to watch your step with all of the snakes around.

The old alignment of Route 66 then travels south, and travelers today will find **Becky's Barn** on Snell Road, just north of Auburn, a Route 66 snack shop, information center, and antique store. Visitors can sign the "guest book" when they arrive – an actual bus where you can sign your name on the inside.

Motoring into Auburn

Just in front of Becky's Barn, travelers will find one of the remaining oddities of Route 66, a bypassed brick portion of the road that is listed in the National Register of Historic Places. This segment of road is actually two parts – a 1932 brick road and a 1921 Portland cement road. Both are almost perfectly preserved examples of Route 66's early years of construction. Both of them were part of Route 66 until the bypass rerouted traffic to the less populated area to the east, through Litchfield, so that traffic would be able to speed up by not passing through so many small towns.

The Auburn "Brick Road"

The concrete section, located on Alpha Road between Highway 4 and Curran Road, was abandoned in a 1932 relocation of the state road. The **"Auburn Brick Road"** is located between Chatham and Auburn on Snell and Curran Roads.

Returning to Highway 4, which is old Route 66 through this area of Illinois, it curves around to the small town of Auburn, which was first settled by farmers in 1818. A few years later, a grist mill, water mill, and a tanning yard followed and the settlement began to grow. The first school was established in 1828, and Presbyterians built the first church in 1835. Auburn was laid out later that year by brothers, Asa and George Eastman, who had purchased land all along Sugar Creek. The village was named by their sister, Hannah, in honor of their hometown of Auburn, Maine.

Although the town was heavily promoted, by 1840, it only contained about six houses and a handful of residents. However, it was home to a two-story tavern, owned by William S. Swaney, who had bought several lots in the town. Swaney, who had settled in Illinois from Ohio with his family, was a blacksmith by profession, but he was often absent from home for weeks at a time. Rumor had it that he was a professional gambler, working in the towns along the Illinois River. With neighbors and local farmers already speculating about his mysterious trips out of town, things became especially heated when he failed to return in 1843. His wife soon learned the sad news that her husband was dead. The stories had been true. Swaney had been killed by a disgruntled loser, who had taken back his money from the slain gambler.

With few industries to market, the Eastman brother's project to develop the new town was deemed a failure, and they closed their mill and moved to Springfield. The town continued on, though, primarily because it was a stop on the stagecoach line from Springfield to St. Louis and because of the Sugar Creek post office, which was established in 1839.

When it was announced that the Alton and Sangamon Railroad planned to build tracks through the area, the people of Auburn were excited, convinced that the village would finally begin to grow. Anticipating the new arrivals who were sure to flock to the town, William Roach and George Organ built a large store in Auburn in 1852. The village plans were thwarted, though, by a man named Phillip Wineman, who owned 200 acres of land about a mile south of town. He offered a free donation of land to the railroad on the west side of Sugar Creek and even laid out a plan for a new town to support the railroad, which he named after himself. A struggle began between the new and old factions in town, but Wineman prevailed. Although there was no reason barring the railroad from passing through Auburn, Wineman had obviously cut a deal with the railroad.

In a short time, most of the businesses from the original site of the town had picked up and moved to the new town, which had been renamed "Auburn." The old town, which was largely abandoned by now was referred to as "Old Auburn." Later, after a fire destroyed many of the buildings and many others were torn down or hauled off, the old town site was turned into a cornfield.

Located along the new railroad line, the town finally began to grow. A store was established by Ham & Poley in 1853, and Morse's Wagon, Carriage and Agricultural Implement Manufactory set up a factory in town in 1856, employing 20 men. Auburn became an "official" city in 1865. In 1872, the Auburn bank was organized and two years later, the *Auburn Herald* newspaper began publication. By the 1880s, the community boasted eight schools, eight churches, four grocery stores, two dry goods stores, three saloons, two hardware stores, three restaurants, a furniture store, brick factory, and a number of small businesses. By the turn-of-the-century, the town was mostly supported by manufacturing companies, which were producing flour, carriages, and farm equipment.

Over the years, the town continued to develop, welcoming Route 66 motorists as they passed through until the new alignment came along in 1930. Today, most of the bustle of days gone by has vanished from town, but it still has the advantage of being a quiet small town that's just a short distance away from the state capital.

Motoring through Illinois Coal Country

After leaving Auburn, old Route 66 traveled on toward Thayer and passed through what was once a major part of Illinois' coal country. Starting in the 1860s, coal mines and the towns that sprang up around them began bringing immigrants from all over the world to Central Illinois. By 1910, there were 22 operating mines in Macoupin

County, south of Thayer, that were shipping hundreds of train cars filled with coal to large industrial centers across the country.

Thayer only had one mine, but Virden had 21, Girard had nine, Nilwood had 16, Carlinville had 14, Gillespie boasted seven, and Staunton had 12. During the heyday of the coal mines, the region became an area of unrest and violence. Life was often difficult for the miners and their families. The dangerous and dirty working conditions, stale and dusty air, noxious fumes, and low pay all combined to lead the miners to form unions. During the turbulent decades of the early twentieth century, a number of strikes occurred, leading to violence, riots, and deaths.

The coal mines of that era are now a thing of the past, but the highway that served as Route 66 from 1926 to 1930 still passes through many small towns where their coal mining roots are still very visible. From Thayer south, the highway is dotted with small villages, public squares, and haunting reminders of the lost highway.

Thayer came along late in the coal-mining era. Founded in 1900, it came about thanks to the Chicago, Wilmington & Vermillion Coal Company buying up mining lands in southern Sangamon County. Mine Superintendent Ruffin D. Fletcherson oversaw the building of the mines and laid out the town of Thayer. He also supervised the building of 86 tenant homes for the miners, a 26-room hotel, a large company store, and a handsome residence for himself.

The coal company had been formed in 1866 by investors from Chicago and Boston. Having had a number of other successful operations in the area, they sank their first coal shaft in June 1900. By the following January, the mine was producing 250 tons each day. By December 1901, the mine's daily capacity had increased to 2,000 tons. It was a "first class" mine, considered one of the best in the state, but, in time, it played out and the mine closed in 1914. Thayer would never truly be a thriving town again.

But it does have a minor place in the gangster history of the 1930s. Thayer was home to Byron "Monty" Bolton, a member of the infamous Barker-Karpis gang, and during an FBI investigation his boyhood home in town was searched. He was arrested in January 1935, and started talking about pretty much everything that he'd ever done, including the

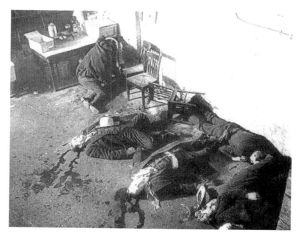

Was Thayer native "Monty" Bolton part of the infamous St. Valentine's Day Massacre?

location of Ma and Fred Barker's hideout in Florida and his role in the St. Valentine's Day Massacre six years earlier.

According to Bolton, he had been working with a criminal crew organized by Fred "Killer" Burke in 1929. Burke had been suspected of having a role in the Chicago massacre by the police, but he'd never been named publicly as a suspect until he was convincingly fingered by Bolton.

Bolton was an expert machine-gunner in the U.S. Navy before turning to a life of crime and kidnapping and stated that the planning for the massacre was carried out at a resort owned by Fred Goetz on Cranberry Lake in Wisconsin, in October or November of 1928. Al Capone was present, as was Burke, and several other mobsters. Bolton himself claimed to be a lookout man, waiting in a rooming house across Clark Street from the garage where the massacre took place. His story was backed up by the discovery of a medicine bottle and a letter, both with his name on them, found in a rooming house during a neighborhood canvass. Bolton claimed that Burke and fellow gangster Fred Goetz were disguised as police officers during the massacre and three others were the assassins dressed in plain clothes.

Bolton was under arrest in St. Paul, Minnesota, for the ransom kidnapping of Edward Bremer, along with members of the Barker Gang, when he made the confession. Informed of his statement, Chicago police captains John Stege and William Shoemaker, probably the most honest crime fighters in the city during the Prohibition era, believed Bolton. Lieutenant Otto Erlanger of the homicide bureau added that he thought Bolton's story was "true in every word."

But not everyone was convinced. FBI director J. Edgar Hoover, who had Bolton in custody on the federal kidnapping charge, dismissed his claims. His information about the massacre was never acted on, but FBI agents did use his testimony to track down the Barkers in Florida. They were shot to death by lawmen in their Florida hideout on January 16, 1935.

Just two miles south on old Route 66 is **Virden**, a former mining town that was originally established as a stage stop in 1852. The stagecoach stand was opened by John Virden at the point where the Springfield and St. Louis line intersected with the Springfield and Vandalia stage.

The completion of the Chicago and Alton Railroad spurred the establishment of Virden. The first lots were sold in 1852 and John Virden himself but the first commercial building: a hotel called the Junction House. The first homes and stores soon followed, along with a post office the following year, a blacksmith shop, and the first school. Before long, there were several churches, more businesses, and a local doctor.

In 1869, the first coal shaft was sunk near Virden, and the following year, the people of the village voted to spend $30,000 for the building of the Jacksonville and Southeastern Railway. The whole length of the road was 31 miles and was finished by

Virden, Illinois in the late 1890s

the end of 1871. Soon, freight was coming into town and carloads of coal were being shipped out by the Virden Coal Company. Over the next few decades, Virden supported 21 different coal mines.

By the 1890s, coal had helped Virden to grow substantially. The town boasted a tile factory, two railroads that passed through the community, new businesses, and area mines that employed hundreds of men. Virden was prospering, but at the expense of many of the residents. For the miners, life was often brutal. Work in the mines was dangerous – and often deadly – but the biggest complaint was usually about the low pay and the monopoly of company stores, which forced the miners and their families to purchase goods and supplies from them using "scrip," which was not actual money. It was only good in stores owned by the mine company they worked for. Miners also had to rent their homes from the company and the rent was deducted from their pay, often leaving little left over. Making matters worse, mine workers accused the coal companies of recruiting men from Europe to take their jobs since the immigrants would work for less.

The complaints led to organized unions, and in 1890, the United Mine Workers of America was formed. In addition to joining the unions, miners also elected sympathetic politicians who would pass laws dealing with safety, company stores, and fair pay. But the most successful tactic was a strike, several of which occurred in Illinois mines in 1874 and 1877. Strikes were often accompanied by violence, as company property was destroyed, trains derailed, and railroad bridges burned to stop the coal from being shipped out. In retaliation, miners were sometimes shot by gunmen hired by the company.

In 1898, a bitter coal strike began in Virden when the Chicago-Virden Coal Company fought the unionization of its mines and refused to pay the workers union-scale wages. The strike began largely through the activities of Alexander Bradley, who had been involved in the organization of Coxley's Army, a march of unemployed

An 1898 illustration of the "Virden Massacre," which became a pivotal event in the history of mine labor relations in America.

workers down Pennsylvania Avenue in Washington, D.C. in 1894. He assumed the role of primary organizer for the United Mine Workers in Central Illinois and soon started a series of meetings in the nearby woods to organize area miners in a strike. Once it began, the coal industry in the region came to a virtual standstill.

Undaunted, the coal company built a timber stockade around the mine and began recruiting African–American workers from the South as strike breakers. When striking miners learned of this, and the mine company's plan to re-open the mine on October 5, an estimated 2,000 union miners converged on Virden to prevent the mine from opening again. On October 12, 1898, when a train loaded with "scab" workers pulled into Virden, it was surrounded by strikers. To protect their property, mine owners had hired security guards, Chicago police officers, veterans, and 40 heavily armed Pinkerton detectives to be posted on the stockade and on the train.

Fearing violence, Virden's sheriff petitioned Governor John Riley Tanner for troops to help keep the peace. The governor refused and ordered the sheriff to move the strikers to the outskirts of town and disarm them.

A damaged switch in the rail yard prevented train engineers from carrying out orders that had been given to them by railroad executives, who wanted the train to continue on to Bloomington and not stop in Virden at all. As the train slowed, the strikers flooded into the rail yard, and gunshots fired by security guards started a pitched battle between the company men and the striking miners. In the all-out gun battle that followed, six guards and seven miners were killed. Another 35 men were wounded. After 20 minutes of gunfire, the train finally pulled away with the strike breakers huddled for cover in their cars.

Conflicting reports went out over telegraph and telephone lines. Fueling rumors and conjectures were requests for Springfield, Mt. Olive, and other communities to send doctors, and for the governor to send in the state militia. The governor immediately complied this time, and the first troops arrived the following evening.

On October 13, Virden was under martial law. Investigators worked to sort truth from rumor, and conjecture from outright lies.

It would be early November before the coroner's inquest was completed. Martial law was lifted, and the troops finally left town. The Virden incident resulted in the creation of the United Miners Cemetery in nearby Mt. Olive, is credited with the winning of the eight-hour workday, and is regarded today as a pivotal incident in the American labor movement. A large granite and bronze three-dimensional memorial in the town square commemorates the battle.

By the way, a month after the battle, the coal company finally granted the wage increase.

In the early 1900s, Virden continued to grow. There were soon four churches, a bank, two newspapers, flour mills, brick and tile works, a machine shop, and nearly two dozen coal mines. The mines operated until the seams were diminished. Today, only one mine remains near Virden, however, Macoupin County remains one of the state's largest producers of coal. Virden's economy today revolves around another kind of product taken from the ground – corn and soybeans.

Route 66 cruises along just four more miles to the town of **Girard**, named for one of the first settlers to the area, a Frenchman who built a sawmill on the banks of Mill Creek. By 1834, more people had settled in the area and with the increase in population came the stage line from Springfield to Alton. Built along an old Indian trail, this road would later become Route 66.

In that same year, a local doctor named Edwards and George Mather laid out a town site and called the place "Girard." However, the plat was never recorded and the town would not become official for another two decades. It took ten of those years before there were enough people in the area to warrant a school house, but in 1852, when the Chicago and Alton Railroad came through, interest was revived in establishing the place as a "real" town. During the following spring, another town site was laid out and this one actually stuck.

The first homes were located near the square, the first of which was brought in from the country by Barnabas Boggess. Another was built by Sam Boggess and it also served as the town's first boarding house. A blacksmith shop was established, as was a private school. In 1854, several businesses were erected, including a general store, owned by Alfred Mayfield, and W.E. Eastman's drug and merchandise store. J.W. Woodruff built a warehouse and shipped out the first carload of wheat from Girard. Daniel Macknett started a lumberyard, which he owned until 1893. It would operate for more than a century. The post office and the first hotel, the Girard House, were also established in 1854.

The town was incorporated on February 14, 1855. That same year, the first flour mill was built on Mill Creek by H. Hall and the first church was built. A brickyard soon followed, and in 1857, the *Girard Enterprise* newspaper first began to be published. It was later replaced by the *Girard Gazette*. A public school was built in 1858, and the wooden building served all grades until it burned in 1870.

For many years, the oldest business in Girard was the Deck Drug Store. It was first established by a Dr. Clark in 1865, and he kept his office on the upper level. He was joined by Lewis Deck in 1884. He ran the pharmacy and later become the sole owner. Passing the business on to his sons, the drug store was family owned and operated until 2001. It was then sold and operated by new owners until it closed a few years later. This was the first time that Girard was without a hometown pharmacy. Today, the building operates as **Doc's Soda Fountain** and **Deck's Pharmacy Museum**.

In 1867, Bowersox Clothing Store opened. It changed ownership several times over the years, but it remained in business until 1976. That same year, F.W. Ring came to Girard and opened a bakery and restaurant. In addition to a talented cook, he was also an accomplished musician, and he organized a band that became known as the best in Central Illinois. They traveled by train to every major celebration in the region to furnish entertainment.

By 1870, Girard was home to the St. Nicholas Hotel, a bank, three steam flour mills, a butter and cheese factory, numerous merchandise stores, a lumber yard, and five churches. Dodson's Opera House opened in 1893 and became the cultural center for the town. Road shows, vaudeville companies, and musical troupes, appeared there regularly. Later, it served as a movie theater.

The town saw its greatest growth after the opening of the Girard Coal Mine in 1869. As the years passed, Girard became home to nine different mines, employing nearly 600 men during peak times. When most of the mines closed in 1922, it dealt a terrible blow to the town's economy. Only one mine still operates in Girard today.

The mines in Girard were also the center of one disaster and another near disaster in the town's history. In 1879, a fire started in a coal mine shaft while all the men were down below. Extremely frightened for their friends and loved ones, the townsfolk rallied and every bit of salt in the city was dumped into the shaft, saving the men from certain death.

But they wouldn't all be so lucky the next time. In 1922 – the same year that the Girard Coal Mine shut down – a mine disaster occurred in December. When gas ignited an explosion of an unused part of the mine, several men were riding through the tunnels to the bottom of the shaft. The men in the first car were terribly burned. One man died from his wounds and 16 men were seriously injured.

One of the first cement highways in Illinois came through Girard. It was State Route 4, which passes all the way through Macoupin County from north to south. It was built through Virden and Girard in 1921. Girard then began to work on its streets, first around the square, which was paved, and the other roads were oiled and rocked. In 1926, Route 4 became Route 66, bringing scores of travelers to town who never would have visited otherwise. For the next four years, the town boomed again, offering services to travelers, but then in 1930, the highway was realigned through less populated areas to the east.

Time marched on and Girard declined. The People's Bank, with its handsome building on the north side of the square, was a casualty of the Great Depression, and by the end of World War II, many of the stores and services once found in town were gone. People began driving into larger cities to do their shopping.

Girard is a quiet little town now, but it does offer intriguing glimpses into its past.

Just about four more miles down old Route 66, you will come to the tiny little town of **Nilwood**. Today, travelers can find one of the most humorous reminders of Route 66 along this stretch of road. It is here where the pavement has a section of the road that is imprinted with turkey tracks. After the road was poured, and just before the Portland concrete hardened, a group of wild turkeys trooped across the road and left an indelible mark on the highway. A sign has been posted to alert travelers to the spot.

The history of Nilwood revolves, like so many other towns along this part of Route 66, around farming, the railroad, and the coal mines. The town was supposedly named by train engineers in the days of steam locomotives, and means "no wood." There were no trees in Nilwood, so when the steam engines approached, they knew there would be no wood to take aboard and burn to produce steam.

The first settler to the area was a man named John A. Harris, who settled a part of the township called "Harris Point," in 1829. Three brothers – John, Samuel, and Edley McVey – followed, as did Judge John Yowel and his son, James, that same year. William Street from Kentucky arrived in 1831 and opened the first general merchandise store. Most of the settlers were farmers and grew corn. Lewis Pitman built a gristmill on Macoupin Creek in 1838. He attached a blacksmith shop to it.

The Chicago and Alton Railroad came through town in 1852 and made Nilwood a station stop. The railroad owned land in the far southern part of Nilwood and provided a home there for the railroad section boss.

This began the "boom" time in Nilwood. The village had been officially laid out in 1855, and homes and stores began to appear. The Methodist Church was built in 1862 and the Baptist Church in 1869. On the same block, between these two churches, a two-story school house was constructed a short time later.

The first coal mines opened in Nilwood in 1873. The Carbon Coal Mine, owned and operated by John Bennyworth, was started in February. The coal mine – and the 15 others that followed – brought scores of workers to town, boosting the population to over 500 people.

Those numbers would climb and, by the early part of the twentieth century, Nilwood had a post office, a brick high school and grade school, three physicians, two grain dealers, wheelright shop, shoe shop, six grocery and dry goods stores, blacksmith shop, tavern, several restaurants, and a number of other businesses. The Nilwood State Bank was incorporated in 1908. When gasoline cars came along, the small town boasted five filling stations.

When telephones came to Nilwood, not many residents had one. Jenkin Davis, who ran a grocery store, had a telephone. Many of the residents used his telephone and put down as a reference that they could be reached at Jenkin Davis' store.

The coal mines closed in 1908, reopened for a time, and then closed permanently in 1920. The main shaft was sealed but the steeple, engine house and boiler room remained for many years until it was finally abandoned in 1927 by the Union Fuel Company, which owned it at the time.

Nilwood's bank closed during the Great Depression and little by little, the town began to dwindle in size. The closing of the mine marked the end of an era for Nilwood. The population was cut in half and the stores and schools vanished until only one gas station and a post office remained. It became a "blink and you'll miss it" town on Route 66.

Motoring into Carlinville

Named for former governor and Macoupin County politician, Thomas Carlin, the town of Carlinville has played a number of roles in Illinois history, largely thanks to its location on the railroad and the coal industry. The largest and most important hallmark of the town's history, though, is its famous -- and some say infamous – "Million Dollar Courthouse." Built in 1870, it became well-known for the huge cost overruns, missing funds, and charges of corruption associated with it, leading to the end of several careers, creating unsolved mysteries and stories of ghosts.

Carlinville thrived for many years on the number of railroad lines that ran through the community, offering freight and passenger service to points all over the country. The coal industry played a major part in its development, and in 1837, it became home to **Blackburn College**, a four-year liberal arts college that was started by Presbyterian minister Reverend Gideon Blackburn. Blackburn is one of the oldest colleges in Illinois and, since 1913, the college's student-managed Work Program has made an education affordable for many students, who have built Blackburn – literally brick by brick. In fact, Blackburn enjoys the distinction of being the only college campus in the United States to have been largely built by its students. Today, students carry on this tradition by staffing mission critical jobs as plumbers, carpenters, painters, landscapers, cooks, servers, computer technicians, graphic artists, security officers, assistant coaches, tutors, and teaching assistants.

One of the most unique aspects of Carlinville is the abundance of Sears, Roebuck & Company mail-order catalog homes in the small community. In 1918, Standard Oil of Indiana constructed an entire neighborhood of 156 Sears Catalog homes for their mineworkers at a cost of nearly $1 million. It was purported to be the largest order ever received by the Sears Modern Homes Department. In gratitude, Sears named one of its house models the "Carlin." Today, 152 of the original homes still exist in a part of town dubbed the **"Standard Addition."** It is the largest single collection of Sears Catalog Homes in the United States.

When travelers on Route 66 arrived in Carlinville, the town had much to offer America's first real tourists, including motels, supper clubs, restaurants, and the only town square in Illinois that Route 66 actually went around, instead of bypassing.

Carlinville was the original home to the **Ariston Café**, a Route 66 landmark. When the restaurant was opened by Pete Adam in 1924, it was a quiet place with two gas pumps out front. But when Route 66 was given its designation in 1926, Adam's business began to thrive. In 1930, though, Route 66 was re-routed east through

Carlinville's "Standard Addition" of Sears Catalog Homes

Litchfield and business suffered. Refusing to give up, Pete moved the Ariston to Litchfield, creating a new history for the place, explored later on in this volume.

Another classic spot that is still in business today is **Taylor's Mexican Chili**, which has been in Carlinville for over a century and, quite literally, put the town on the national map. It all started when Carlinville native Charles O. Taylor took a job working for the Mexican National Exposition at the 1904 World's Fair in St. Louis. It was there that he got his first taste of Mexican food. Anxious to bring the taste back home, he began making and selling tamales on a two-wheeled cart that he would push around the Carlinville square and sell at the saloons.

Business was so good that he couldn't keep up with demand. Desperate, he needed help, and when he heard that a Mexican had gotten himself arrested and was jailed in town, Taylor knew that he was in luck. He decided to pay the man's $3 bail and to pay him back, the Mexican worked for Taylor and paid him 50-cents out of his pay each week to cover the cost of the bail. While he was repaying the loan, he taught Taylor how to make *chili con carne frijoles*, a recipe that he later bought from the man and turned into Taylor's Mexican Chili.

The first location for Taylor's Chili was at 218 West Main Street and business boomed. The people of Carlinville couldn't get enough of his unique use of red beans and the fire of his chili sauce. But Taylor wasn't always easy to get along with. He had strict rules of behavior for his establishment and if the rules were not followed, patrons were unceremoniously kicked out.

His first rule was that, when getting ready to order, a customer had to have his or her money ready to pay. There was no fumbling in pockets and purses allowed. They had to have their nickel or dime – depending on the size of order they wanted – in hand when Taylor bought the chili. If the payment wasn't ready, the chili was taken away. Taylor also did not tolerate people talking, conducting business, flirting or hanging around the chili parlor. Customers were expected to eat and leave. Asking for ketchup was also prohibited. If a customer asked for ketchup, they had to leave. He also did not allow coffee to be served in the restaurant. He believed that the chili had all of the heat that anyone needed and coffee would ruin the flavor.

The chili parlor stayed in the family for decades and even survived the Great Depression by offering vegetable and butter bean soup and also began canning their products. The canning operation was only stalled during World War II during shortages. They stopped canning the chili altogether in the 1980s.

In 1976, President Gerald Ford visited Carlinville and among the gifts he received was a can of Taylor's Mexican Chili, which means that a small bit of Taylor's made it all the way to the White House.

The chili parlor remained in the Taylor family until 1992, when it was purchased by Joe Gugger. He loved the product and happily began canning it again. In 2004, Joe moved the parlor from Main Street to a location on the square, next door to the Anchor Inn. Since that time, the business has thrived, appearing on the *Food Network*, *Travel Channel*, and bringing in people from all over the country to Carlinville. Taylor's Mexican Chili has been shipped as far away as Japan and sales continue to grow.

In 2015, Taylor's, and the adjoining Anchor Inn, was purchased by Bobby and Chaney Whitlock and they continue to use the same classic recipe. There are many restaurants on Route 66 that are "must visits," and Taylor's ranks right up there with the best of them.

Judge Loomis & the "Million Dollar Courthouse"

There is no question that Carlinville can proudly boast one of the most beautiful town squares in the state. Many of the nineteenth century buildings have been preserved and restored and are now home to shops, restaurants, antique stores, and art galleries. The wide streets circle a picturesque little park, and a gazebo in the center of it completes this Norman Rockwell-like view of small town America. Dominating the northeast side of the square stands a silent sentinel that looms above the streets and the passing automobiles. The stark white structure is known as the Loomis House, a once-grand hotel, and it's a place where time seems to stand still.

Just beyond the Loomis House, silhouetted against the sky, is the stately dome of the Macoupin County Courthouse, which will be forever linked to the hotel that stands just a block away. The Loomis House was named for its builder, Judge Thaddeus Loomis. There was a time when Loomis' name garnered great respect in Carlinville, but that was before the construction of the opulent courthouse mired him in scandal and forever sullied his name.

Is it any wonder that many believe that his ghost still walks in this little town?

Thaddeus Loomis was descended from Joseph Loomis, who had come to America from England in 1638 and was one of the original settlers of Windsor, Connecticut. The family prided itself on their education and became prominent in science, literature, and politics, and one family member became a professor at Yale University. Horace Loomis, Thaddeus' father, was born in Connecticut and later moved to New York where he married Julia Tuttles. The couple had three children, all boys, the oldest of which was Thaddeus, born in 1826.

In 1838, Horace Loomis packed up his family and moved west to Illinois, settling in Chesterfield Township. He became a successful farmer, raising livestock, and running a large dairy until his death in 1850.

After arriving in Illinois, Thaddeus, age 12, began a rigorous education. Studying through the winter months and helping his father on the farm the remainder of the year, he gained a reputation as an intellectual and something of a prodigy. At 19, he entered Illinois College in Jacksonville and attended for one year. The following year, he entered the law department at the University of Kentucky in Louisville, graduating in March 1849.

Returning home to Illinois, though, he soon found himself restless. Like so many other young men of the time, he was struck with "gold fever." Rich deposits had been discovered in California and Loomis struck out for California. Accompanied by eight other young men – one of which was future Illinois governor Richard J. Oglesby – he set out from St. Joseph, Missouri, for his westward trek. After an arduous 90-day journey, the wagons reached California and Loomis remained there, working as a prospector, for the next five years.

Loomis returned to Illinois in 1854, never gaining the fortune that he had hoped for in the California gold fields. On December 13, he married Sarah Dukels and purchased a farm near Carlinville. For the next six years, he lived much the same life as his father had. In addition to tending his farm, he contracted with the Chicago and Alton Railroad to cut timber to make ties for the rail line. He also purchased land around Carlinville and laid out an addition to the town known locally as "Loomis' Addition."

In 1861, the Democratic Party nominated Loomis to run for county judge, and in November, he was elected by a large majority. Loomis served as a judge for the next eight years. During his tenure, he was able to levy, collect, and pay off the county's debt of a staggering $200,000. But that accomplishment, unfortunately for Loomis, would soon be overshadowed by the scandal wrought by his involvement with what would be called the "Million Dollar Courthouse."

The Illinois General Assembly created Macoupin County on January 17, 1829, its name derived from the Native American word "macoupiana," which meant "white potato." There was a type of white artichoke that grew along the creeks of the county.

Thomas Carlin, who was a state senator at the time and later become governor, worked hard to pass the bill that created the county. His efforts were later rewarded when the town of Carlinville was established in his honor. It was also chosen to be the seat of the new county. The first county courthouse was a small log building, which was soon obsolete. A second, larger courthouse was built on the square in 1830 and served the county for the next three decades.

By 1865, the county was in need of a larger courthouse, and it became understood that a vote for Judge Loomis, then up for re-election, was a vote for a new courthouse. Loomis carried the election and he immediately put his places for the new building in effect.

Architect Elijah Meyers created a new design for the courthouse – as well as for the new jail that would be included in the project – and construction began in 1867. It was completed over the winter of 1869-1870 with Judge Loomis playing a major role in the work. As construction was taking place on the courthouse, Loomis also began building the hotel that he would name for himself on the nearby square.

Almost immediately, charges of corruption were leveled against Judge Loomis. One angry citizen wrote an open letter to several area newspapers, asking Loomis: "Who pays the courthouse contractors for the building of your house?"

Why were people so angry and suspicious about what was going on with the courthouse and Judge Loomis' hotel? It was undoubtedly due to the unbelievable cost overruns, construction delays, and missing funds connected to the courthouse project. Almost as soon as construction began, clouds of controversy began to swirl about the endeavor and, as one might expect, it involved money – lots of it. Immediately, a 50-cent levy on each $100 of property value was established and bonds were issued in the amount of $50,000 to pay for the project. By September 1867, with little more than the foundation underway, the new courthouse had already cost the taxpayers $13,000. By the time the cornerstone was laid in October, the costs was already exceeding the estimates that architect Meyers and Judge Lewis had provided for the entire project.

As January 1869 rolled around, the cost for the courthouse had risen to an astounding $449,604 and an additional $125,000 was still required to complete the roof and the building's magnificent dome. The county issued more bonds to meet the ballooning costs. When the building was finally completed in 1870 the bill was a whopping $1.3 million!

Taxpayers were enraged and accusations of corruption were hurled at a number of people, but mainly at Loomis and the County Clerk, George Huston Holliday.

Holliday was born in Harrisburg, Kentucky, on August 5, 1824, and came to Illinois with his family sometime between 1834 and 1836. George earned an early reputation as a scholar. He was fluent in Latin, Greek, Hebrew, and was a respected orator. In 1845, he graduated from McKendree College in Lebanon, Illinois, and returned home to Carlinville.

In April 1852, Holliday married Cinderella Chism, a Macoupin County native who was 10 years his junior. The marriage produced six children, four boys and two girls. As an outlet for his "keen intellect" and political interests, Holliday became the publisher of the *Carlinville Spectator*, a Democratic newspaper. The venture was short-lived, but, after selling his own paper, Holliday continued to write for several others in the area.

In 1868, he purchased the *Conservative*, another Democratic vehicle, which only ran from March to June of that year. During this time, Holliday was acquiring one of the largest private libraries in the state. His next position was a political one, serving as the County Surveyor. In 1850, he and John Shipman laid out the town of Shipman, Illinois. Additionally, Holliday served as a school commissioner during the 1855-57 term of the Illinois Legislature.

When County Clerk Enoch Wall died in office in 1858, Holliday was appointed to finish out his term. He was re-elected in 1860, and soon after, he became part of the so-called "Courthouse Crowd," and later invested in Loomis' hotel. Both situations, as it turned out for Holliday, were very bad decisions.

The staggering costs outraged local citizens, and in November 1869, three men formed an investigative panel to look into the exorbitant costs of the building project. Their submitted report laid blame squarely on the members of the building committee who had let spending run amok. Thaddeus Loomis, who was the first judge to preside in the new courthouse, George Holliday, and the rest of the old committee members resigned in disgrace as talk of illegal activity began to filter thru the citizenry.

Loomis seems to have taken the brunt of the abuse, likely because he never publicly answered all of the claims of corruption made against him. It was suspicious to many that his magnificent hotel should be constructed at the same time as the new courthouse. Fueling this suspicion was the fact that the building was also designed by E.E. Meyers and built from the same limestone as the courthouse. Although Meyers had received the commission for the fortress-like jail, across the street from the courthouse, in the initial contract, the hotel was part of an additional agreement between Loomis and the architect. The details of that agreement have never been discovered. Like much of the association between Meyers and Loomis, they remain a mystery.

For his part Loomis agreed that the limestone was, indeed, taken from the courthouse project, but he argued that the stone had been leftovers, and that he had obtained the material legally. Though many called for it, proof of this was never forthcoming from Loomis, Meyers, or anyone else involved. Eventually, Loomis was

The "Million Dollar" Macoupin County Courthouse

cleared of any wrong doing --mainly due to lack of substantial evidence --and life went on for the judge. His name had been tarnished, but he survived.

But what of the county clerk who had overseen the project's finances? George Holliday, just as the investigation was reaching its most heated period, skipped town in 1870, and was never seen again. Holliday's sudden disappearance convinced many of his guilt, but he was forgotten and no proof of his wrongdoing was ever confirmed. Many years later, in 1879, a man claiming to be Holliday arrived in Carlinville. He was immediately arrested and locked up for questioning. "Holliday" had been living in Washington state, he claimed, under the name S.W. Hall and working as an attorney. Holliday's wife denied the man was her missing husband and since no one else could identify him, the matter was dropped and the county paid to have the man sent back to Washington. It was later learned, though, that when Hall returned to Washington, he abruptly sold his law firm, settled his accounts, and fled the area. Could he have been George Holliday after all?

It took the residents of Macoupin County 40 years to pay off the debt left by Loomis and company for the grand courthouse. On September 7, 1904, the town of Carlinville held a great celebration when the last of the bonds was paid off. Today, the lavish building stands proudly in place, its past long over but not quite forgotten.

Over the years, stories have circulated about the courthouse's resident spirits. It's not uncommon for staff members, clerks, and visitors to encounter eerie phantoms from years gone by. Footsteps are heard in empty rooms and corridors, voices and whispers echo off the walls and floors when no one else is there, and apparitions are often spotted, crossing the hallways or lurking in the historic main courtroom.

Over the nearly century and a half of its existence, dozens of horrific trials have been held at the courthouse. Could some of the lingering spirits be the ghosts of the killers and thieves who received their sentences here? Or could they be the specters of their victims, hoping for some kind of justice after death?

Some believe that at least two of the spirits are those of Judge Loomis and George Holliday, the two men who faced the greatest controversy after the building of the magnificent structure. Do they remain here, doomed to revisit their crimes for eternity?

But the courthouse may not be the only place where the spirit of Thaddeus Loomis lingers.

After his resignation, Loomis retreated to his new hotel and devoted his time to making it a showplace in Carlinville. When it opened in 1870, it boasted three floors with 50 guest rooms and a large dining area. Over the course of the next 11 years, the Loomis House played host to travelers from every walk of life, from traveling salesmen to actors, circus performers, politicians, railroad men, and a number of shady characters. A man named William Siemens was known to entertain patrons in the saloon on the hotel's ground floor while, according to rumor, another type of business was carried on upstairs. It was said that travelers and gentlemen from town could hire "fair ladies" employed by Siemens for more discreet entertainment in the rooms on the upper levels.

It was Siemens who led to the downfall of the Loomis House. In 1881, Siemens was convicted of violating Illinois liquor laws and the saloon was closed down. Profits began to shrink and Loomis was forced to surrender the hotel to the banking firm of Chestnut & DuBois, which held the mortgage on the property. But the bank firm was facing problems of its own. They had also been deeply involved in the controversy surrounding the courthouse and, eventually, the firm folded. The hotel was sold to William A. Robertson, a wealthy farmer and businessman who also happened to be the bank's largest creditor. Robinson was strictly anti-liquor and he vowed that the "devil drink" would never be served at the Loomis House again. A short time later, Robinson died and his family took over operations. Unfortunately for the travelers and locals who might want to have a drink at the Loomis House, they shared his views on alcohol.

The Loomis House during the time when it was known as the St. George Hotel

The hotel was closed for six months, it's future in doubt, but then it re-opened – and no one came. The self-imposed ban on liquor kept the customers away and the building was finally put up for sale at public auction.

The winning bidder was a man named Simonson from Decatur. Simonson believed that the name of the hotel had an "unsavory reputation" and he changed its designation to the St. George Hotel. He spent a large amount of money remodeling and refitting the place with all of the latest luxuries. But he didn't hold the deed for long.

In 1909, Simonson sold the hotel to Theodore C. Loeur, a druggist, who opened a pharmacy on the ground floor. Today, much of the pharmacy fixtures remain intact and offer a wonderful look at what was then an ordinary store – that seems out of the ordinary today – in that bygone era.

In time, Loeur's nephew, Ralph Surmon, took over the pharmacy and became a longtime fixture on the square. Surmon sold the hotel to the Carlinville Elks Club in 1953, and they operated it for nearly two decades under the name of the Elk Hotel. Men who were down on their luck always had a place to stay in the now fading hotel, which was starting to fall into disrepair. The roof had started to leak, and over time, each hard rain sent torrents of water into the upper floors and inside the walls. The damage caused peeling paint and crumbling plaster on the top two floors.

In 1975, Alex and Fern Perardi purchased the old building from the Elks and changed the name back to the Loomis House. The saloon was re-opened as the St. George Room, which still operates today. But the hotel itself was too far gone to be opened again, so the Perardis closed off the top two floors and set about converting the second floor into a restaurant. The spacious dining room was a welcome addition to Carlinville's downtown business community at the time and it operated for nearly a decade.

The restaurant is long gone now, but it was during its time in operation that the tales of ghostly happenings first began to be reported at the Loomis House.

The staff in the restaurant were among the first to report an unnerving presence in the hotel. A waitress was working alone one night after the restaurant had closed. She was preparing the dining room for customers the next day. As she walked out of the kitchen and into the dining room, she was startled to see a man standing in the middle of the room. At first she thought that someone had stayed after hours and she started to tell him the kitchen was closed, but the man turned and started to walk away. Halfway across the dining room, he vanished! The waitress ran screaming from the building. She didn't stop working there, but she never worked alone in the Loomis House again.

The waitress could never give a clear description of the man, but a patron at the restaurant's bar was able to do so. He was drinking with friends one night and happened to glance toward the back of the room. He saw a man standing there, looking very out of place. He claimed the man was wearing a turn-of-the-century (early 1900s) style suit and had a thick, white beard. The man turned to point out the odd-looking fellow to his friends, but the old man just as quickly turned, and vanished into a brick wall! None of his friends had seen the man, but later, when he had the chance to identify the man from a photograph, he learned the identity of the ghost – he identified a photo of Judge Thaddeus Loomis.

And Loomis apparently does not haunt the place alone.

A woman was in the abandoned hotel section one evening and encountered a man standing alone in one of the rooms. He was tall, in his mid-40s, and was wearing a dark suit with a pocket watch chain across his vest. The woman said that the man looked at her and spoke. "Find me in an armoire," he said. A moment later, he vanished into a wall. At the time, the woman had no idea what the man could have meant. However, an old armoire was discovered on the second floor of the building and inside of it were three men standing in front of a dry goods store on the square. The photograph had been taken in the late nineteenth century and the men were identified as F.L.J. Breymann, Albert Muller, and William Grotefendt. The woman was sure that the man she had seen was F.L.J. Breymann. It was later learned that he was a local businessman who had run a men's clothing company adjacent to the Loomis House.

One of the most widely known hauntings of the Loomis House was the staircase that led from the sidewalk outside to the restaurant on the second floor. The marble staircase can be very imposing, especially if a visitor is aware of the ghostly reputation that it has. Legend has it that an older man, a transient, was staying at the Elks Hotel in the 1960s. One night, he took a fall on the staircase, tumbled down the marble steps, and broke his neck when he hit the bottom. He died at the foot of the marble staircase and ever since that time, visitors have reported an odd feeling on the stairs.

The Loomis House on the Carlinville Square

Some say that they feel as though they are being watched. Others speak of eerie cold spots that cannot be explained, while others say that they have caught a glimpse of a shadowy figure lurking on those stairs. It is often seen from the corner of their eye, but it always quickly vanishes.

Other strange things have been reported in the former hotel, including in the basement. When the Loomis House first opened, a number of businesses rented spaces below street level. A flight of steps led patrons from the street down to the shops below and the pathway was lighted by glass panels that were embedded in the sidewalk overhead. One of the first businesses below the street was a barbershop that opened in 1870, operated by two men named Winn and Hinton. They were two of Carlinville's earliest African-American business owners and they enjoyed a long, successful run in the basement shop.

Another long-time tenant under the building was a bakery. It was said that, during the early morning hours, the smell of warm, fresh bread and hot, sweet rolls would waft up the stairs to the street, filling the air along the whole east side of the square with wonderful aromas. A year after it opened, though, a fire swept through the bakery. Fortunately, no one was injured in the blaze, but the damage was severe.

Repairs were made, and the business was re-opened, but even today, charred ceiling beams remain as a reminder of the fire.

Memories of those former businesses make themselves known today in the basement. In addition to phantom smells of baking bread and the clatter of metal objects, footsteps, and eerie voices, witnesses claim to have encountered areas of terrible cold that they cannot explain. Two people who were once exploring the basement, discovered a liquor storage closet for the hotel's saloon. The door had a padlock, which was not latched, and as they walked toward it, the lock began to rattle violently, shaking back and forth. When they opened the door, they found no one inside.

The Loomis House – along with the Macoupin County Courthouse – are symbols of Carlinville from days gone by. They are places with long histories, colored by crime, corruption, and the inevitable passage of time. Many of the people who walked the hallways and corridors, and spend time in the offices and rooms, left little bits of themselves behind – a passing history that has returned as a haunting.

Doing Time at the Old Macoupin County Jail

During the time when the courthouse project was underway, construction was also taking place on a new jail for Macoupin County. Earlier incarnations of the jail had been slipshod affairs at best and escapes were common. Architect Elijah Meyers, who designed the courthouse, also drew up the plans for the jail. It was built using the "cannonball method," which meant using stones of the same size that were closely-packed, intended to make escapes from the jail impossible. A tunnel at the south end of the courthouse led underground to the jail, which was directly across the street.

The jail opened for prisoners in 1869. It was built to house 17 male prisoners and one female prisoner, while also offering a home to the jailer and his family in an upstairs apartment. At one time, there were 33 prisoners packed into the small space, four of which were accused of murder. The jail lacked most modern amenities and conditions were rough, to say the least. Over the years, there were several suicides and deaths in the prison, and even though the conditions of the place deteriorated, it remained in use until 1988. Today, a fund has been established to try and renovate the old jail as a historic site.

There have been a number of stories told about ghosts and hauntings, but one of the most chilling dates back to when the jail was still in operation. In fact, it had been open only a few years when the strange tale appeared in the *St. Louis Democrat*. The 1874 article told the story of a Spiritualist medium from Mendota, Illinois named Betty Smith, who became troubled by a spirit that she considered to be evil. The spirit was plaguing her, causing her to speak occasional "wild utterings" about hatred, murder, revenge, and remorse.

Betty was eventually overwhelmed by this spirit, the account said, and on October 23, the spirit appeared before her in the shape of a young man with long hair, and "German features." The newspaper article reported that there were a dozen or more people present, all of whom saw him, and saw that Betty was in a trance. The spirit made a confession, which

The old Macoupin County Jail

was heard by all in the room. The spirit stated that his name was Carl Reystadt, and on the night of May 8, 1872, he had murdered a man named Andrew Garrity. It was for this crime, he said, Martin Fynes had died in the Alton prison. He told those present, "I was in spirit form at the time, but assumed the likeness of Martin Fynes when the deed was done, in order that he might be suspected of the crime and hanged for it. I stole his knife; I purposely encountered two men who knew him, that they might honestly swear to have seen him near the scene of the murder. I hid the bludgeon where it was found at his house." According to the spirit, he had done this so that he might be revenged for a great wrong that Fynes had done to him. But, in the after-life, he regretted what he had done and wanted to make sure that his testimony was given to clear Fynes' name.

The spirit then disappeared and was never seen again. It was discovered that there had been a man named Andrew Garrity, that he had been murdered as the confession claimed, that Martin Fynes had been arrested for murder, and that he had died in Alton, Illinois. It was also learned that Carl Reystadt and Martin Fynes had disliked one another, and that he was dead when Garrity had been murdered. During the trial, the evidence was conflicting. Two men swore that they had seen Fynes on the night of the murder, near the place where the body was found, with a bludgeon in his hand. They had spoken to him, they claimed, but he had not answered – and acted as though he was not himself. But four other people had testified that he was somewhere else at the time of the murder and they accounted for his movements that night. Even so, it was proven without a doubt, that the knife found near the murdered man belonged to Fynes. The evidence was so puzzling that the jury couldn't agree on a verdict and were discharged. Fynes was tried twice, each ending in a hung jury, and died in jail before the third trial could take place.

Fynes did die in Alton, but he also spent time at the Macoupin County Jail and, while there, he claimed that he was haunted by the ghost of Carl Reystadt, who appeared to him and taunted him. He became so frightened while there that he begged his jailers not to leave him alone.

While most refused to believe that Fynes was haunted, one of the jail officers became convinced the man's story was true. He actually claimed to see the ghost after Fynes' cellmate was removed. He described the phantom intruder as looking exactly like Martin Fynes, standing next to him, but completely separate. The officer was so startled by the appearance that he quickly slammed the cell door shut and called for help. When the cell door was opened a few minutes later, the spirit had vanished, but Fynes was lying on his bunk unconscious. Fynes believed that the murder of Andrew Garrity had been committed by a spirit that had taken his form – and then continued to visit him while he was locked up in Carlinville.

Spirit of the Marvel Theatre

During the days when Route 66 passed through Carlinville, one of the popular stops in town was the Marvel Theatre, located just two blocks off the highway on Main Street. The Marvel was built in 1920 by Frank and Freida Paul as a playhouse and movie theater and opened the doors on August 26. The theater not only brought movies and live theater to the area, but acrobats, comedians, and even live animal shows. There was something for everyone at the Marvel Theatre.

And all of that was thanks to Freida Paul, perhaps the most glamorous woman in Carlinville's history. She was not your average farm girl of the early 1920s. Frieda had been well-schooled in theater and music and in 1914, had gone west to Hollywood. She worked in a Los Angeles theater, where she played piano as a musical accompaniment to silent films, a skill that she brought back to Illinois and introduced to the Marvel with the $10,000 pipe organ that was purchased for the theater.

Freida was known for her passion for the Marvel Theatre and became one of the first prominent businesswomen in Carlinville. She took the lead in the theater's business and was not easily discouraged by business setbacks.

In 1925, three armed bandits followed the Pauls home from the theater one winter night, bound and gagged them, and stole jewelry and cash valued at over $1,200 before fleeing the scene. Frank was able to get free and untie his wife and their son, but the police never found the robbers.

During the early morning hours of December 18, 1926, another tragedy occurred when police officers discovered the Marvel engulfed in flames. Although the fire department worked valiantly to save the theater, it was a total loss. Many suspected arson. Someone had tried to set fire to the theater a few years before, but nothing could be proven.

Freida was determined to keep the theater alive and assured the public that the Marvel would be rebuilt. On the same morning that the Marvel burned, Freida leased the old Grand Theatre building and even arranged a show for that same night.

The Marvel re-opened on January 19, 1928. Soon after, it became one of the first theaters in the area to feature sound pictures. The first show was Al Jolson's, "The Jazz Singer."

The theater changed hands several times over the years. In 1977, it was split into a twin theater, dividing the balcony from the main floor. Sadly, the Marvel closed down in February 2014 and, as of this writing, remains dark. Dark, but according to the stories, not empty.

According to former staff members, the ghost of a woman has been seen, watching over the activity that takes place at the theater. She keeps a watchful eye over things, pleased or displeased with what she sees taking place. It's believed that this lingering spirit is that of Freida Paul, who remains behind at the place where she was the happiest in life. You see, not all ghosts remain behind because of tragedy and horrible events.

Some of them stay behind because they simply don't want to leave.

The Final Stretch of the Old Alignment

Like so many other towns between Springfield and Hamel, the fortunes of **Gillespie** were built on coal. The town followed a familiar pattern: settlement, the railroad, the coal mines, and a sad decline.

The first settlers to the area were farmers, who arrived to work the black soil of the region, which was nourished by the Dry Fork and Little Cahokia Creek. The first to settle there was Michael Dodd in 1825, but no one followed him to the area for three years, when Dennis Davis, B. Nowlin, and J.G. White each purchased nearby

Early days in Gillespie, Illinois from a local postcard, date unknown

land. More families followed over the next few years, and in 1833, George Harlan but the first mill. A school was built, then a church in 1834.

The settlement was just a loose collection of houses and a few stores until the early 1850s, when the railroads made plans to pass through. The town site was surveyed in 1853, and the first real building in town was erected that same year by B.F. Clark. The lower floor was a dry goods store and he and his family lived upstairs. A year later, the makeshift post office, which had been in the home of Giles Adams, was moved into the store and Thomas Chandler was named as the first postmaster.

The new town was called Gillespie and it was named in honor of Judge Joseph Gillespie by the managers of the Indianapolis & St. Louis railroad. The city grew after the railroad passed through it, but it was the coal mines that brought a short period of boom times to the town. In the early 1900s, three of the largest coal mines in the world were located in Gillespie. They were owned and operated by the Chicago & Northwestern Railroad Company.

The first mines were started in town around 1880 with the Dorsey Mine and Gillespie Mine shaft. The railroad being built across the state created a need for more coal, causing more mines to be sunk, and more men and their families arriving to bring the coal to the surface. The mine companies built housing additions for the miners, each cottage nearly identical, and the miners were required to purchase their food and supplies from the company store.

As mentioned, the Chicago & Northwest Railroad started mines as a fuel source for their operations. They sunk four shafts in all. In 1910, they also established repair yards at Gillespie for its coal cars. They were, at that time, using 2,000 cars each day to handle the coal. There were 75 men working full-time in the shops, just to keep the cars in good repair.

Gillespie survived a number of tragedies over the years, from a fire that wiped out the entire business section in 1905, to the deaths of miners in mine accidents, but it could not avoid the inevitable changes that came when the railroads declined and most of the mines were played out. But even so, Gillespie has endured. The locals still celebrate the heyday of the mining era today with the annual "Black Diamond Days" celebration and still honor the miners who fell during the labor strife in the 1920s. It may not be the "boom town" of days gone by, but most can agree that it's still a pleasant place to live.

"Auld Lang Syne" at the Coliseum Ballroom

As the original Route 66 alignment rolls on, it took travelers to the legendary **Coliseum Ballroom** in Benld. The ballroom's long and often mysterious past has been linked to big band history, bootlegging, gangsters, murder, and more, and it remains one of the great old landmarks of the region. The ballroom stopped being a dancehall many years before the fatal fire that destroyed it in 2011, but it still managed to attract people from all over the region who came looking for a little history – and for its resident ghosts.

The Coliseum stood for more than eight decades in the small town of **Benld**, a once-prosperous mining community that was known as a melting pot of nationalities who came to south-central Illinois to work in the coal mines. Situated in the middle of three mines, Benld furnished residences, churches, schools, and more to the immigrants who settled the area. They came from many countries, including Austria, Bohemia, Croatia, England, France, Germany, Greece, Ireland, Italy, Lithuania, Russia, Scotland, Slovakia, and Sweden.

The history of the area began in the late 1800s with the arrival of the Dorsey family, who settled the Cahokia Township of Macoupin County. In the early 1900s, the Superior Coal Company, a subsidiary of the Chicago & Northwestern Railroad, bought 40,000 acres of coal and mineral rights from the Dorsey family and began to sink mines to furnish coal for their locomotives.

In 1903, the town of Benld was established, taking its name from its founder, Ben L. Dorsey. Legend has it that the name was actually a mistake. The story goes that a sign once existed outside of town that had Dorsey's full name on it. A storm came along and tore off the end, leaving the letters "Ben L. D." By default, this became the name of the town. No one seems to know if there is any truth to this tale, but it's an odd bit of possible history for this fascinating town.

Benld was laid out in the middle of the three mines and soon began to grow. The original town was platted so that North Sixth and Seventh Streets would be the hub of the community, with growth spreading in every direction. At the western edge of town, a station was built and tracks were laid by the Illinois Traction System for their trolley. The Chicago & Northwestern Railroad also laid their tracks to the west of town, creating a surge of business toward Central Avenue, where a rail yard and a roundhouse were developed, creating additional employment for the area. In 1916, a fourth mine, the No. 4, was sunk west of Benld and more people came to the area. By the early 1920s, the population of the town had grown to over 5,000.

The town boasted a racetrack, a football field, where a professional football team played, and a city band that consisted of coal miners who played every Sunday, their only day off. Benld also had barbershops, blacksmith shops, dairies, a feed store, hardware and grocery stores, laundries, a hemp factory, a soda factory, a lumber yard, a bowling alley, a theater, taverns, and numerous other establishments during its heyday.

One unusual incident in Benld's history occurred on September 19, 1938, when a local resident named Edward McCain was surprised to find that his garage and automobile had been damaged by a falling meteorite. The meteorite, which was about four inches in diameter, fell from space and penetrated the roof of the garage. It ripped through the top of the car, through the car's upholstered seat, and the floor of the car before coming to rest on the garage floor. The "Benld Meteorite," as it came to be known, is now on display at the Field Museum of Natural History in Chicago.

But it wasn't a meteorite that gave Benld its lasting infamy; it was liquor. During the years of Prohibition, the town of Benld was home to more than 40 taverns, which operated wide-open, even though it was against the law to sell alcohol anywhere in America. In Benld, alcohol wasn't just sold, it was also manufactured. In a wooded area east of town and along Cahokia Creek, was a place known locally as Mine No. 5. Of course, it was not a coal mine at all but a large, well-funded, alcohol distillery with three 50-foot smokestacks and the capability to produce hundreds of gallons of whiskey each week. The distillery was one of the largest illegal operations of its kind in the United States at the time and it was owned either by gangsters from St. Louis, Springfield, or by Al Capone himself, depending on the stories you hear. There are some pretty solid recollections of Capone actually visiting Benld later in the 1920s, so it's possible that the distillery was connected to his Chicago operations in some way.

Illegal liquor operations in Benld would also give birth to what remains as the town's greatest historic landmark, the Coliseum Ballroom. The large brick ballroom, with a main floor that could hold up to 800 dancers, was opened on December 24, 1924. It had been built for the grand sum of just over $50,000, an exorbitant amount

The Coliseum Ballroom in Benld, Illinois

for the time period. The Coliseum was constructed and operated by Dominic Tarro, a local businessman, but rumors spread that the funding for the project had come from unsavory pockets, namely those of gangsters who planned to use the ballroom as a hideout for syndicate gunmen and as a way station for liquor runners between Chicago and St. Louis.

And as it turned out, the rumors apparently had some basis in truth. In January 1930, Tarro was one of many people indicted by a U.S. Department of Justice investigation into bootlegging in Central Illinois. Indictments were returned against the Corn Products Co. and the Fleischmann Yeast Co. for supplying materials for making liquor and, in addition, 17 bootleggers were charged with conspiring to violate the Volstead Act, which enforced Prohibition as law. This was the first time that the government criminally charged the companies that made the supplies used in illicit distilling, but investigators believed they could make a case against them. Prohibition agent James Eaton was able to track more than 200 carloads of corn sugar that were sent from a St. Louis plant of the Corn Products Co. to bootleggers in Benld. He also believed that the Fleischmann Yeast Co. had sold products to distillers in Benld, a town where, prior to Prohibition, there was little market for their product.

The alleged go-between for the bootleggers and the suppliers was Dominic Tarro, owner of the Coliseum Ballroom, and according to the indictments, the purchasing agent for the raw materials and a distributor for the illegal finished product. On January 30, Tarro posted a $30,000 bond and was freed from custody. Rumors began to circulate that Tarro planned to offer testimony about the Benld operations in exchange for immunity when a few days later, he disappeared.

On February 5, Tarro's automobile was found near Mason City. He left home that morning in Benld and was on his way to see his attorney, but he never arrived. The car was discovered later on that same day. It had been riddled with bullets and left on the side of the road. Tarro was nowhere to be found and while his lawyer publicly stated that he feared his client had been murdered, the prosecutor in the case surmised that he was hiding out because someone had heard that he planned to be a government witness. He was sure that Dominic Tarro would turn up soon, alive and well.

Tarro did turn up, on May 2, but he was neither well, nor alive. His body was found in the Sangamon River and was positively identified by his cousin, Fazzio. His arms and feet had been tied together with wire, a strand of which had been looped around his neck to draw his head down almost to his knees. He had been badly beaten and the clothing stripped from his body before he was thrown in the river. The corpse was badly decomposed and the coroner surmised that the body had been in the water since the day that Tarro had disappeared.

Dominic Tarro had learned the hard way that it didn't pay to turn informant against the mob.

Following his murder, Tarro's wife, Marie, took over management of the ballroom, and in the years that followed, the Coliseum gained legendary status for the big name groups that were booked to play there. The ballroom drew top talent of all types, dating from the 1930s all the way into the 1970s.

Some of the bands and acts that played at the Coliseum included Sammy Kaye, Tommy Dorsey, Count Basie, Lawrence Welk, Duke Ellington, Lionel Hampton, and Guy Lombardo, who treated patrons to what became one of his signature tunes, "Auld Lang Syne." Years later, former customers would remember this song as a special favorite from the heyday of the Coliseum.

After the Big Band era, the Coliseum wholeheartedly embraced rock-n-roll. Performers that came during the 1950s, 1960s, and 1970s included Ray Charles, Ike and Tina Turner, Fats Domino, Chuck Berry, Chubby Checker, the Everly Brothers, Jerry Lee Lewis, Bill Haley and the Comets, Fleetwood Mac, Ted Nugent, Bob Seger, and many others. People came from all over the region, even the state, to see the acts that Marie, and later her daughter, Joyce, booked into the Coliseum. The ballroom had the largest dance floor in the state of Illinois, outside of Chicago, and could seat hundreds on the main floor and the balcony.

The place enjoyed great success for many years, especially after Joyce Tarro took over operations after her mother's death in 1955. She was a tough, hard-headed businesswoman who, her friends always said, would never back down from a fight. She had a habit of carrying around the ballroom's weekend receipts with her, which could amount to several thousand dollars, a fact that was commonly known in the small town of Benld. But what was also well-known was the fact that Joyce also carried a gun, and she was not afraid to use it. Unfortunately, the gun was not enough to save her life in February 1976.

On February 16, a huge party was held at the Coliseum to celebrate St. Valentine's Day. It was packed for the event with over 800 people in attendance. Bartenders at all five of the ballroom's bars were kept busy throughout the evening. With admission prices set at $2.50 per person, and thousands of dollars made from the free-flowing drinks, Joyce had a very good night. When she got home, though, she surprised two robbers who had broken into her house and was shot five times. Joyce returned fire but died moments later. The killers, a long-time criminal and his girlfriend, were later captured by the police. After a trial, each received sentences of 50 to 150 years on the murder charges, plus 25 to 75 years for the armed robbery, and an additional 10 years for theft.

It was a fitting end to a bloody chapter in the history of Benld and the Coliseum Ballroom. This second violent death brought down the curtain on the Tarro era at the Coliseum.

Many feared that, after Joyce Tarro's death, the ballroom would be closed for good. In her will, Tarro had left the Coliseum to Bonnie Anderson, a former Benld resident who had gone on to become a singer and entertainer in Ft. Lauderdale, Florida. The ballroom was operated for a short time by Tarro's cousin, Bud Tarro, who owned a grocery store in town, but his tenancy was short-lived. After the Coliseum was closed for two months, Anderson began leasing it to Patty Ferraro, a close friend of Joyce's, and Hiram Franzoi, the owner of a construction company. Sadly, their occupancy of the ballroom would also not last for long. Ferraro had vivid memories of the night that Tarro was killed and she remained at the ballroom for as long as she could. She said, "It's not the same place with her gone, and the atmosphere to me, is different. The ballroom business isn't the ballroom business without Joyce."

As the years passed, times turned tough for the ballroom. New owners attempted to revitalize the place a time or two with music acts and even as a roller rink but it never again enjoyed the success of its earlier days. However, it was during these days of decline that employees began to report strange incidents in the building. Eerie footsteps were often heard and shadowy figures were sometimes reported in dark corners. One former employee, George Luttman, who worked there from 1977 to 1981, told me that he often came in to clean in the mornings and on several occasions he saw people in formal clothes who looked as if they were ready to swing to the sounds of Tommy Dorsey or one of the other big bands of the era. When approached, the figures always vanished.

The Coliseum fell into years of abandonment and further decline, but then, in the late 1990s, it was re-opened as an antique mall and a roadside attraction on Route 66. The new owners bought the building in October and had a lot of work to do before they could make their planned opening in February. Almost immediately, they later reported, a woman was spotted upstairs who should not have been there. The figure had short dark hair and was there one moment and then gone the next. No one had any idea who she might be, but she was seen in the building many times after that.

Customers, visitors, and even antique dealers who came in to stock their booths reported a litany of odd happenings. A local carpenter, who helped renovate the building, saw a man ascend a back stairway that the owners had blocked for safety reasons. When he went up the rickety stairs to investigate, he found that the bottom of the stairs were actually inaccessible. There was no way that anyone could have climbed up the staircase.

Dealers and customers experienced cold spots among the booths and in hallways and told of a misty woman who was often seen near a former bar area. In spite of the fact that the owners paid to have the place re-wired, lights frequently turned on and off without explanation. Others told of feeling a presence as the hair on the backs of their necks stood on end. They also talked of a breeze that moved past them as if someone had just walked by. In every case, no one visible was near.

Eventually, the owners closed the Coliseum, likely discouraged by the lack of traffic that ventured off the interstate, and moved their operations a few miles south to a former school building in Livingston. The Coliseum was closed, dark, and empty for several years, but then re-opened again, first as an antique mall and then as a venue for live music once again. It seemed that things were finally starting to happen again at the legendary ballroom, but then disaster struck. On July 31, 2011, a fire broke out during a music show and the Coliseum was gutted by flames. The building was beyond repair, marking the end of another icon on Route 66.

Motoring Down the "New" Route 66

In 1930, Route 66 was changed. Even though the highway had not existed before 1926, it had been assigned to follow the route of State Highway 4, which had been built in 1924 from existing roads and new pavement to provide an "all-weather road" between St. Louis and Chicago. When Route 66 was designated, Illinois became the first state to be able to boast that Route 66 was paved from end to end.

The paved road also had other benefits as well. Prohibition was in effect from 1920 until 1933 and the paved road made the transportation of illegal alcohol possible virtually all year long. Production stills located in Central and Southern Illinois could easily ship alcohol on Route 66 to speakeasies in Chicago and St. Louis.

Back in those days, the average speed of an automobile was 25 mph and cars shared the road with horse-drawn vehicles and travels. Since mechanical problems with frequent were the newfangled automobiles, it was necessary for the highway to pass through many small towns. But soon, that would all change.

Cars began to get faster and people started looking for speed. They didn't want – or need-- to have to stop so often in small towns, so Route 66 was aligned to a more sparsely populated area of Illinois. By the early 1930s, cars now had top speeds of 60-80 mph and the nickname of "Bloody 66" began to be used by police officers who witnessed what happened when poor drivers got behind the wheels of fast cars. Even so, this didn't stop the top speed on the highway to be set at 70 mph.

By the late 1930s, Route 66 between Chicago and St. Louis was the heaviest traveled long-distance highway in the state and the alignment added a new series of memories to the Illinois stretch of America's Main Street.

Route 66 passes through quiet farm communities like **Glenarm**, where a restored covered bridge crosses over Sugar Creek; **Divernon**; **Thomasville**; and **Farmersville**, which was home to iconic **Art's Motel and Restaurant**.

In 1932, Art McAnarney and Marty Gorman became business partners, operating everything from illegal gin joints to gas stations to dance halls and casinos around Farmersville. In 1937, Art decided to go into business for himself and sold his share of the business to Gorman. Art leased a building that had once been home to a two-story filling station called Hendricks Brothers Café and Gas Station and went into business. He continued operating the gas station and restaurant, but also opened six cabins for overnight guests, until a fire in 1952 destroyed the buildings second floor. With the main dining room still in one piece, Art started all over again and rebuilt the place on a single level.

Art died in 1957, leaving the business to his sons, Elmer and Joe. By that time, Route 66 had been expanded into four lanes and more and more traffic was coming past the location. So, in 1960, they expanded, building a 13-room L-shaped motel that still stands today. When Interstate 55 was

159

completed in the mid–1970s, it luckily ran right in front of the property. An exit for Farmersville was constructed and, as more luck would have it, Art's was conveniently located near the exit ramp. It was the first place that most people saw when they exited the interstate.

Art's continued to operate for many more years, although as of this writing, it's closed and looking for a new owner.

"Our Lady of the Highways"

Along Route 66 in Illinois, travelers will find scores of monuments. There are statues of men like Abraham Lincoln – even a watermelon in his honor and a great bronze cast at his tomb that tourists rub for good luck – and obelisks for miners who died defending the rights of the working man. There are towering spacemen and lumberjacks, wielding axes and oversized hot dogs, and much more. But there's a monument of a different sort on the highway, just a few miles west of a little town called **Raymond**. It's a marble statue of the Virgin Mary on the edge of a cornfield. Some call her the "Queen of the Road," but most Route 66 buffs refer to her as "Our Lady of the Highways."

At night, there are lights shining on the statue, so she's very difficult to miss, even on Interstate 55, which lies to the east of what was once Route 66. She stands on a concrete pedestal, protected by an alcove of wood and stone. A priest helped lay the stone walk that leads up to her site. She has been standing there, looking out over the road with her hands grasped in prayer, since 1959. The group included kids from Raymond, Litchfield, Staunton, Mt. Olive, Hillsboro, Morrisonville, Divernon, Farmersville, and Taylorville, among other places. Farmer Francis Marten, whose oldest daughter, Loretta, was one of those farm kids, offered to have the stature placed on his land.

After $400 was raised to buy the Carrara marble statue and ship it from Italy, they came up with another $500 to pay for the concrete, lumber, and lights to create the shrine. Marten kept his promise and he donated the land along Route 66, which was still a thriving, busy highway at the time. At the dedication, two priests came out and blessed the statue and locals prayed and sang songs. A plaque was placed below the statue that read: "Mary, Loving Mother of Jesus, Protect us on the Highway."

Marten allowed the kids to put up a dozen hand-painted placards (Burma–Shave style) that read off the "Hail Mary," phrase by phrase, on successive posts for about a half-mile along the highway.

After the shrine was erected, there were the pilgrims. People would meet up on the road and walk to the statue, saying the rosary. They'd stand around the sign and sing hymns and perhaps have a picnic. The kids returned every years to paint, rake up the dead leaves, and keep the place looking nice. But after five or six years, the pilgrimages and all of the attention mostly stopped. The kids grew up, got married, and moved away, so Marten and his wife, Ruth, took over. They cared for the shrine, paid the light bill, trimmed the trees, and kept fresh flowers at Mary's feet.

When Interstate 55 was built, the government tried to make Marten take down the "Hail Mary" signs, but he refused. He knew that the signs were four inches inside his property line and there was nothing that anyone could do about it. The signs stayed put, and they still stand today. Marten passed away in 2002, but his sons, Carl and Lee, continue to maintain the shine and passersby on Route 66 can still view the tribute, which stands as both a bit of highway history and a testament to the faith of those who believed that the Virgin Mary would guide them on a highway that was then known as "Bloody 66."

Getting Your Kicks in Litchfield

Travelers that rolled on southwest toward St. Louis found a lot of places to get a hot meal and a cold drink in Litchfield, a town that got its start solely as a town site along the proposed line of the Terre Haute & Alton Railroad. The original platting of the town came first, however, and the planners called the place Hadinsburg in 1849. But a year later, a man named Electus Bachus Litchfield formed the Litchfield Town Company, a consortium of businessmen, and chose the fledgling community as the perfect spot for a railroad crossing. A name change was proposed and in March 1855, the town became known as Litchfield.

In the years after the Civil War, the town moved away from farming and began attracting industries. In 1867, a blind, sash, and door factory opened, and that same year, the first coal mining company on nearby Rocky Branch began operating. The organization of the Litchfield Mining Company took place in February 1869.

The Wabash Railroad ran a line through Litchfield in 1870, beginning an era of prosperity – and disaster. In the early spring of 1867, three stores burned in town, but it was the burning of the McPherson Mill in 1870 that did the most damage. In 1871, fire swept through the central business district, and in 1873, the Boxberger Mill was leveled by fire.

The founding of the Litchfield Car and Machine Company in 1876 truly transformed the community, however. Formed from the reorganization of the Litchfield Car Manufacturing Company and H.H. Beach & Company, a machine shop and foundry, the new company quickly became an industry leader in the manufacture of railroad freight cars, coaches, locomotives, and steam engines.

And more changes were coming. In 1878, oil discoveries, and in 1885, the discovery of large pockets of natural gas brought about increased development in the area. With the establishment of gas mains, Litchfield became the first town in the state of Illinois to have gas lighting.

Growth and development continued into the early years of the twentieth century, in spite of a major disaster in 1893 when the Planet Mills, one of the largest flour mills in the country, exploded and burned.

Sadly, fires and explosions in flour mills happened often in the nineteenth century. Flour dust in the air can be highly combustible and, on many occasions, obliterated entire factories and killed scores of people. This is exactly what happened in Litchfield in 1893. Even though initial accounts of the explosion blamed the fire on a boiler malfunction, evidence discovered later pointed to employees overlooking a major safety precaution: the dust machine. The machine had not been properly secured and allowed flour dust to escape into the confines of the rolling room. When a fire broke out, a night watchman tried to put out the fire, but with no success. Apparently, the water pipes to the emergency hydrant were not in working order and he was unable to get enough water. The fire quickly spread to adjoining rooms and when it reached the rolling room, the airborne dust exploded. The shock of the explosion was heard 25 miles away, and window glass was broken, and chimneys blown down for several miles in every direction. All the plate glass in the stores on Main and State Streets was blown out. About 40 homes were wrecked and many others slightly damaged. Two blocks of local businesses were destroyed, one man was killed, and 12 others were seriously injured.

And that was not Litchfield's only calamity. On July 5, 1904, a Wabash train known as the *Exposition Limited*, which was ferrying passengers to the World's Fair and to a Democratic convention in St. Louis, was running about 20 minutes late and trying to make up the time when it struck an open switch outside of Litchfield and overturned. In an instant, almost the entire train was demolished. Seven of the nine cars caught on fire. As the steam from the engine began escaping, it killed the engineer, J.B. Sanford, fireman W.L. Smith, and the train dispatcher, Howard Groves, who was riding in the cab. It was asserted in the aftermath of the crash that the red signal light had been on, showing that the switch was open. The engineer, if he noticed that fact, was unable to stop the train, and when it overturned, it plowed into a long line of box cars that were on a separate track in the yard. The baggage car, a smoking car, and a day coach crashed into the engine and the fire swept through the train. Only two Pullman cars at the rear were saved from the flames.

Just moments after the crash, the city wreck whistles began to blow and the fire bells began to ring. Residents were quickly on the way to the scene of the accidents. The newspapers reported, "The screams of the injured and the groans of the dying were horrifying as the bruised and blackened bodies were taken from the wreckage. The dead and injured were frightfully mangled and identification in many cases was extremely difficult." There were 22 people killed and 37 more injured in the terrible accident.

In the days that followed, wrecking crews worked hard to clear the tracks of overturned cars and debris. Thousands of people arrived from surrounding towns to help with the grim work, or simply to stare at the carnage. Local residents assisted the police in making sure that no souvenirs were carried from the scene by curiosity-seekers. Money, jewels, and other property of those who were killed were closely guarded, and the authorities reported no trouble with those who came to the scene.

At that time, it was regarded as the worst disaster in Wabash Railroad history.

Litchfield's connection with Route 66 began in 1930, when the new alignment of the highway was put into place. This added another facet to the town's economy. The American Automobile Association (AAA) consistently found places to recommend in Litchfield and nearly everyone listed **Brubaker's Garage** as a place for auto repairs, if the worst happened on the road, of course.

The Ariston Café was moved from Carlinville to Litchfield after the new alignment of Route 66 was opened.

Litchfield may have made its fortunes by industry, mining, and oil production, but it made a name for itself as a great place to stop along Route 66. One of the best places to eat in town was the **Ariston Café**. As mentioned earlier, Litchfield was not this iconic restaurant's first location. It had its start in Carlinville in 1924, but when business died after the highway was re-aligned, Pete Adam moved his café to Litchfield in 1931 and re-opened it as "the most up-to-date restaurant between Chicago and St. Louis." The place did so well that Pete had to construct a new building in 1935 that is still there

The Overhead, home of "Chicken in a Basket"

today. Hubert Humphrey once ate at the restaurant, and so did Tommy Dorsey, who was playing just down the road at the Coliseum Ballroom in Benld. The place still looks pretty much like it did in the 1930s. Over the years, Route 66 was rerouted several times through Litchfield and each change made it necessary to move the front door of the restaurant to keep it facing the road. As fate would have it, with the last realignment, the restaurant entrance wound up at the original front location.

A favorite stop for truckers was **Skinny's Café**, and people who traveled back and forth on Route 66 always knew to stop at the **Gardens Restaurant and Motel**, the **Blue Danube**, and many others.

The **Overhead**, a café near a bridge on the north side of the city, was started by Charles Aikman and Truman L. Felts in the summer of 1948. Located just north of the Chicago, Burlington & Quincy Railroad bridge, it was a landmark for years. The restaurant, one of the busiest on Route 66, introduced a specialty, "Chicken in a Basket" shortly after opening and reportedly served over 40,000 chickens in their first two years in business. Felts sold his interest in the business to Francis "Lum" Fleming in July 1950, but no changes were made to the menu of delicious road food and cold drinks. They also opened a souvenir store, one of the first on Route 66 in the area.

The **Belvedere Motel and Café** became a Route 66 landmark in the 1950s, even though it was built a number of years before and, like many other businesses in Litchfield, was remodeled to match the various alignments through town. The

The Belvedere, long past its Route 66 heyday

business dated back to the late 1920s when Vincenzo "James" and Albina Cerolla purchased several lots along the highway and started things up with a one-room gas station and a single pump. As money permitted, they expanded to include a motel and a café, both built in 1936. The small, four-unit motor lodge was originally designed to include individual garages next to each unit. They also built a larger, brick gas station at this same time.

The new four-lane highway was completed through Litchfield in 1940. Located west of the original two-lane road and on the opposite side of the motel property, the couple hurriedly had new signs made and moved the motel's office to the other side of the lot.

James passed away in 1945, and Albina died four years later. The property was willed to their daughter, Edith, and her husband, Lester "Curly" Kranich. Around 1950, they remodeled the hotel by enclosing the garages and making room for additional guest units. At this same time, two additional buildings were added behind the gas station, each containing four more units. Each building housed one- and two-bedroom units. Lester and Edith also built a residence for themselves on the property during this same time period. All of this new construction proves that demand for tourist services on Route 66 skyrocketed after the end of World War II, when people really began taking to the roads. It was a golden era for Route 66 and for the Belvedere Motel and Café.

After the interstate was completed in the early 1970s, business disappeared. The gas station closed, but Edith and Lester remodeled the café and kept it going until they retired in 1975. The property changed hands many times in the years that followed, until it became a shadow of its former self. Remnants of the place remain today, but it's nothing like it was in the fading years of Route 66.

Rut's Corner Tourist Camp was built in Litchfield in 1929 by Russell "Ruts" Brawley, just a few years after the decision had been made that Route 66 was going to be re-aligned to run through town. A single row of gable-roofed cottages were built on one side of Brawley's property, while another structure was added that contained five guest rooms. For the customer's convenience, each unit had a covered garage and a private entrance. A community bathhouse was set up between the cabins and the rooms. In time, a café was also added to the property, but it burned in 1936. It was

quickly rebuilt, bigger and better than ever. It now had room to serve up to 150 hungry diners, offering T-bone steak dinners for 40-cents.

It became one of the busiest and most popular stops between Chicago and St. Louis. People loved the food, but they loved the slot machines even more. Employees later recalled having wash basins so heavy with change that it took two men to lift them.

A filling station was later added to the operation, making Rut's a full-service tourist stop. It closed down in 1951 and became the **Annex Café and Motel**, a classic diner-style restaurant with large, slanted glass windows. The guest house was turned into a motor lodge, and the old gas pumps were removed. It's long gone now and today is unrecognizable as the place that it used to be. It's been replaced by a local tavern, just steps away from the decaying ruins of the old Belvedere.

The **Varner Brothers Motel** was started on Route 66 in 1950. The two brothers, Shirley and Ellis, were machinists and farmers, but with land along Route 66, they saw the demand that had been created in Litchfield by the re-alignment of the highway. They built a new "ultra-modern," (according to the postcards) motel, doing most of the work themselves. They opened up with eighteen brick units, each with radiant heat. They later added a café and service station to the property.

The **Dearduff Roller Rink** was a fun stop for overnight Route 66 travelers with children. Located at the junction of the highway and Route 16, it was designed and built by Virgil A. Dearduff in 1946 and opened one year later. It featured a full-scale roller-skating rink and a snack room that served sandwiches, soft drinks, and ice cream, Curb service was available for drivers in the summer months.

Sky View Drive-in, the oldest continuously operated outdoor theater in Illinois and on the entire stretch of Route 66, can also be found in Litchfield. The theater was opened in June 1950 by the Frisina Amusement Company, which was based in Springfield. At the time, they also operated two other theaters in town, the Capitol and the Ritz. At the time, they also operated 60 other theaters, including eight drive-ins in Illinois, Iowa, and Missouri.

The Capitol Theater had been built in 1918 by W.D. Kneedler and was taken over by Frisina in 1931. Seven years later, in 1938, they built the Ritz, a 400-seat theater located on State Street. In 1949, they began construction on the Sky View Drive-in. It had a capacity for 750 cars when it opened and during the heyday of the drive-in theater, it was often packed.

In 1980, the Sky View was purchased by Norman and Del Paul of Carlinville. They also owned the Marvel Theater in Carlinville and the Orpheum in Hillsboro. The Paul's also once owned the Diane, another drive-in theater in Carlinville, but it closed down in the middle 1980s. The drive-in, which was named for their firstborn daughter, still remains just outside of Carlinville. The ticket office and concession stand are now shuttered and dark and the screen is crumbling under the Central

166

Illinois sky. Luckily, its abandonment has not spread to the Sky View, which still offers bargain-priced tickets to movie-goers today. It's a place where it's still 1955 all summer long.

"Mother Jones" and Mt. Olive

As Route 66 rolls on to the south, travelers soon arrived in the little town of Mt. Olive. The land that the town now occupies first belonged to a German immigrant named John C. Niemann, who purchased 40 acres in 1846. After he established a farm and bought more land, he wrote to his brothers, Fred and Henry, in Germany and urged them to join him on the Central Illinois prairie. After they arrived, they purchased land that adjoined their brothers' farm.

Soon, more Germans came to the area and Niemann built a store to service the new settlers. The store was also home to a post office and Niemann became the postmaster of what was then known as "Niemann's Settlement." In 1866, a man named Corbus J. Keiser purchased a half interest in the store and it was re-named Niemann & Keiser.

It was Keiser, along with another man, Mient Arkebauer, who laid out a town plat on Niemann's original acres. The town was called Oelburg, which means "Mount of Olives." In 1870, when the railroad came through, the settlement's name was changed once again to Drummond Station. A few years later, Niemann sold his interest in the store, and another decade passed before the town would finally settle on the name Mt. Olive.

In the meantime, Corbus Keiser was making a fortune in coal mining. In 1875, he had opened his first shaft, started a mill business in 1876, and opened one of the first banks in town in 1882. He was one of 12 original stockholders in the mine works, which attracted hundreds of immigrants to the community.

Of course, mining brought prosperity to the region, but it also brought violence, grief, and turmoil between union activists and mine owners. After the United Mine Workers of America was formed in 1890, the workers began standing up against unfair wages and company stores. The men lived in company-owned homes and were often paid in scrip or coupons that were redeemable only at stores owned by the mine company. Workers had to buy their own tools, maintain them, and even buy the oil for the lamps they used in the mines. In the beginning, the union had little effect on company owners because if union members went on strike, the company just took away their homes. But over the next decade, even after the union was defeated time and time again, the activists continued to rally. Starting on July 15, 1892, in Mt. Olive, a group of miners began to march south through one coal town after another, calling miners off the job. They held impromptu rallies, winning moral and material support from the communities and their residents. Even so, it was difficult to get the men to join the union. Wages were low, but they were better than nothing, which the men expected to end up with if they incurred the wrath of mine owners. By the time of the great strike of 1897, only about 400 out of 35,000 Illinois coal miners belonged to the union. However, the dedication of this small group began to make a difference, and by early 1898, an agreement was made between the union and management that workers would receive an eight-hour work day, receive a mutually agreed upon age, and company stores would be eliminated.

However, in the fall of 1898, the Chicago-Virden Coal Company, along with many others, sought to be exempted from the agreement. Failing in that effort, management locked out the union workers and began importing strike breakers to work the union men's jobs. This provoked an immediate reaction about the union activists. Violence began at Virden, some 40 miles from Mt. Olive, and the melee became known as the "Virden Massacre."

Four of the miners that were killed were from Mt. Olive and were originally buried in the town cemetery. However, the owner of the land objected to the burials and the Lutheran cemetery barred them from burial because the local minister denounced the miners as "murderers." In response, local union members purchased a one-acre site and the bodies were moved to the new **Union Miner's Cemetery** in 1899. Over the years, additional land was purchased and a monument was dedicated on October 11, 1936.

These four miners were viewed as martyrs by the union, but not many recall their names today. But there is one person buried in the miner's cemetery that became a household name in the bloody years of mine strikes in Illinois. Her name was Mary Jones, or as the miners knew her – "Mother" Jones. She called the miners "her boys" and she asked to be buried in the cemetery at the time of her death in 1930, at age 93.

Mary Harris Jones, or the "grandmother of agitators," as she was denounced on the floor of the U.S. Senate, was born in Ireland on May 1, 1837. Falling victim to the Irish Potato Famine, her family left Ireland for Canada in the 1840s. Persecuted as immigrants and Roman Catholics, they managed as best they could and Mary received an education at the Toronto Normal School. At the age of 23, she moved to the United States and became a teacher in a convent in Monroe, Michigan, in 1859. She later moved first to Chicago, then to Memphis, where she married George E. Jones, a member and organizer of the National Union of Iron Moulders and Foundry Workers of America. The union's members specialized in building and repairing steam engines, mills, and manufacturing equipment. Mary decided to leave the teaching profession and opened a dress shop in Memphis, just before the start of the Civil War.

There were two turning points in Mary's life. The first, and most tragic, was the loss of her husband and their four children – three girls and a boy, all under the age of five – in 1867, during a yellow fever outbreak in Memphis. After that, she returned to Chicago to start another dress-making business.

Then, four years later, she lost her hard-earned home, shop, and possessions in the Great Chicago Fire of 1871. But Mary, like so many others, joined in helping to rebuild the city and it was during this time that she joined the Knights of Labor. She started organizing strikes and fought for justice for workers. At first the strikes and protests failed terribly, ending with the police firing and killing a number of protectors. The Haymarket Riot of 1886, coupled with the fear of anarchism and revolution incited by many union organizations, led to the end of the Knights of Labor. With the United Mine Workers, she frequently led strikers in picketing and encouraged the men to stay on strike when the management brought in strike breakers and

Mary Harris "Mother" Jones – the "Most Dangerous Woman in America"

militias. She strongly believed that "working men deserved a wage that would allow women to stay home to care for their kids." Over time, the strikes became better organized and began to see changes for the workers in the form of better pay and better working conditions. Soon, "Mother" Jones, as she began to be called, led so many successful strikes and protests that she was known as "The Most Dangerous Woman in America," a phrase coined by a West Virginia district attorney, Reese Blizzard, in 1902, at her trial for ignoring an injunction banning meetings by striking miners. He added, "She comes into a state where peace and prosperity reign ... crooks her finger twenty thousand contented men lay down their tools and walk out."

Mary was ideologically estranged from many of the other female activists of the era because she had little interest in the right to vote. She was quoted as saying that "You don't need the vote to raise hell!" She became known as a charismatic and effective public speaker, livening her speeches with real and folk-tale characters, with participation from the audience, and with humor-driven profanity, name-calling, and wit. By age 60, she had effectively assumed the persona of "Mother Jones" by claiming to be older than she actually was, wearing outdated black dresses, and referring to the male workers that she supported as "her boys."

In 1901, she became involved with her "Children's Crusade," a strike to help young female workers in the Pennsylvania silk mills earn adult wages. In those days, one of every six American children were employed and conditions were often harsh and dangerous. Mill owners claimed that they would not be able to do business if they paid adult wages and would be forced to shut down. An agreement was eventually reached that sent the young girls back to the mills, but with better pay. Mary continued to fight child labor for the rest of her life, including in 1903, when she organized children working in mills and mines to march from Philadelphia to Oyster Bay, New York, the hometown of President Theodore Roosevelt, with banners demanding, "We want to go to School and not the mines!" When Mary tried to get the facts about child labor reported in the newspapers, she was told that the mill owners held stock in essentially all of the newspapers and the stories would never appear in print. Mary refused to give up and in time, the issue of child labor reached the public and conditions began to improve.

In 1912, Mary was involved in the Paint Creek–Cabin Creek Strike in West Virginia. She arrived that summer, speaking and organizing through a shooting war between United Mine Workers and a private army hired by mine owners. Martial law was declared in the area and rescinded twice before Mary was arrested on February 13, 1913, and brought before a military court. Accused of conspiring to commit murder, among other charges, she refused to recognize the legitimacy of her court martial. She was sentenced to 20 years in the state penitentiary, but after 85 days of confinement, she was released at the same time that Indiana Senator John Worth Kern initiated a Senate investigation into the conditions of the West Virginia mines.

Several months later, she was in Colorado, helping to organize coal miners. Once again, she was arrested, served time in prison, was escorted from the state in the months leading up to the Ludlow Massacre, in which a private militia hired by mine owners slaughtered dozens of striking workers. After the massacre, Mary was invited to Standard Oil's headquarters to meet with John Rockefeller, Jr., a meeting that prompted Rockefeller to visit the Colorado mines and introduce long-sought reforms.

By 1924, Mary was in court again, this time facing charges of libel, slander, and sedition. In 1925, Charles A. Albert, publisher of the fledgling *Chicago Times*, won a $350,000 judgment against her. But Mary was undaunted. She remained a union organizer for the United Mine Workers into the 1920s and continued to speak on union affairs until the time of her death. In her later years, Mary was largely retired, living on a farm in Maryland, where she wrote:

When the last call comes for me to take my final rest, will the miners see that I get a resting place in the same clay that shelters the miners who gave up their lives of the hills of Virden, Illinois on the morning of October 12, 1898, for their heroic sacrifice of their fellow men. They are responsible for Illinois being the best organized labor state in America. I hope it will be my consolation when I pass away to feel I sleep under the clay with those brave boys.

Mary died in Silver Spring, Maryland, at the age of 93, although she claimed to be 100. She was buried in the Union Miner's Cemetery, and in 1936, a granite obelisk was placed on her grave. The stone bears a great medallion that bears the likeness of "Mother Jones."

On the day of her funeral, tens of thousands of people traveled to Mt. Olive to join her funeral cortege. Father John Maguire of Bourbonnais, Illinois, someone who had assisted Jones in the steel strike in Illinois in 1919, gave the eulogy, suggesting that Jones' death caused "strong men and toil worn women" to cry "tears of bitter grief." Meanwhile, in "mahogany furnished and carefully guarded offices in distant capitals wealthy mine owners and capitalists are breathing sighs of relief" at Jones' death, he said.

Mary's belief that ordinary people had the capacity to control and manage their economic destiny was shared by the miners of Illinois, whose struggles against the coal companies set the standard for a role that could be taken on by workers everywhere. Even after all of these years, Mother Jones remains a symbol to union workers across America, and the Union Miner's Cemetery has become a place of pilgrimage for those who want to see where it all began.

A few years after the tumultuous times of the bloody mine strikes in the area, a coal miner named Henry Soulsby lived and worked in Mt. Olive. He followed in his father's footsteps and became a coal miner, but an injury in the 1920s forced him to leave the mines and look for another trade. In 1926, betting his life savings that Route 66 was going to pass through Mt. Olive, he purchased two lots on which he planned to build a gas station. With help from his young son, Russell, he built a small place of his own design, and in 1926, the **Soulsby Shell Station** opened. After high school, Russell joined his father in the business full-time, and later, Henry's daughters, Ola and Wilma, also helped out.

The original station was a small building with barely enough room for a desk, battery charger, and a few supplies. In 1937, it was doubled in size, but was never large enough to offer a garage for repairs. Instead, the station offered a drive-up ramp on the side of the building for oil changes and minor fixes. When Henry retired, Russell and Ola, who were both adept at pumping gas, checking oil, and doing small tune-ups, took over the station.

Following a stint in the military during World War II as a communications technician, Russell returned home and began using his war experience to repair radios and televisions at the station. In the 1950s, he devoted the north side of the station to his new business and placed an antenna on the roof to test his repairs. In the late 1950s, when Interstate 55 was finished and pulled away most of the Route 66 traffic, the Soulsby station ended up a mile away from the new road. Russell found that this television repair business became the most profitable venture.

Regardless, he and Ola continued pumping gas until 1991, when the pumps were finally removed. Over the next two years, though, the station remained open selling soft drinks, checking oil, and greeting a new and ever-growing legion of Route 66 travelers. The station finally closed its doors for good in 1993. Four years later, Ola passed away and Russell sold the station and all its contents to Mike Dragovich at a public auction.

With Mike's encouragement, however, Russel came to the station as often as he could and greeted visitors. He did this several times each week, until his death in 1999. As a tribute, his funeral procession passed under the station's canopy on the way to the cemetery.

In 2003, Mike led volunteers in a major restoration effort that took the station back to the look and color scheme that it had just after World War II. It remains today in Mt. Olive as a time capsule and fitting tribute to the Soulsby family and the heyday of Route 66.

Staunton's Rabbit Ranch

After leaving Mt. Olive, the later alignment continued on to Staunton, a town that was also crossed by the original alignment of Route 66, and is today home to one of the quirkiest roadside attractions on the Illinois stretch of highway.

Staunton was of the first areas to be settled in Macoupin County and was platted in 1835. A man named Staunton first owned the property and he donated the land for a village square. When new settlers applied for a post office, they unanimously approved the name "Staunton" for the community.

The town was officially organized in 1846 and, at that time, farming was the main way of life. But, like so many other towns in this region, that changed in the 1880s when coal mining came to the area. Before long, hundreds of European immigrants came to town, all looking for jobs. By 1910, there were four coal mines operating in town and while it remained in Staunton until fairly recently, it began its decline decades ago. The town's population declined along with it, although today Staunton is a pleasant community of about 5,000 people with a historic downtown – and one rather strange attraction.

A few years ago, Rich and Linda Henry were taking a trip on Route 66 and noted a lack of visitor's centers and souvenirs along the Mother Road. They decided to rectify the situation, at least in their part of the county, and set about opening up a roadside attraction in their hometown of Staunton. But what kind of attraction? They began pondering this about the same time that their daughter got a pair of rabbits and was surprised by the resulting rise in the rabbit population at their home. The question of the attraction was quickly solved and **Henry's Rabbit Ranch** was born.

But there's more here than just rabbits. Rich and Linda, being Route 66 enthusiasts, opened a visitor's center that looks so much like an authentic old-time filling station that the EPA wanted to know where there buried gas tanks were. Rich had to convince them that the structure was not a real gas station at all. Inside of it, though, visitors find a wide array of Route 66 memorabilia and souvenirs. Outside, the ranch is home to hundreds of rabbits, each with its own name and personality. Some of them have even been trained to do tricks for the travelers who stop by.

Continuing on south of Staunton is the old DeCamp Junction. Once a small coal mining settlement, it's all gone now, except for an old house that was built from a Montgomery Ward catalog kit. It was purchased in 1931 by Alois and Elnora Duda and they moved it to the opposite side of the road and added a north wing, south wing, and upstairs living quarters. Taking out the old living space and replacing it with a dance floor, they soon opened **Duda's Restaurant** and it became a frequent stop for Route 66 travelers. One night in the late 1930s, a large black sedan pulled up in front of the place and unloaded several gangsters who burst into the restaurant with guns

A scene from DeCamp Junction before it became a Route 66 ghost town

drawn and ordered everyone outside. They then ransacked the place, stealing cash, slot machines, and liquor.

On the next road south of DeCamp Junction is the old **Riddel Store**, which is now a private residence. At one time, it was the only place in town to buy groceries and other staples.

The "Neon Cross"

Just a few miles beyond Staunton is the small village of Livingston. The former coal mining community was founded in 1904, and was surrounded by farmland. When the Staunton Coal Company was established that same year, workers began to settle near the railroad tracks that ran alongside the mine site. The mine attracted workers from all over the country and immigrants from all over Europe. The new settlement was called "Livingston" after the farm family that owned the land where the rich coal veins had been found.

The Livingston family laid out the town site and the first post office was operated from the Livingston Lumber Company. David G. Livingston was the first postmaster and, as the years passed, also served as a deputy sheriff, deputy coroner, and school treasurer.

In 1907, Livingston gained telephone service, a school, and the village hall and jail. In 1911, the first bank and first church were established, but in 1912, a fire broke out in a downtown store and destroyed the village hall and jail. They were rebuilt soon after, this time using brick. Over the years, more businesses and churches were built, but in 1930, the New Staunton Coal Company was closed, signaling the first decline in the industry. Businesses and people came and went throughout the years as more mining operations closed.

Today, one of the most popular businesses in town is the **Pink Elephant Antique Mall**, located in the former Livingston High School, which saw its last graduating class in 2004. The mall boasts a large pink elephant in front, as well as an ice cream shop, and a scattering of fiberglass giants on the grounds. Travelers who think this display seems familiar may be recalling the same figures outside of the Coliseum Ballroom in Benld a few years ago, when it was being used as an antique mall.

Just eight miles down the road is the small town of Hamel. Before reaching it, travelers will pass the **St. Paul Lutheran Church** and its large, blue neon cross. It was placed on the building by the Brunworth family for a son that was killed at Anzio during World War II. It's become a landmark for Route 66 travelers, wistfully sending thoughts of safe travels for those who journey past.

Across Interstate 55 is the restored **Hamel Meramec Caverns barn**. It's one of only two on the Illinois stretch of Route 66 and it's not to be missed.

As a traveler motors into Hamel, it's impossible to miss that the town embraces its Route 66 heritage with banners and Burma-Shave signs. Even though Hamel got its start in 1918, it wasn't officially incorporated until 1955, but it presents a nice picture of small-town America today. While in town, a great place to check out is **Scotty's Route 66 Bar**. Built in the 1930s as Ernie's Roadhouse, the old tavern continues to serve up hot food and cold beer to highway travelers.

Route 66 to Edwardsville

Eight miles down the road is the third oldest city in Illinois – Edwardsville. The first building in what would become Edwardsville was a log cabin that was built around 1805 by a settler named Thomas Kirkpatrick. Other settlers soon followed, and in 1812, Ninian Edwards, the first Illinois territorial governor, created Madison County and designated Kirkpatrick's farm as the county seat. Three years later, Kirkpatrick surveyed the settlement and named it "Edwardsville" in honor of the governor.

More settlers arrived over the next few years and by 1816, the village had two stores, including one owned by Abraham Prickett. He had arrived in the area from Kentucky in 1808 and became the town's postmaster. His son, George, was the first white child born in the settlement. The other store was owned by Benjamin Stephenson, who built a home in Edwardsville in 1820 that still stands today. John T. Lusk was the proprietor of the first hotel in town. In its early years, Edwardsville continued to grow, and eventually, Governor Edwards made his home there.

By 1834, much of the town's trade was being drained away by nearby St. Louis and Alton, and Edwardsville's population began to decline. At the time, the city had four stores, two saloons, a castor oil factory, and a female academy. By the end of the Civil War, Edwardsville had started to grow again, thanks to a new railroad line and the building of several new factories. In 1890, N.O. Nelson relocated his plumbing and fixture factory on the outskirts of town. Surrounding the factory, he also constructed his own model town for workers, based on the cooperation movement and profit-sharing with the workers. The workers chose the name of "Leclaire" for the model town, named for Edmund Leclaire of France, one of the pioneers of profit sharing.

Today, Edwardsville is a thriving community with scores of new businesses, restaurants, and two historic districts, including the Leclaire district that

A & W Root Beer stand in Edwardsville in the 1950s

encompasses N.O. Nelson's company town, and the St. Louis district, a tree-lined residential neighborhood filled with preserved old homes. The city also boasts a downtown area that is filled with commercial buildings that have survived since the late nineteenth century.

Edwardsville was also the home of two separate restaurant and lodging legends – one that came before Route 66 and one that came along during the heyday of the Mother Road. One of those places became known as one of the most haunted places in the entire region and memories of it still spook those who remember it before it burned down in 1985.

The Three Mile House

Even though it burned to the ground on a cold March morning over 30 years ago, the historic Three Mile House has long been considered to have been one of the most haunted places in the area. This reportedly ghost-infested building was once located on Illinois 159, a little outside of Edwardsville, and just a short distance off Route 66. Even though it has been gone for years, the stories about the place continue to be recalled today, and those who had experiences there still get chills from the retellings of the ghostly events that occurred.

The history of the Three Mile House began in 1858, when it was built by a St. Louis barber named Frederick Gaertner. It opened its doors along the St. Louis–Springfield stage road and the inn and tavern proved to be a popular roadside establishment. The first brick section of the Three Mile House was ready for business by 1860. The place had been built to primarily serve as a tavern or inn where travelers could eat, rest, and spend the night. Those to whom the inn offered hospitality were mostly individuals traveling by horseback or buggy, and most importantly, farmers and cattle drivers taking their stock to the markets in St. Louis.

Gaertner's business increased enough to justify enlarging the original building to include a dining room, kitchen, tavern, grocery store, and post office on the first floor and between 10 and 15 sleeping rooms on the second.

Thanks to the thriving trade from travelers and the stagecoach line, a blacksmith shop was opened next door to the tavern in 1863. The two buildings served as a social and business center for the surrounding area for many years. Frederick Gaertner was well-known and liked throughout the area and became famous for his generous hospitality. He became friends with many of the upscale citizens of Edwardsville and threw lavish parties and receptions at the Three Mile House, drawing visitors from around the area. In addition to the friendships that he cultivated with members of local society and politicians, he also made many friends among the common people, farmers, and cattlemen, who made up the largest part of his business. Because of this,

The infamous Three Mile House became known as one of the most haunted buildings in the entire region.

the Three Mile House was known all over the region and became a destination point for travelers.

The inn remained prosperous for more than two decades, although things began to decline by the 1880s. By this time, the railroads had begun to make stagecoach travel, at least in the east, obsolete. The rail lines were also able to provide a more economical way to take cattle to market, thereby eliminating the need to take the herds by an overland route to St. Louis. After a few seasons of declining trade, Gaertner decided to close the inn and he returned to his birthplace in Pittsburgh, Pennsylvania. When he passed away, the land, and the now abandoned tavern, was left to his son, Tony.

The Three Mile House stood empty for the next 25 years, slowly deteriorating, until Tony Gaertner sold it to an Illinois road contractor named Orrie Dunlap. Dunlap was in possession of some very lucrative contracts with the state to build and pave Route 112 (now Route 159). In order to more easily service the contracts, he wanted to find a building along the highway project that could be used as a headquarters for his construction crew. He discovered the empty Three Mile House and decided to buy and renovate the building for this purpose. Offices could be set up in the old building and his men could be fed and even quartered during the many months it would take for the road to be built.

After the highway was completed, several others leased the inn until Roy Mohrman of Collinsville bought the land outright. In the years prior to this, and during a period in which a succession of different owners claimed the property, the house was allegedly used for a variety of notorious purposes. The Three Mile House was said to have been used as a gambling house, a bordello, and a bootlegging operation during Prohibition. As all of these activities were obviously illegal, no records remain to say exactly who ran these operations and only rumor and legend exist to tell us what went on there during these lost years. The decades of the 1920s and 1930s are lost, but we do know that in the 1940s, the house operated as a roadside tavern.

In 1970, the Three Mile House was purchased by a real estate developer named Merrill Ottwein, who hoped to renovate the place and open it again for business. Rumor had it that Ottwein planned to turn the place into a nightclub, which upset local residents, but the developer consistently denied the story. According to Ottwein, he merely wanted to restore the historic site and open the place as a restaurant. At some point later, he did begin some of the work on the building, which had fallen into a state of disrepair. Much of the old plaster was stripped and two attic dormers were added. Some old photographs showed that the dormers had been present on the original structure. He also replaced many of the windows with modern glass.

Unfortunately, though, Ottwein never had the time to devote to the project and the house was placed on the back-burner, where it remained for five years until it caught the attention of Doug and Beverly Elliot. They had noticed the building some time before and always expressed an interest in renovating the place and opening a restaurant.

As luck would have it, they were in the market for a new home and discovered the Three Mile House was for sale. At that time, it was still in pretty bad shape and it had been more than 12 years since anyone had lived in it. Still, the Elliots felt drawn to the building and decided to buy it, having no idea how the house would change their lives.

The Elliots' oldest daughter, Lori, was the first to encounter anything unusual about the house. It happened on the day they were moving in. She was carrying a large box into the basement and was suddenly hit on the leg by a brick which seemed to fly through the air by itself. She decided right then and there that whatever inhabited the house was going to have to put up with the new arrivals. She became the first member of the family to accept, and to literally make contact with, the spirits in the house. It would be some time later before the rest of the Elliot family came to the realization that they were not alone in the Three Mile House. By that time, there would be no way to deny it.

The family spent the next year carefully renovating the house. It was back-breaking work that would eventually pay off by getting the house listed in the

National Register of Historic Places. They reinforced floors, put in first floor rest rooms, a scullery was added to the kitchen for dish washing, they installed modern plumbing, and cleaned and repaired the place from top to bottom. During the work, they discovered the mysterious tunnels extending out from the basement. Apparently, other excavation work had been done in the tunnels in the past because the Elliots discovered that some of the brick walls in the basement were hollow, leading to secret rooms. They also found names and dates carved into the old wooden beams. Doug Elliot later heard a story that a previous owner had found a skeleton between the walls in the 1930s. Stories had long circulated that the Three Mile House had once been a stop on the Underground Railroad. These new discoveries seemed to confirm it.

While the discoveries in the basement were strange, they weren't nearly as strange at the small balls and sparks of light that flickered about in the building each night, or the fact the Elliot's younger daughter, Lynn, swore that dark shadows were chasing her about her room. There had to be a logical explanation for what was going on, but what was it?

At this point, only Lori suspected that the house might be haunted. So, one night she and some of her friends decided to conduct a séance in the attic. Believing that spirits were present, they planned to use a Ouija board to find out for sure. Not long after their impromptu séance began, eerie things began to occur. Loud banging sounds began to be heard on the third floor, along with tapping and rapping on the walls. The unexplainable noises continued for a long time and wouldn't stop, confirming for Lori that the place was inhabited, and possibly infested, by ghosts.

The weird events continued, and soon, the balls of energy, strange sounds and weird tapping and knocking noises became everyday events to the Elliots and they got used to them. Slowly, they were beginning to accept the idea that the Three Mile House might truly be haunted. They could learn to live with the inexplicable little events, they thought. It was just a part of life in the old house. However, as opening day for the new restaurant approached, they started to wonder if the customers would be so forgiving? Would they scare the business away? Would the new restaurant fail before it even got a chance to get started?

On opening night, in the spring of 1976, Bev Elliot's worst fears seemed to be coming true. The first evening, a little while before the customers arrived, the heavy dining room chairs began sliding away from the tables and rocking back and forth. Each time a chair was replaced and the staff member turned her back, the same chair (or another one) would mysteriously rumble away from the table again. Then, dishes began rattling in the china cabinet, vibrating as if they were about to fly across the room. But, as soon as the first guests arrived, the activity suddenly stopped and the house remained quiet for the rest of the evening.

At first, the spirits only seemed to perform for the Elliot family, but then odd things started to happen around the restaurant workers as well. One of the cooks claimed to see a misty-looking man in a derby-style hat, who appeared at the top of the stairs. Another waitress saw a face in a mirror (that wasn't hers) and others saw candles lifted off tables under their own power. Another cook reported seeing a tray filled with coffee mugs hovering about a foot above a table. Water taps were also turned on and off, stove knobs were twisted, and even the piano played by itself.

A former employee, who I spoke with, told me of many nights when she would feel the tug of an invisible hand on the back of her shirt. Each time she turned around, she would find no one there. Apparently, this was a regular occurrence, along with dishes that would move about from place to place, water glasses that would suddenly empty their contents onto the floor, and napkins which would somehow fold and unfold with no one around to assist them.

After about the year, the ghosts began to perform other tricks and started entertaining the customers, too. While many of them were fascinated and intrigued by the bizarre events, others were not amused. Tables jumped and hopped across the floor, dishes were reported to levitate, and on occasion, customers had to keep scooting their chairs forward just to keep up with their food. One past customer of the restaurant explained to me that he was having dinner one night and the table kept sliding away from him as he tried to eat. He kept moving his chair forward, thinking that he must have inadvertently moved backward on the wooden floor. Then he finally realized that his table was almost directly on top of the table next to him. Needless to say, the nearby diners were almost as surprised as he was.

In October 1977, Doug Elliot got his first really good scare in the house. The Elliots had an apartment on the second floor of the building and he woke up one night and realized that something was not right in the bedroom. He looked down to the end of the bed and saw the hulking figure of a massive, African-American man, well over six feet tall, who was wearing rough gray work clothes. He was terrified to think that a burglar had broken into the house, so terrified that he was unable to even call out. Elliot waited for the man to do something and then he did -- he turned and walked out of the room. Still shaken, Doug found his gun and searched the entire house. He found no one there and discovered that nothing had been disturbed. The whole house was dark, silent, and empty. All of the doors and windows were locked and secured. Doug fell asleep with his gun in his lap that night.

When his wife awakened him the next morning, he was still shaking and unnerved. He told her about the prowler and when they told their daughters, they were in for quite a surprise. Lori explained to them that the man her father had seen was "Herman," a ghost that she was very familiar with and who inhabited the house. He was completely harmless and may have simply been checking on her parents or trying to communicate with them. She also explained that after Doug's reaction to him, Herman was now frightened of her father.

After the restaurant had been open awhile, newspapers in the area began giving them good reviews and they later won several awards. However, with every article written also came mention of the ghosts. The stories helped business and put the Elliots in contact with psychics and ghost hunters from around the country, many of whom traveled to the Three Mile House. Among them were Chris Mitchum, the son of actor Robert Mitchum, and Cyril Clemens, the cousin (several times removed) of author Mark Twain.

In 1977, several members of the cast of the movie *Stingray*, which was filmed in the area, decided to hold a séance in the house. They wanted to try and get in touch with Herman, the ghost of the man who had so frightened Doug Elliot. According to psychics, Herman was the unofficial leader of the ghosts in the house.

What they learned was that the spirit's name was actually "Tom" and that he had been an escaped slave who had come to the Three Mile House along the Underground Railroad line. In fleeing from the south, he had accidentally killed a white woman. A group of men somehow managed to track him down and had brutally murdered him. He was buried in one of the tunnels beneath the house, but his spirit was not at rest. Tom had been a deeply religious man in life and as he had not received a proper Christian burial, his spirit was disturbed. Doug Elliot was moved by this story and spent quite a bit of time looking for Tom's grave. There were just too many tunnels, though, and sadly, the grave was never found.

Psychics who came to the house told stories about the other ghosts, too. One of the resident spirits was said to be a lady in black who had caught her fiancée with another woman. She had killed them both and then hanged herself in the attic. In the basement was said to be the ghost of a Civil War deserter who had also hanged himself, this time on one of the beams in the cellar. Interestingly, the beam was inscribed with markings which read... "died here..18.." The tunnels were also said to be haunted by the ghosts of slaves who had not survived their flight to freedom. Many of them were reportedly buried in the basement and their spirits had remained close by.

As time passed, the ghosts remained a constant part of the business. Tom was perhaps the most active and playful of the spirits, leaving faucets running and flooding the kitchen and the bathrooms, and generally being a nuisance. One day, an upset waitress informed Bev that she would not be able to work in the afternoons any more. When asked why, she stated that Tom had found a new toy: an antique coffee grinder. He had been amusing himself by turning it all day and the clanking noise that it made was driving the waitress crazy.

One Saturday afternoon, the Elliots were in town on errands, but Bev's mother was upstairs reading a book. There was no one else in the house with her -- but she was certainly not alone. At some point that afternoon, a skillet in the kitchen caught fire. Her mother reported that a ribbon of white mist floated between her face and the book. She put the book down and watched as the mist floated past and then slide under the door. She blinked her eyes and imagined that she was seeing things, but the mist soon came again, this time fuller. She watched it disappear under the door, but this time, she followed it to the kitchen. She found the room was filled from smoke from the burning fry pan. If she had not found the pan, the house may have burned down.

But the ghosts were not always so helpful. They provided the restaurant with a lot of good press, but the Elliots had never been sure the haunting was well-received by new or potential customers. It also seemed that problems with the restaurant had started to multiply. Despite a reputation for fine food, the restaurant began to see a slow-down, thanks to its rural location. It also seemed as though power bills had become astronomical, thanks to the fact that the large, old home was so hard to heat. Plus, operations costs for the restaurant continued to increase monthly.

To make matters worse, a frightening incident took place in 1980 when radio personality Jim White of KMOX in St. Louis asked to broadcast his popular Halloween show from the Three Mile House. The Elliots agreed, with the condition that no Ouija boards were to be used and no séances take place for the show. Unfortunately, one of the guests either forgot about this stipulation, or ignored it, and brought a Ouija board along anyway.

According to the Elliots, the result was chaos. A loud scream frightened everyone in the restaurant as a cook ran from the kitchen, claiming to be terrified by a green-faced, red-eyed monster that had appeared in their midst. Soon after, psychics worked to try and clear the house of this spirit. Eventually, they announced the malevolent ghost had been expelled and order was restored to the place. Even so, the incident left the Elliots wondering if the continued cost and stress of running the restaurant was worth it.

Soon, they decided to put the place up for sale. The tension, pressure, and exhaustion of running the business had just become too much for them, they said. Regardless, they were heartbroken when they left the house for the final time.

In 1982, the Three Mile House was sold to John Henkhaus, who also operated the house as a restaurant. He continued the renovation of the building and added a new kitchen and some additional plumbing. In an article dated from around the time that he opened the place again, Henkhaus admitted that many people came to the house because of the hauntings. "People swear by it," he said. "Ninety-percent of the people that come in here have stories of it being haunted. A lot of this is not documented, but it could very well be true. There's a lot of fact mixed with fiction."

Henkhaus, who also lived in the second-floor apartment, stated that he had not had any contact with the spirits, but added that things seemed to disappear quite often. He also said that the restaurant staff reported some pretty bizarre encounters, like the feeling of being tripped just before taking a fall. He also acknowledged the stories of Tom and his lack of a proper burial. He said that a number of clergymen and curiosity-seekers had come to the house, hoping to find where Tom was buried. Many holes were dug in and around the basement, but the burial site was never found.

A short time later, Henkhaus was also added to the list of previous owners of the Three Mile House. The building was then bought by Steve and Mitzi Ottwell, who owned the house at the time of the fire in 1985.

Today, all that remains of the Three Mile House is a large, grassy mound, a few scattered bricks and, of course, an enduring reputation as the most haunted place in the area, a title that it will most likely hold for many, many years to come.

Legate's Curve

Traveling southwest of Edwardsville, travelers may look closely and see a rusted sign pole as they go around a curve in the road. It was on top of this pole that the sign for the **Hilltop House Restaurant** used to hang. The sign pole is surrounded by empty land, but it wasn't always this way. Few traces remain of the once-popular restaurant and motel that once stood there. Even the highway that passes the site has changed. Once a busy stretch of Route 66, it's now a bustling four-lane stretch of Route 157. A major highway project a few years ago altered the landscape and the look of the curve that served as a landmark for motorists during the golden years of Route 66.

The restaurant and motel were built by Orval and Virginia Legate, who met in high school. The Legate family came from the Grafton, Illinois, area, where they owned large fruit orchards. Orval was born in 1923, and when it came time for him to go to high school, he assumed he'd go to Jerseyville, since Grafton didn't have a high school at that time. However, a basketball coach in Pittsfield had seen Orval play, and he arranged for the young man to transfer to Pittsfield and play for the team. Orval graduated in 1941. Virginia McCulloch lived in Pittsfield, and was two years behind Orval. The two met in high school and married as soon as Virginia graduated in July 1943. They lived in Florida while Orval served as a staff sergeant during World War II and then moved back to Illinois. They settled in Edwardsville and Orval worked as the manager of an automobile agency for a man named Robert Knetzer.

It turned out to be the worst decision that he could have made.

When the war ended, there were acute shortages of consumer goods like sewing machines, radios, refrigerators, stoves, and automobiles. Due to pent-up demand, new cars were selling at a premium and the wait was often a year or longer.

In Edwardsville, the country's most audacious and crazy "Ponzi scheme" was started by a man named Robert Knetzer. In 1946, he devised a scheme that made him rich beyond his wildest dreams. His scheme was dangerously simple. Knetzer, who was born in Carlinville, told people that he could get them new – or almost new – cars cheaper than they could get them from a dealer. Buyers had to pay him most of the money up front, but he promised to deliver the car in three or four months. Legitimate dealers were telling people it would take as long as a year to get a car. Knetzer seemed trustworthy and customers responded. His income was fantastic, netting him sometimes as much as $40,000 a day.

But this is where the scheme turned crazy. Knetzer bought cars from other dealers and actually lost money on each sale. But he had so many people paying in advance that he always had money coming in. And he actually delivered enough cars to make his operation seem legitimate. Happy customers spread the word and people flocked to Edwardsville from as far away as Quincy and Peoria.

Knetzer became the talk of the town. He built an impressive two-story brick house, starting buying fancy suits, took expensive vacations, and became a bigamist when he married a Chicago chorus girl without divorcing his red-headed Sunday School teacher wife, Dolores Choate. After two years of high living, Knetzer began failing to make deliveries. He was taking more orders than he could possibly fill, and soon, a backlog began to develop.

Angry customers began showing up at his office, demanding their money back. But Knetzer, always sharp, pulled open a desk drawer filled with cash and cheerfully refunded the money. As news spread that some impatient customers were getting their money back, this seemed to pacify those who had started to worry.

It all began to unravel when a reporter for a St. Louis newspaper did a story about Knetzer. He discovered that Knetzer was buying Chevrolets, slightly used, from people who had bought them from dealers in Chicago and surrounding states. Knetzer offered them more money than what they had paid for the car, and they couldn't resist making a quick and easy profit. Once word spread about Knetzer's scheme, a lot of people who had given him money found themselves with no way to get it back. Knetzer filed for bankruptcy and claims against him amounted to well over $4 million. Creditors ended up settling for about two-cents on the dollar.

During court proceedings that lasted over four years, an IRS claim was made against Knetzer for over $2 million in back taxes. Ironically, the judge in that case had to dismiss the suit when it became apparent that, while Knetzer had had a tremendous amount of business, he had no income whatsoever. Knetzer told an astonished judge, "There wasn't any profit in it, your honor, just an awful lot of money."

Knetzer ended up with a five-year prison sentence, but was released on bail, pending an appeal. He decided to take a vacation to a ranch in Montana but died of

Legate's Hilltop House Restaurant and Modern Cabins in the 1950s

a heart attack while having lunch in a Bozeman drug store. He was only 39 years old, but he lived several lifetimes by then.

Knetzer did a lot of damage to a lot of people, including Orval Legate, who had innocently taken a job with the swindler's auto agency. After Knetzer's scheme came crashing down in the fall of 1948, Orval was out of a job – and really wanted to get out of the public spotlight.

Orval and Virginia decided to buy a 13-acre property on the north side of the curve on Route 66. The property already had a gas station on it, which they soon leased out. They built a row of tourist cabins – Legate's Modern Cabins – and later on, they joined the cabins together and renamed it Legate's Modern Motel. They also added the Hilltop House Restaurant, which became very popular with travelers and locals, who dubbed that small stretch of road "Legate's Curve."

The motel was located in a peaceful setting with a lake that offered fishing, swimming, and boating. The rooms earned high marks and a number of famous guests stopped in, including members of the Jimmy Dorsey band and numerous professional wrestlers who had matches in St. Louis, when wrestling first became wildly popular in the 1950s.

The Hilltop House boasted "fine foods" on the sign and backed up those claims with fried chicken, steaks, open-faced roast beef sandwiches, spaghetti, and an assortment of homemade pies.

In the big parking lot, motel and restaurant customers could buy produce during the summer months. Peaches and apples from the Legate orchards in Grafton were for sale, along with watermelons brought up from Arkansas.

Spaces were added on the property for trailers to accommodate construction workers building Southern Illinois University-Edwardsville and workers from the nearby oil refineries. At its peak, there were three rows of spaces for 55 trailers behind the restaurant. There was a separate bathhouse and a large laundry room for the trailer court residents.

In 1964, the Legates sold the businesses on Legate's Curve and moved back to Florida. By 1969, the restaurant and motel no longer appeared in Edwardsville city directories. Eventually, the buildings were torn down. Orval and Virginia lived in Florida for 25 years before retiring and returning to Illinois. Orval died in 2012, but Virginia continued to live in the Edwardsville area.

But the businesses at Legate's Curve? Only the old sign post, and the memories, remain today.

Dinner and "Dessert" at the Luna Café

As Route 66 leaves Edwardsville, it drops down below the bluffs to travel along the old floodplain of the Mississippi River. Around this point, over the course of years, Route 66 took three separate paths to St. Louis. The earliest went down Chain of Rocks Road and into the town of Mitchell.

At this point, today's motorist starts to notice that the farmland of Illinois has been left behind and the suburbs of St. Louis have started to appear. However, even on the outskirts of the city, there are still numerous remnants of the old highway.

Nearing Mitchell, a traveler should watch for the old **Bel-Air Drive-in** sign on the right side of the highway, just after crossing Route 111. Opened in the 1950s, the drive-in entertained audiences along Route 66 until 1987. Over the years, its old screen has fallen down and the parking lot

has been reclaimed by the grassy fields, but its sign remains as a souvenir of better times.

Just about where the original route through Mitchell turns left is the famous (or infamous) **Luna Café**, a well-known night spot on old Route 66. Founded in either 1924 or 1926 (depending on the version of events you believe), the bar and grill was once said to be the hangout of mobster Al Capone, who used the Luna as one of his haunts when he came down from Chicago. While this may be an apocryphal tale of crime from the place's history, it is well known that the basement of the café was once a popular gambling parlor.

The woman given credit for the creation of the Luna Café is Irma Rafalala, who used hired mules and an old-fashioned scoop to dig the building's foundation. A restaurant and tavern were located on the first floor and bedrooms – allegedly to be used by railroad workers – were located upstairs. It would be the spacious second floor that added to the legend of the café. Stories claimed that the second floor was actually a brothel. The tales of prostitution are also connected to the Luna's famous neon sign. The sign, which bears the café's name, is decorated by a martini glass that holds two cherries. Legend has it that when the red cherries in the sign were lit up, girls were available and waiting upstairs. There was a bell in each room and the proprietors would ring from downstairs to let the girls know who was wanted. The wiring for the individual bells is still intact today.

In the early days, the Luna Café catered to an upscale crowd and much of the clientele came from nearby St. Louis. It was said that the food was so expensive that law-abiding citizens couldn't afford to eat there. Those who made the trip across the river stayed around after dinner to gamble in the basement – or for "dessert" in one of the rooms on the second floor.

Today, the Luna Café is a neighborhood tavern that caters mostly to locals. However, during the summer months, when Route 66 tourist season is at its peak and people come from all over the world to experience the legendary road, the place draws a steady crowd. The café has changed hands many times over the years, and while it offers drink specials and free chicken-wing nights these days, instead of illegal booze and ladies of the evening, it remains a piece of illicit history on Route 66.

Leaving the Land of Lincoln

After leaving the Luna Café, this first route jogged south along Route 203 and then west along Madison Avenue in Granite City, passing many of the town's landmarks, including its famous steel mills. When Route 66 had been designated in 1926, two important factors determined its path through Illinois. One of these was the location of its major cities and industrial centers, with Chicago in the north and St. Louis in the south, just across the river. The other was Illinois' freshly-paved Route 4, running from Chicago to St. Louis, roughly following the old route of the Chicago and Alton Railroad line. The race was on to pave Route 66 in all eight of the states that it passed through, but Illinois was ahead of the game and State Route 4 soon became Route 66.

Although Route 4 was later altered just east of Worden, its original path was through Edwardsville, Mitchell, and Granite City. In 1926, the newly-designated Route 66 (using Route 4) turned southwest from Mitchell and Madison Avenue to follow its path through Granite City to Madison and then Venice. It then went on to the McKinley Bridge, which crossed the Mississippi into St. Louis. The McKinley Bridge was owned by the city of Venice (named for Venice, Italy since it flooded so often) and was originally a walking and streetcar bridge into north St. Louis. It was named for Illinois congressman William B. McKinley, who was responsible for building a large number of streetcar lines in Southern and Central Illinois. The bridge has been closed for a number of years, after falling into terrible disrepair, but it is scheduled to be re-opened some time in the future.

Some of Granite City's best-known landmarks were new in the 1920s, when Route 66 passed through. Along, or near, this section of the highway motorists passed the new Granite City Community High School, Wilson Park, St. Elizabeth Hospital, and the steel plants. The steel mills, and other huge manufacturing facilities, were undoubtedly the most recognizable landmarks in Granite City. The city had been established as a company town by the German immigrant Niedringhaus brothers as a home for their granite ware factory and steel mills. The National Enameling and Stamping Company, Granite City Steel Works, and numerous other industrial plants attracted huge numbers of immigrant workers, swelling the city's work force and population.

A second route, known as the bypass, was established around 1936 across the Chain of Rocks Bridge. As Route 66 dropped below the bluffs at Edwardsville, it followed the old Chain of Rocks Road, which today runs alongside Interstate 270. It went north of Granite City and passed by the old **Bel Air Drive-in**, the **Luna Café**, heading toward St. Louis.

When the Chain of Rocks Bridge was first designated as part of Route 66, a slew of motels sprang up along the Illinois approach to the bridge. The last portion of road prior to crossing the Mississippi became a logical location for overnight tourist facilities, just on *this* side of St. Louis. By the mid-1950s, the Illinois approach to the bridge was flooded with service stations, restaurants, campgrounds, and motels. In fact, many locals dubbed this stretch of highway "motel row." Among the lodging spots were the **Chain of Rocks Motel** and the **Canal Motel and Restaurant**.

The Canal Motel was located on the south side of Route 66. It had 12 units configured into an L-shape, with the office and restaurant fronting the property. The motel's amenities included tile baths, radiant heat, air conditioning, and a television in every room. A classic 1950s-era sign was out front, tempting the potential guests. Parts of the original sign survive today, including the frame and the very 50's-looking piece that advertised the TV's. The Canal Motel could also brag about being the closest motel to the Chain of Rocks Bridge, making it the last stop before Missouri.

The steady stream of traffic across the toll bridge kept all of the businesses on "motel row" hopping. They enjoyed a parade of tourists for just over a decade, but then, in 1967, a newer, safer toll-free bridge was built to the north. The **Chain of Rocks Bridge** was closed down, but it had already earned its place in history.

The trussed toll bridge was named for a stretch of rocks in the river that were long regarded as a hazard to river travelers. The bridge was constructed by the Scott brothers in 1929 and they started work on the Missouri side of the river before they ever found any bedrock to anchor it to on the Illinois side. When they did find the bedrock, it was necessary for them to build a sharp bend in the middle of the bridge to reach it. The bend was so severe that two large trucks, coming in opposite directions on the roadway, could not pass one another at this point in the bridge. Unfortunately, highway officials in Illinois and Missouri failed to place the bridge on their maps, jeopardizing the Scott brothers' investment. Taking a huge risk, they extended the bridge route until it linked up with Lindbergh Avenue and it not only became the most often used bypass around St. Louis, but it also became one of the most famous bridges on the entire run of Route 66. The Scott brothers never recovered from their financial setbacks, though, and they sold the bridge to the city of Madison in 1939. As luck would have it, it became a major money maker for the city. Route 66 travelers went out of their way to use the bridge and thanks to its popularity, the Chain of Rocks Amusement Park was built on a bluff over the river in Missouri in the 1920s.

The Chain of Rocks Bridge itself closed down in 1968, but remains open today as a foot bridge that attracts bird watchers, bicyclists, and Route 66 enthusiasts. It is regarded as the "world's longest pedestrian bridge," stretching over a mile in length.

The Catsup Bottle in the Sky

Around 1940, a third route was created that entered St. Louis from East St. Louis and over the Municipal (later McArthur) Bridge. It connected with East St. Louis by splitting off at Hamel and brushing the edge of Troy and Maryville before arriving in Collinsville, which was once known as "Downing's Station."

The first resident of what would someday be Collinsville was a man named John Cook, who came west from Shepherdstown, Virginia, in 1810. In 1817, the three Collins brothers came to the area and bought Cook's property from him. They were later joined by their parents, their sisters, and their families. The family established the first store, distillery, flour and saw mills, blacksmith shop, carpentry business, and wagon shop in the region. Before long, more and more settlers began to arrive, and in 1822, the brothers renamed the settlement "Unionville." However, this name only lasted a short time as another post office by the same name already existed in Illinois. The residents voted in 1825 and dubbed the town Collinsville in honor of the men who truly developed it.

The town was platted in 1837 and officially incorporated in 1850, with Judge D.D. Collins as the first president. Although his family and the Collins family that developed the town were friends and fellow Presbyterians, they were not related.

Like many other towns in this part of Illinois, Collinsville became a coal mining town. In 1857, the first mine was sunk by Peter and Paul Wonderly. Another was opened by John Maull and David Williams in 1862. A man named Dr. Lumaghi arrived in town in 1865 and opened a zinc works and the first of his mines in 1871. The Lumaghi Coal Co. lasted the longest of any of the local coal operations and closed its last mine in 1964.

As the miners poured in, the city began to grow, establishing more and more businesses. In 1885, a new city hall, designed in the Italianate style, was built and it continues to be used today. By 1922, more than 3,000 coal mines and their families made up almost one-third of the city's residents. More mines were opened over the course of the next 50 years, as well as other industries like lead works, a knitting mill,

cow bell factory, and canning plants. Most of these were closed by 1950, though, as Collinsville became a "bedroom community" for St. Louis, which was only nine miles away.

But, unlike so many other towns, Collinsville did not fade away after the mining industry closed down. It has continued to grow in population as people seek a quieter place to live outside of the hustle and bustle of the big city to the west.

Just off old Route 66 through Collinsville is what many roadside attraction enthusiasts like to call **"The World's Largest Catsup Bottle."** Located along Route 159, this 70-foot-tall water tower was built by the W.E. Caldwell Company for the C.S. Suppiger catsup bottling company – bottlers of Brooks Old Original Rich and Tangy Catsup.

Plans were started for the water tower in 1947, when the W.E. Caldwell Company of Louisville, Kentucky, was contracted to build the 100,000-gallon structure. The water tower was needed for plant operations and to supply water to the new sprinkler system. Gerhart S. Suppiger, then president of the company, suggested that the tower be built in the distinctive tapered shape of their catsup bottles. Final drawings were approved in 1948, and the World's Largest Catsup Bottle was completed in October 1949.

In the late 1970s, Brooks Foods left town and relocated to Indiana, but their massive condiment bottle stayed in place. By the early 1990s, the bottle had deteriorated and started to fade and peel. In 1995, volunteers raised money to restore it, just in time for its 50th birthday, modeling it after an original 1949 bottle, provided by a collector.

Although it's been up for sale a few times over the last few years, it remains where it's been standing since the late 1940s, looming over Collinsville and allowing us to imagine the size of the cheeseburger needed to put the massive catsup bottle to use.

"I Must This Day, the 5th of April, Die..."

The most infamous event in Collinsville history occurred on April 5, 1918. America was embroiled in the bloody events of World War I and anti-German sentiment in the country was at a fever pitch. It was on that day that Robert Prager, a German coal miner, was lynched by an angry mob just outside of the city. Twelve men were tried for his murder, but all were acquitted.

Robert Prager

Prager had been born in Dresden, Germany, in February 1888. He came to the United States in 1905 at the age of 19. A drifter, who spent a year in an Indiana reformatory for theft, he was living in St. Louis when America declared war on Germany in April 1917. Prager showed patriotic feelings toward his adopted county. He took out citizenship papers after the declaration of war was announced and even tried to join the U.S. Navy, but was rejected for medical reasons. He also had a German baker in St. Louis arrested after the man objected to Prager displaying an American flag. But none of that would matter one year later in Collinsville.

After being fired from his job in St. Louis because of his "stubborn, uncompromising personality," he moved across the river to Illinois, hoping to find work in the coal mines. He applied for membership in the United Mine Workers union and got work at a mine in Maryville. However, he was rejected for membership in the union, not only because he was German, but also because he was "unmarried, stubbornly argumentative, given to Socialist doctrines, blind in one eye," and, according to a letter, "looked like a spy to other miners."

Word spread about Prager's rejection from the union, and many men who heard the story latched onto the last words of the rejection note and began spreading the rumor that Prager was a spy and that he intended to blow up the mine where he was working. On April 3, 1918, Prager was confronted by a group of miners and was warned away from Maryville. As more rumors spread, plans were hatched to have Prager kidnapped. Local UMW leaders Moses Johnson and James Fornero, who feared for the German's safety, tried to get the Collinsville police to put him into protective custody, but they declined. The two men then took Prager back to his home in Collinsville. The next day, Prager returned to Maryville, where he prepared a letter that attacked Fornero for suggesting that he was a spy. He posted copies of the document around town and returned to Collinsville that evening to find his house surrounded by an angry mob of miners. They grabbed him and began parading him around town until he was finally rescued by a police officer, Fred Frost, who took him to the jail. The mayor, John H. Siegel, calmed the crowd for a time, and it was decided to close the town's saloons early. However, the officer who was sent to close the saloons brought the news that "a German spy" was being held in the jail.

A mob converged on the jail. Finding only four policemen on duty, they battered down the doors and restrained the officers. The mob found Prager hiding under a pile of rubbish in the basement and dragged him outside. Prager was then marched through the streets, was forced to kiss the American flag, and to sing the national anthem. He was taken outside of town, beyond the edge of police jurisdiction, and in the early morning hours of April 5, 1918, the men stripped him naked, wrapped him in an American flag, and decided to hang him. Over 200 people witnessed the event, and did nothing to help.

The mob cheered and waved flags as they led him to the tree, where a rope and noose had been strung. When he was asked if he had anything to say, Prager replied in broken English, "Yes, I would like to pray." He then fell to his knees, clasped his hands, and prayed for three minutes in German. He was allowed to write a short note:

Dear Parents, I must this day, the 5th of April, 1918, die. Please pray for me, my dear parents. This is my last letter. Your dear son.

The noose was dropped over his head and he was quickly pulled into the air. However, since his arms had been left unbound, he was able to support himself, so he was lowered, bound, and hanged again. He slowly strangled to death, his feet kicking and twitching until he finally stopped moving.

On April 25, a grand jury indicted about a dozen of the men who were present at the hanging for murder. The trial commenced on May 13, and supporters wearing red, white, and blue ribbons gathered outside of the courthouse, singing patriotic songs. Vendors sold food and drinks. Inside, the judge refused to let the defense try to demonstrate Prager's disloyalty, and the case for the defendants amounted to three claims: no one could say who did what, half the defendants claimed they had not even been there, and the rest claimed they had been bystanders, even a man named Joe Riegel, who had confessed his part to newspaper reporters and a coroner's jury. In its concluding statement, the defense argued that Prager's lynching was justified by "unwritten patriotic law." When the defense was finished, the judge declared a recess. After deliberating for between 25 and 45 minutes (accounts vary), the jury found the defendants "not guilty."

A week after the trial, an editorial in the *Collinsville Herald* newspaper, by editor and publisher J.O. Monroe, said that, "Outside a few persons who may still harbor Germanic inclinations, the whole city is glad that the eleven men indicted for the hanging of Robert P. Prager were acquitted." Monroe noted, "The community is well convinced that he was disloyal.... The city does not miss him. The lesson of his death has had a wholesome effect on the Germanists of Collinsville and the rest of the nation."

But Monroe's opinion was a bit skewed. Not everyone in the country shared his bloodlust for disposing of alleged German spies. An editorial in the *New York Times* said, "A fouler wrong could hardly be done in America," which would be "denounced as a nation of odious hypocrites," as a result.

In hindsight, the story of Robert Prager is a case of anti-German sentiment during the war spinning out of control because of anger and drunkenness. It could have happened anywhere, some say. Others feel that Prager was killed by men who feared being accused of disloyalty themselves. It was a way to prove that they were unquestionably American at a time when local miners were in the midst of divisive labor struggles between the working men and the mine company owners. Accused of their own anti-American beliefs, the killing of a "German spy" was the perfect way to show that they were absolutely loyal to their country. Did they consider this in the heat of the moment? Probably not, but it was undoubtedly in the back of their minds and at the root of their actions when they pulled Prager out of the jail that night.

Regardless, the lynching of Robert Prager remains one of the darkest moments to occur on the American home front during World War I and a terrible incident that will be part of Collinsville's history forever.

The Mystery of Cahokia Mounds

As Route 66 left Collinsville, it followed Route 157 for a time before heading west on Collinsville Road, past Evergreen Gardens and to Cahokia Mounds, one of the most mysterious sites in North America. The site, which once covered more than six square miles, was named after a tribe of Illiniwek Indians, the Cahokia, who lived in the area when the French arrived in the late 1600s. What the place was called in ancient times is unknown. The city was in a strategic location. Not only was it on the banks of the Mississippi River, but it was near the confluences of the Missouri, Illinois, Kaskaskia, Meramec, and Ohio Rivers. Thousands of people lived there, working, creating, farming, and trading, and it must have been a bustling place during its heyday.

Who built the mounds, and why did they build them? No one knows for sure. The great mounds of Illinois have long been a source of debate and mystery. Most likely, they were the ancestors of the Native Americans who lived in the region when the

A vintage postcard of Cahokia Mounds

white settlers came, but they could tell nothing to the explorers that might explain the meaning and use of the man-made earthen structures.

The site boasted well over 100 mounds, but the centerpiece was "Monk's Mound," named for Trappist monks that farmed the terraces of the structure in the early 1800s. It is believed to have been built in stages over a period of what was probably close to 300 years. It is the most colossal, entirely earthen prehistoric mound in the New World. It covers 15 acres of land and rises with four terraces to a height of 100 feet above the surrounding bottomland. At the summit of the mound was found the buried remains of some sort of temple, which further added to the mystery of the site. Excavations uncovered extraordinary artifacts like pottery, carved pipes and stone trinkets, effigies of birds and serpents made from copper and mica, and vast numbers of human bones. It came to be believed that – existing at the same time – Cahokia was a larger city than London.

In its heyday, Monk's Mound dominated a plaza, or town square. Bordering the plaza were lesser mounds that were arranged in two rows. In every direction were smaller plazas, also surrounded by mounds, as well as avenues where clusters of one-family dwellings were located. The houses, mostly rectangular in shape, were built of closely placed upright poles interlaced with reeds, with steeply pitched roofs of thatch. A coating of mud or plaster was used to cover and insulate the houses. The interior walls were sometimes hung with matting or were painted with earth-red, black or grey-blue pigments. Although the houses had fireplaces for warmth, most of the cooking was done outside. Houses that belonged to the elite members of the Cahokian society were similar to those of the common people, although slightly larger.

Although the understanding of the hierarchy of the city has been based on historic accounts of the Natchez Indians (as close to the Cahokians as is known), it is believed that the city was ruled over by a king or monarch of some type. He lived in the temple at the top of Monk's Mound and delegated his younger brothers or other male relatives as his council. They presided over the day to day operations of the city, while the chief was in charge of games, festivities, and religious ceremonies. Just what those ceremonies may have consisted of is anyone's guess, although there has been a lot of speculation over the years.

It is believed that one of the major aspects of the Cahokian religion was the observance of the solstices and equinoxes and the related seasonal changes that affected the planting and harvesting of crops. Excavations of the city have revealed that there was once a succession of large circular arrangements of wooden posts, located about a half mile north of Monk's Mound. It is believed to have been a horizon calendar for solar observations and are aligned with the sunrise at the solstices and equinoxes. Dubbed "Woodhenge" because of its similarity in form and, possibly, function, to Stonehenge in England, it may have served as the only such solar observatory in prehistoric America.

The religious beliefs of the Cahokians likely played a role in the burials, too, segregating the dead by way of class. Mound #72 was one of the best examples of the ritual involved with burying the upper class. When discovered, archaeologists noted that it was a rather small, insignificant-looking mound, but because it was placed on a north-south axis with Monk's Mound, they were intrigued by it. When it was opened, they found the skeleton of a man in his early 40s, laid out on a blanket with over 20,000 conch-shell beads. He was surrounded by a huge quantity of grave goods, including rolls of cooper, two bushels of mica, and 800 arrowheads of different types and materials. Nearby were several burial pits that were believed to belong to his wives and servants – killed and buried with him at the time of his death. In one of the pits were the bodies of 53 young women. In another were four males, lying side by side with their arms overlapped and with their heads and hands missing.

Another chief was also found buried in the same mound. His body was surrounded by 700 bone arrowheads and more than 30,000 shell beads. Altogether, 300 bodies were discovered in Mound #72, more than half of them sacrificed young women between the ages of 15 and 25.

The discovery of the Cahokians practice of human sacrifice had led to a lot of speculation as to whether or not the deterioration of their society may have led to Cahokia being abandoned in the late 1300s. We know that this was the start of the city's collapse, for by the time the first Europeans set foot in America in the early 1500s, Cahokia was already deserted. According to records left by the French explorers, the strange mounds bore no signs of life when they arrived and began claiming the Mississippi Valley for their own. The people who had once lived in the great mound city had long since disappeared ---but where had they gone?

Time marched on after the vanishing of the Cahokians and the French settled the region where the city once thrived. After the Revolutionary War, trade between French residents and Americans invigorated the business interests in the region and a store was opened by two traders, Isaac Levy and Jean-Baptiste La Croix, near the base of the pyramid at Cahokia Mounds. The post was eventually abandoned because the "Indians grew too troublesome." The land was sold and re-sold, and in time, fell into the hands of Trappist monks, who fled to the New World after the revolution in France. They established a monastery at Cahokia on what was called the "Big Mound." The order introduced a good breed of cattle to the region, planted vegetable gardens, fruit orchards, and a vineyard on the upper terraces of the pyramid. Unfortunately, illnesses caused from drinking bad water, terrible harvests, and the New Madrid Earthquake in 1811 forced the monks to leave Cahokia behind. The site of the once great city was abandoned again.

The first real expedition to explore the Mounds complex came in 1819, under the leadership of Major Stephen H. Long. Outfitted with state of the art scientific equipment and accompanied by a geologist and a botanist, Long spent months in the area. His final report contained metrological records, latitude and longitude positions, vocabularies of seven major Indian languages, accounts of Indian customs, dress and architecture, and lengthy scientific descriptions. He also detailed measurements of 27 Mississippian mounds that were located north of St. Louis and also wrote of those at Cahokia. This was the first time that the Mounds would appear in a scientific report. He wrote: "In the prairies of Illinois, opposite St. Louis, are large numbers of mounds. We counted 75 in the course of a walk about 5 miles ... including La Trappe [Monks Mound] but it was so overgrown with bushes and weeds, interlaced with briars and vines, we were unable to obtain an accurate account of its dimensions."

In the years to come, as the Native Americans in the east began to surrender their lands to the government, writers, travelers, and settlers began coming into the region and exploring the mounds near the Mississippi River. Around this time, the first professional "archaeologist in the making" came to Cahokia. His name was Charles Rau. He had been born in Germany and attended Heidelberg University, where he had studied mineralogy and chemistry. He came to the Midwest in 1848 and settled in Belleville, where he taught German and became interested in the many Indian artifacts that were found in the area.

One day, while strolling along Cahokia Creek, Rau ran across an old Indian potter's site and found hundreds of pieces of broken and discarded pottery. Fascinated, he began a careful excavation of the site and the discovery occupied him for years. He drew many careful diagrams of his findings and wrote detailed reports based on his earlier scientific training. Despite not being a schooled archaeologist, his articles about the pottery site were published in the *Annual Report of the Board of Regents of the Smithsonian Institution* in 1864. His reports would shed the first light on the earliest inhabitants of the Mounds complex.

Meanwhile, others came to the region as well, including many farmers, who found the rich lands along the American Bottoms, the flood plains of the Mississippi, to be to their liking. In the early days, with so much land around Cahokia available that did not contain mounds, the farmers followed the path of least resistance and simply went around the large and intrusive mounds with their plows. The mounds would be difficult and costly to raze, they believed, and abundant land was available and was relatively cheap. Later, as the cities and towns expanded and grew, developers found it more cost-effective to destroy the mounds and to use the dirt to fill low areas that impeded the cycle of progress. Mounds located in rural areas, like Cahokia, were outside the interest of real estate developers --- for the time being at least.

By the middle 1800s, American transportation systems were shifting from the rivers and waterways to land travel, especially travel by rail. As the railroads began arriving in southwestern Illinois, they began to threaten the very existence of the Cahokia Mounds. As the railroads converged on the St. Louis area, Cahokia soon found itself on a direct route to the city. The mounds that lined the new rail lines were not only in the way of the railroad's "progress," but they were also irresistible sources for free dirt fill to make causeways across the often swampy land. The great mounds began to be destroyed, but few noticed. Only a handful of professional and amateur archaeologists raised their voices in alarm. The general public was indifferent and the Native Americans were unable to protest. Thanks to this, the destruction continued as lines of the Litchfield and Madison, Illinois Central, Alton and Southern, the Illinois Terminal Electric, Baltimore and Ohio, and Pennsylvania Railroads crossed Cahokia.

One of those to be alarmed by the railroad's incursions into the region was John Francis Snyder, the son of a pioneer farmer, who was born in St. Clair County in 1830. Snyder eventually earned degrees in both medicine and law, but archaeology was the passion of his life. He devoted much of his time to a study of the nearby mounds, produced careful descriptions, maps, and historic research material about these ancient wonders. He published 30 articles based on his findings with the Smithsonian and the *Journal of the Illinois State Historical Society*. Snyder also collected and studied hundreds of pieces of Indian artifacts that were found widely around Cahokia. Many of them appeared at the Columbian Exposition, the 1893 World's Fair, in Chicago.

In January 1897, Snyder took over as the editor of the *American Antiquarian* magazine, a journal aimed at amateur archaeologists. Through the magazine and in his daily life, Snyder worked tirelessly to encourage research into Illinois' prehistory. He was also one of the first to try and make Monks Mound into a state park. He organized a group called the "Monks of Cahokia" and wrote a booklet called "The Prehistoric Mounds of Illinois" to try and further the effort. Snyder had seen the mounds being torn apart by scavengers looking for Indian relics and also knew the dangers they faced from developers, as well. He argued passionately for the preservation of the site and sought state financial aid for it. Snyder was indignant over the fact that Illinois universities subsidized archaeological expeditions to foreign lands while prehistoric sites in Illinois were virtually ignored. With his arguments, Snyder planted the seed for state-supported research, and later, Illinois began sponsoring archaeological work within its borders.

Interestingly, it would be two World's Fairs that would shine the spotlight on Cahokia Mounds for the first time. In 1893, during the World's Columbian Exposition, John Francis Snyder would donate many of his collected artifacts to be put on display during an exhibit known as "The Stone Age in Illinois." In that era, world's fairs were not just commercial and tourist attractions, but major scientific events, too. They provided a forum for international meetings of scientists, religious and social leaders, and offered displays of the arts. International conventions, or congresses as they were called, were held in fair cities and gave the groups the chance to exchange ideas and information. The Columbian Exposition offered advances in electricity, music recording, early motion pictures, women's suffrage, and much more. The fact that Cahokia was also "put on display" there for the first time brought attention from all over the world. A little over a decade later, the next world's fair, this time in St. Louis, would expose even more of the mysterious past of the region.

In 1904, the world came to St. Louis and the region was more than ready for it. Like the Columbian Exposition, the fair in St. Louis was more than just a place of commerce and amusement. One of the most popular attractions turned out to be the excursions that were taken to Cahokia. The Great East Side Electric Railway System was set up for trips across the Mississippi to East St. Louis and then on to Monks Mound, or as the advertising called it, the "Grand Central Shrine of the Mound Builder's Empire." Special trolley parties and charters could also be arranged, and groups could rent private cars for the day. Each car, which could hold as many as 60 passengers, was supplied with "portable tables" that could be placed at the windows and the conductors and motormen wore special uniforms. Rates for a chartered car over the entire system, from East St. Louis to Belleville and then on to Edwardsville via Caseyville and Collinsville via Monks Mound, was $50, less than a dollar per person.

For Cahokia, this sudden attention as a tourist attraction was both good and bad. In the long term, knowledge about the mounds contributed to the preservation of the site. In the short term, though, the effect was devastating. According to photographs taken before and after the 1904 fair, visitors literally picked the site to pieces, digging up the ground, and even shredding the surrounding trees by taking leaves for souvenirs. The trees seemed to be the most alarming loss at the time. There were no souvenir shops at the Mounds, and it was a common Victorian practice, as a way of preserving memories, to press leaves within the pages of books and display them later with other trinkets or photographs.

Fortunately, many of the 1904 readers chose to preserve their thoughts in printed form and Cahokia became even better known as a result of the fair. Interest was aroused in international circles, and while interrupted by two world wars and a national depression, scholarly interest in the mounds began in the early 1900s and picked up again in the 1960s. It has intensified in recent years, as local antiquarians, laypeople, and archaeologists have worked together to try and preserve the site, which was something nearly impossible to do in the past. Prior to 1910, dozens of groups rallied to save the mounds, even trying to get the site turned into a national park in 1909. The measure failed but it did cause the locals to realize that preserving Cahokia was something that was only going to be accomplished by the people of Illinois alone.

Within a few years of the St. Louis fair, the destruction of the Cahokia Mounds seemed to be unbelievably imminent. Although Monks Mound was safe for a time, there were many of the mounds, all located on privately owned land, which were destroyed by plows and by businessmen. Urban growth began to encroach on the old Indian land and developers began eyeing the property for commercial use. St. Louis was beginning to grow and with the expansion of the railroads and traffic from new automobiles, engineers wanted direct access to the city. The Mounds were now doubly in jeopardy. They were not only in the way of the new highways but they were also readily available sources for dirt to build railroad and highway embankments.

In 1913, an electric railway company proposed building another spur through the Mounds site, and this time, the local community was incensed. Norman Flagg, the state representative in Springfield, proposed making the Mounds into a state park. People in Edwardsville formed a "Save the Mounds" society and were joined by the Kickapoo Club in Bloomington. Everyone waited anxiously for news reports of the debate over the state park proposal that was going on in Springfield. It was a representative from Cook County who killed the proposal. "My district needs parks for live people," he said. "All of the guys in that mound are dead ones."

It would be World War I that would give Cahokia Mounds some breathing room. As the nation was directed toward war efforts, plans for new railroads and highways were put on hold. As soon as the war ended, though, real estate prices began climbing and "empty" land was again highly prized.

Fearing the worst for the Mounds, David Kinley, president of the University of Illinois, contacted eminent archaeologist Warren K. Moorehead and asked him to come to Illinois for a serious investigation of the site. Moorehead had long been interested in Cahokia and was one of the leading scientists in the country. In 1908, President Theodore Roosevelt had appointed Moorehead a commissioner of the United States Bureau of Indian Affairs. Moorehead arrived at Cahokia in 1921, but by this time, the climate of public opinion was so heated that it was clear from the beginning that his work would not be confined to archaeological research alone.

As soon as Moorehead stepped into his new position at the site, he realized that he was fighting a battle to save Cahokia on five separate fronts. First off, he needed to secure permission from the various owners of the property to conduct limited explorations. Secondly, he had to interest the press in the story of the Mounds in order to enlist help in turning the site into a state park. Third, he had to ascertain the culture of the Cahokia people so that he could get support for preserving the artifacts of their culture. He also had to persuade the University of Illinois, or some other institution, to continue excavations on an extensive scale. And finally, and perhaps most importantly, he had to raise the funds to support all of the other battles that he faced.

It was obvious to Moorehead, and others, that to lose on any of these fronts meant disaster for the entire enterprise and that a successful outcome was therefore unlikely. In spite of this, Moorehead began to fight with full intensity on all five fronts.

After hiring several local former servicemen, Moorehead directed the digging of a 60-foot wide trench on the north face of Kunnemann Mound. When a number of artifacts were discovered, he was able to settle the question once and for all as to whether or not the Mounds were man-made or natural. Until that time, A.R. Crook, the director of the Illinois State Museum, had been maintaining the mounds were geologic formations. Although Crook was in favor of making Cahokia into a state park, his position on the origins of the mounds had been a major obstacle in the campaign to save them. The new dig also garnered the support of the Raney family, who owned so much of the nearby land, and a good relationship was formed between them and Moorehead that would last for years.

Although he won a major fight, Moorehead was not content to rest on his successes. Soon after, he hired a team of horses to drag a slip to unearth shallowly buried artifacts, workers to dig new trenches, and assistants to describe and classify the findings. He kept the artifacts in cigar boxes that were labeled according to the levels at which they were unearthed. Moorehead's methods seem crude to modern archaeologists, but they were cutting edge at the time, especially under the volatile conditions that Moorehead's team was forced to work under.

Moorehead knew that publishing his findings was important in ways that went beyond his professional responsibilities of disseminating information and maintaining his reputation. He knew that much wider public support was needed if he wanted to save the Mounds and so he quickly published a report in the University of Illinois Bulletin about the 1921 excavations.

Archaeology work was finally off to a tremendous start at Cahokia Mounds ---- but then came a violation of Monks Mound from a place that no one would have expected.

On the night of May 26, 1923, an army of 12,000 masked members of the Ku Klux Klan descended on Monks Mound in all of their "glory." Attracted by the enormity of the site, and hoping to appropriate it to their cause, the Klan burned a gigantic cross on top of the pyramid as a "guiding beacon" for other arriving Klansmen. Cars blocked the road for three miles on every side of Cahokia and two newspaper reporters were barred from the grounds by Klansmen armed with clubs, but they could see the burning cross and could hear cheering from some distance away. The meeting ended with a midnight ride through nearby Collinsville with participants honking their horns and shouting ----- "creating a din that was heard all over the city." Most of the automobile drivers wore official hooded robes and others simply carried pieces of white cloth to show their allegiance to the Klan.

The Ku Klux Klan was in the midst of a resurgence in the 1920s. Originally formed after the Civil War to fight against the new rights for freed slaves, its resurgence came as a result of Prohibition. The Klan of the 1920s was violently opposed to foreign immigrants, Catholics, African-Americans, and "wets," meaning those who broke the alcohol laws of the era.

Bootlegging was prevalent in downstate Illinois at the time, and with liquor stills and illegal booze shipments came lawlessness, violence and bloodshed. Many in the region believed that they needed more help than local law enforcement could provide and welcomed the arrival of the Ku Klux Klan. The Klan saw the discontent of the people as an opportunity to step in and provide relief, as well as their version of law and order. As most of the bootleggers were "Catholics and foreigners" anyway, this provided the Klan with the perfect opportunity.

The Klan began its movement into the area by appearing at local churches with gifts of money and speeches on law and order and "walking the line of Americanism." Such sentiment was greeted warmly by the mostly Protestant and largely uneducated residents of the area. The local officials did little to curb the lawless elements in the region and the Klan was now offering to put the bootleggers out of business. They were warmly accepted and many joined in the cause, as evidenced by the size of the gathering at Monks Mound.

Although the use of Monks Mound by the Klan must have seemed like a desecration to Moorehead and his supporters, it was actually a blessing in disguise, for it underscored the urgency of preserving the site as a state park where regulations for its use could be imposed.

This may have been the only good thing that came out of it, though. Thanks to the Klan, local support for the project was at an all-time low. In addition, funds were dangerously low. Once again, though, Moorehead rose to the challenge. As a master of both public relations and fund raising, he ordered a local printer to create an impressive letterhead for his stationary, calling cards, and even informational slips about Cahokia that his publisher could insert into his previously published books. The slips read: "You have been kind enough to order some of my books. Will you please consider the appeal with reference to saving Cahokia, the largest mound group in the world?" He solicited local, state, and national groups and agreed to countless speaking engagements in support of the cause. He also constantly cultivated the press, tirelessly sending out releases about any work that was done at the site, and trumpeting their discoveries in newspapers all over the country.

Finally, in late 1923, Representative Thomas Fekete and Senator R.E. Duvall of East St. Louis introduced a bill in the Illinois State Legislature calling for the state to purchase 200 acres around Monks Mound for $250,000. Moorehead and his supporters pulled out all of the stops and newspapers began rallying in support of the park. Letters streamed into legislator's offices in Springfield and distinguished scientists from several states endorsed the plan. In appeal after appeal, local people called on their representatives and senators. Old letters and testimonials were re-submitted and new supporters added their voices to the cause. Moorehead himself made many speeches and a few years later, in a speech before the National Research Council, he admitted that shamed the state of Illinois into action. He issued a release that cast aspersions on the intelligence of southern Illinois people who preferred filling stations, hot dog stands, and dance halls to the greatest monuments north of Mexico and also added that in any other state but Illinois, Cahokia would have been a state park a long time before. The reaction to his tirade was immediate, and while he was roundly denounced by the press, politicians passed a bill to make Cahokia into a state park in just 48 hours.

The dream of the state park had finally come true, but various political negotiations that had taken place while the bill was en route to passage had severely compromised the effort. The legislature would only allow $50,000 for the park and would purchase only just over 144 acres, which was basically just Monks Mound and a small area around it. It became Cahokia Mounds State Park in 1925, but the rest of the ancient Indian land remained in private hands. It was a great victory, but covered only a small portion of the original site, which was about 4,000 acres. Even today, only about 2,200 acres of the original settlement is preserved.

In 1926, as state park employees began planting grass and laying out new drives and even building a "tourist camp" on the Cahokia property, a new threat arose on all sides of the site. The land that was still in private hands began to be marketed and a housing developer started touting the merits of living in "State Park Place," just east of Monks Mound. The lots were divided and 283 of them were offered for $500 each. Several of the lots were purchased and small homes were built, some of them on top of existing mounds, and other developments included a church and a golf course. The biggest problem was that the whole area was on such low-lying land that flooding was a constant problem. The Indians had constructed their frame houses on poles to lift them about the flood plain, but the modern developers made no such concessions. Flooding occurred here many times in the years that followed, and in 1946, the Red Cross provided shelter for 253 victims of the "state park flood" and were forced to inoculate them against typhoid fever.

While State Park Place was still being developed, the Powell family, who owned Mound 86 (Powell Mound), which was outside of state property, wanted to fill a nearby swamp with dirt from the mound so that they could farm both the swamp and the land under the mound. The mound itself was considered the "marker mound" for the western edge of the site and was the focus of the West Mound group. Its historical importance was deemed immeasurable and would be an irreplaceable loss to the site. Moorehead continued to push for the purchase of the rest of the mounds by the state of Illinois.

The Powell's offered $3,000 to anyone who would remove the mound, but there were no takers. In late 1930, they began secretly digging into the mound themselves, but Dr. P.F. Titterington, a St. Louis doctor and archaeologist, raised the alarm. He contacted A.R. Kelly from the University of Illinois, Will McKern of the Milwaukee Public Museum, and Thorne Duel of the Illinois State Museum and all of them dropped everything and came immediately to the site. Their sad duty was to record and salvage what they could while the mound was being razed to make way for farm land. As demolition commenced, they worked frantically and watched the loss of history with dismay.

When the assembled archaeologists met with Moorehead at the ranger's cottage at the base of Monks Mound, with its relic room that they called the "old museum," they must have all been greatly discouraged by what had happened. The Great Depression, which began in 1929, was worsening and little money was available for the site. The little relic room in the cottage would be the only interpretive center at the Mounds for decades to come. Local people loaned parts of their own collection to the park, but for the most part, the site was used only for picnics, camping, and sledding during the winter months. The long delay before the restoration of Cahokia to greatness had begun.

Cahokia remained mostly the same over the course of the next 40 years. By the 1960s, the state of Illinois had acquired several of the houses east of Monks Mound and they were improvised over the next few years as temporary laboratories and field headquarters. On other occasions, they were used as interpretive sites, office, and exhibition spaces. It was a makeshift arrangement but it did allow lay people, staff members, and archaeologists to work together as they continued to study the ancient site.

Despite gains by archaeologists, the site also had to deal with the encroachments of modern life. New highways and interstates in the area brought with them new homes, businesses, and buildings. A drive-in theater was constructed to the west of Monks Mound in the 1950s and was torn down in 1983. Several airports were also built nearby, although were eventually allowed to revert back to nature and disappear into the local swamps. The Raney Subdivision was started across Collinsville Road from Monks Mound in 1941, but gained ground after World War II. A variety of houses sprang up in four rectangular blocks in the shadow of the great mound and many of them remained until the 1970s.

In the latter part of that decade, the state of Illinois reclassified Cahokia Mounds from a state park to a State Historic Site. The state bought up the rest of the houses in the subdivision as they came up for sale and offered them to the highest bidders with the idea that the new owners had to move them. By the time the new interpretive center opened in 1989, only four were left and two of them were moved within a few months and the others were used as site manager residences for a time. Regardless, the removal of the final houses marked the end of an era at Cahokia.

By 1990, Cahokia had gone from an ancient city to a monastery, to a picnic site, and, finally, to a world-class park and interpretive center. As time passed, the sacred meaning of the mounds was lost and was replaced by the greed of railroad tycoons and highway and real estate developers. It would not be until the end of the millennium that a new appreciation would appear for not only the history and preservation of Cahokia but for the very mystery of the place itself.

Many had forgotten the fact that Cahokia marks one of the greatest unsolved mysteries in the history of America: what happened to the people who built this place?

This question has bothered archaeologists since the site gained prominence more than a century and a half ago and has become even more intriguing as new discoveries have been made. Bodies were discovered inside of the mounds and many of them were found to be covered in seashells, namely from the Gulf Coast. This led many scientists to feel that the Cahokians had traded with, or perhaps ruled over, a vast realm. At some of the mounds, they also found finely crafted statues and ornaments that suggested influences from areas as far away as Mexico.

Some archaeologists believe that the last survivors of the Mound Builders became the Natchez Indians of the Lower Mississippi Valley. These Indians were known for being devout worshippers of the sun, which may explain the uses of the mounds at Cahokia and the so-called "Woodhenge" of the site. The arguments have continued over whether the observatories were scientific or religious in nature, but they did seem to suggest that Cahokia had once been a major Native American center. But how did this connect to the Natchez Indians?

Many believe that the residents of Cahokia may have moved south after abandoning their city, and those who remained were the ancestors of the Natchez tribe. It is thought that perhaps they traveled south because of changes in climate at Cahokia. Temperatures in the Midwest became increasingly colder around 1250 and this may have shortened the growing season. Changing rain patterns, leading to floods and drought, may have made the situation worse. Others have argued that the growth of Cahokia itself was responsible for the destruction of the city. The Cahokians cut down trees for farms and lumber, causing erosion to flood the crops. Clearing the forests may have also driven away much of the wildlife, increasing their dependence on corn and causing protein deficiencies.

It has also been suggested that perhaps the Mound Builders abandoned the area because of overcrowding or contamination of the local water supply, while others have theorized that it may have been a breakdown of the civilization itself. Some feel that perhaps war brought an end to the civilization. Although no evidence of any widespread conflict has been found at Cahokia, bodies have turned up with arrowheads in them. And it's possible that the enemy may not have come from outside Cahokia, but within. The wealth and power of Cahokia's rulers may have changed the city's social structure. Some archaeologists have counted bowls and jars found in the area's largest buildings and noted that, starting around 1100, there were fewer buildings and more artifacts within them. It was interpreted that this meant there were fewer communal feasts, perhaps a sign that Cahokia's leaders were increasingly cut off from the common people. It was surmised that the city's destruction may have come from a "peasant revolt."

Or the answers may be even darker than this....

Around 1500, the Mississippi Valley was seized by a religious movement that has been dubbed the "Death Cult." A new type of grotesque artwork became prevalent, portraying winged beasts, skulls, and weird faces. The rituals practiced during this period of decline are unknown, but scholars have imagined them to be quite dark. Some have even hinted at human sacrifice and cannibalism. Regardless, this proved to be the death knell for the civilization.

According to legend, a bearded and robed god had originally visited the Mound Builders and inspired them to love one another, live in harmony with the land, and built the great earthen works. But later, they degenerated to human sacrifice and warfare during the Death Cult period. The possible survivors of the Mound Builders, The Natchez, were described by the French as being the "most civilized of the native tribes," but their tribal traditions sometimes had dark elements to them. It was reported that in 1725, the death of a chieftain touched off a sacrificial orgy when several aides and two of the man's wives agreed to be strangled so they could escort him into the next world.

This story, of course, has connections to what was found at Mound #72 at Cahokia, which proved that the inhabitants did indeed practice human sacrifice. Is this what led to their decline and the abandonment of the city during the Death Cult era? Had the Cahokians destroyed one another in such a way that the remaining members of the society had drifted away to the south, abandoning their mighty city for all time? Perhaps, or perhaps the answers are far stranger. One thing is sure --- we will never really know one way or another. No matter how many theories are put forth, ideas are created, or excavations are carried out, the people of Cahokia will always remain one of America's greatest ancient mysteries.

Gangsters of East St. Louis

Beyond Cahokia Mounds, Route 66 traveled on past Horseshoe Lake and Fairmont City, a region long connected to organized crime, horse racing and book making. The highways then ducked under a railroad underpass and crossed St. Clair Avenue into East St. Louis.

This is a place of fading wonder, crumbling brickwork, broken windows, and the dust and grime of a century of city life that can't completely hide how prosperous this area once was. For those who have an affinity for vintage signs, there is plenty to see along this stretch of the road. Old neon signs still brokenly proclaim that this area was once an exciting place. The **Night Spot Café** in Fairmont City is closed now, but its sign still hangs on. There are the lonely signs – those left behind when the area declined and was abandoned. Old neon and faint vestiges of weathered signs on the sides of brick buildings tell of times gone by. There are a lot of memories that haunt the old streets in East St. Louis.

Route 66 once passed through East St. Louis and crossed the river, entering St. Louis on the south side of the city. Most travelers are encouraged to skip this part of the old highway today. East St. Louis is a depressed area that might not be appropriate for the casual traveler, especially at

night. It is a place of sadness and ruin and illustrates the darker side of American culture.

The time period that Route 66 represents was a period fraught with discrimination. Many former travelers had different memories of Route 66 than white travelers once did. Even though almost every ethnic group used Route 66, some motels and cafes were closed to certain minority groups. Perhaps one of the saddest outcomes of these times and this type of prejudice is a phenomenon known as "white flight." East St. Louis could be a case study for the effects of this kind of migration. The city began its decline when Route 66 faded as an economic force because the new interstate rerouted the flow of traffic. Compounding this decline, this time period also saw the opening of once predominantly white neighborhoods to other ethnic groups. This caused a mass migration of affluent whites away from these old neighborhoods. They took their money with them and the economic base in these neighborhoods collapsed. Poverty, crime, anger, and a feeling of hopelessness settled into the once prosperous East St. Louis and turned the city into what it is today.

But there is still a lot of faded glory to be seen along Route 66 here. One can only imagine what this place looked like in the early days of the Mother Road. If you look closely at the now ruined buildings and homes in East St. Louis, you will begin to understand what fear and prejudice can do to a city. It's perhaps the saddest place that you'll find anywhere on Route 66, but it's an important part of the highway's story – a story that is part of a larger American story, for better or worse.

In the early years of the twentieth century, a number of gangsters operated in the East St. Louis and Collinsville areas who played a large role in the Prohibition violence that occurred in Illinois. This was a rough and often dangerous region in the 1920s, and it was not uncommon to hear of shoot-outs, murders, and arrests taking place on a weekly basis.

Perhaps the best known gangsters of the area were the Shelton brothers: Bernie, Carl and Earl. They were bootleggers who were deeply involved in the violence of the era. In the 1920s, they became nationally-known for the "beer war" that raged between the brothers and the famous Southern Illinois gangster, Charlie Birger. The Sheltons's attack on Birger's "Shady Rest" roadhouse is still considered the only time that bombs have been dropped during aerial warfare in America. It should probably be mentioned, though, that the bombs were so badly constructed that they never exploded.

The Shelton boys grew up in Southern Illinois. Their father had moved to Wayne County from Kentucky, married a local girl, and started farming. The boys were brought up on the farm but from early youth showed an aversion to hard work. As they got older, Carl and Earl began leaving home for months at a time to drive taxicabs in St. Louis and East St. Louis. When he was old enough, Bernie joined them. The boys quickly sought out trouble and all of them were soon mixed up with the law.

In the fall of 1915, Earl was convicted of armed robbery and sentenced to 18 months at the Illinois State Penitentiary at Pontiac. About the same time, Carl was arrested in St. Louis and charged with petty larceny. He was sentenced to a year in a workhouse. Bernie was arrested in a stolen car while Earl was still in prison. He was also sentenced to a year in the workhouse, but was paroled.

After Carl and Earl served out their sentences, both of them went to work in the Illinois coal mines, but around 1920, they moved back to East St. Louis, where Bernie was now living. They went into the bootlegging and gambling business and opened illegal joints in East St. Louis and the surrounding area. Their organization spread and was soon organized to provide liquor and gambling to most of the region.

When the Ku Klux Klan tried enforcing Prohibition laws in the region, the Sheltons teamed up with Charlie Birger to oppose their authority. Once those problems were over, the two rival operations began fighting one another – leading to more bloodshed and murder than Illinois had ever seen.

The men started out as friends. Around 1923, Birger and the Sheltons joined forces. The Sheltons were running bootleg liquor from the south for distribution in the East St. Louis area. Birger allowed the Sheltons to use Harrisburg, Illinois, as a layover and shipping point, and they also worked together to establish slot machines and gambling across the region. Why the bloody rift developed between Birger and the Sheltons is unclear. Most likely, it was simply business that became personal. Once the Klan was wiped out, there was no one left to fight but each other. Regardless of why it started, though, it plunged southern Illinois into chaos. The war began in 1926 and small towns, farms, and roadhouses in the region were terrorized as both sides built armed vehicles to carry out deadly reprisals against one another. Machine guns blasted, speakeasies were torn apart with gunfire, and many died during the fighting. Eventually, Birger was hanged for his role in the murder of West City, Illinois, mayor, Joe Adams.

After Charlie Birger was hanged, the Sheltons moved their operations to East St. Louis, continuing with bootlegging, prostitution, and gambling. They remained there until driven out, making room for Mafia organizers to turn the city into a major gambling spot. The Sheltons then moved north to Peoria, which they found to be much more hospitable. During the late 1930s, they established themselves again and began an operation that comprised most of the illegal rackets in downstate Illinois. Apparently immune to prosecution, they were able to protect themselves from the long arm of the law. There was nothing that they could do, however, to protect themselves from other gangsters. Carl, who had left Peoria to retire to his Wayne County farm, was killed there in the fall of 1947. Earl survived a murderous attack in Fairfield, Illinois, and Roy, the oldest brother, was killed in June 1950, while driving a tractor on Earl's farm. None of the Shelton murders were ever solved. Bernie Shelton survived until 1948. He was killed on the morning of July 26, when he stepped outside the door of a tavern that he owned in Peoria. He was shot to death by a sniper who was hiding in some nearby woods.

Of all of the gangsters who ruled on the east side of the Mississippi River from St. Louis, though, Frank "Buster" Wortman was undoubtedly the most feared and respected. According to newspaper reports, Chicago gangsters allegedly spoke respectfully of Wortman as the "Boss of St. Louis."

Frank Wortman was born on December 4, 1904, and after his parents separated, he was raised by his grandparents in North St. Louis, near the old McKinley Bridge. His father, Edward, had moved to East St. Louis, where he achieved the position of Captain in the East St. Louis Fire Department and Wortman followed him there when he was a young man.

He soon became immersed in the local criminal element, fascinated with the Shelton gang. He worked hard to earn respect within their ranks and while he never rose much higher than a lowly soldier, he acquired a knack for running his own organization. He was often used by the Sheltons whenever they needed some muscle, since he was quick with his fists and could handle a revolver. His only legal convictions resulted from his hot temper and his tendency to throw a punch. In 1933, he was arrested for assaulting federal officers during a raid on an illegal still near Collinsville. He was sentenced to 10 years in Leavenworth, and then Alcatraz, for the beatings. Two decades later, he slugged an Internal Revenue Service agent who came

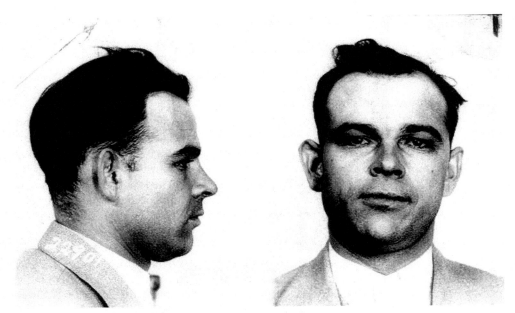

Mug shot of Frank "Buster" Wortman

into a restaurant that he owned. The agent was on routine business (checking to make sure the place had paid their Cabaret Tax) and Wortman punched him out after calling him a "stool pigeon" and a "meddler." For six years afterward, the IRS dogged Buster out of spite and, eventually, he and several of his associates were convicted in U.S. District Court for conspiracy to evade federal income tax laws.

It was the 1933 conviction, and subsequent stretch in Alcatraz, that led to a falling out between Wortman and the Shelton gang. He expected that the Sheltons would use their influence to make his life in prison easy, but to his surprise and bitter disappointment, they forgot about him. Seeing an opportunity, the Chicago syndicate took advantage of the situation by doing favors for Wortman while he was incarcerated. When he was released in 1941, he immediately threw in with the Chicago mob. Wortman became a vital downstate connection, and soon, small-time bookies and criminals could not operate in the region without Wortman's consent.

Within three years, Wortman was firmly in control of East St. Louis and the surrounding region. He had muscled his way into the Hyde Park casino in Venice and had gotten control of the Pioneer News Service, which carried horse racing information in St. Louis. When the authorities clamped down on racing wire services, he moved the company across the river to Fairmount City. Wortman also controlled other gambling establishments, night clubs, taverns and restaurants, and distributed slot machines, jukeboxes, and pinball machines. It seemed that every time he tried to expand his business in East St. Louis, though, he ran into Shelton control and Shelton loyalty. For this reason, he made a trip to Chicago in 1944 for a strategy session with the Chicago mob about how to deal with the Sheltons. Soon, word began to spread that there was a $10,000 bounty out on the heads of Carl and Bernie Shelton.

It would be the death of Ray Daughtery that would really foreshadow the end of the Shelton opposition against Wortman. Daughtery was one of Wortman's men. He was shot to death and his body dumped in Crab Orchard Lake near Carbondale. The rumor spread that his death was a signal that the Sheltons planned to reclaim territory taken by Wortman. Around this same time, some of the Sheltons' prized Angus cattle were stolen and Carl was enraged. Searching for the culprit, he administered a beating to a relative of Charles "Blackie" Harris, an associate of Wortman. Harris was infuriated and a short time later, on October 23, 1947, Carl was shot while driving a jeep on his farm. The coroner removed 17 bullets from his body, fired from three different weapons. Blackie Harris skipped town to Tulsa, Oklahoma, and the killing of Carl Shelton was never solved. Buster Wortman now had a free hand to expand his empire throughout Madison and St. Clair counties – and beyond.

Wortman's criminal enterprise flourished for a number of years and he expanded his territory in Illinois as far south as the Ohio River. He began running into trouble with his gambling establishments in the middle 1950s, butting heads with the Internal Revenue Service and new state's attorney, Dick Mudge, Jr., who had been elected on an anti-gambling platform. Wortman was clever, though, and to keep his favorite casino, the Red Rooster Inn, operating, he hired teenagers from St. Louis to come over after school so that he could offer his customers secluded valet parking. The teenagers would drive the cars into nearby corn fields and hide them so that the authorities wouldn't realize the extent of the club's operations.

His restaurant and night club, the Paddock Lounge, became his base of operations and stories from the place became part of Buster's larger-than-life legend. One story told of four young men who came in one night and started giving one of the waitresses some trouble. She told Buster and he put on a waiter's apron and walked out to their table. When he approached them, he pulled aside the apron and exposed a handgun that he had in his belt. "Who wants to be served first?" he reportedly asked them, and the young men fled from the club.

Thanks to the business that he was in, Buster had every reason to fear for his safety. For many years, he lived well in an expensive ranch-style home in the Morris Hills subdivision, west of Collinsville. When he and his wife divorced, he moved into the Broadway Hotel in East St. Louis and began planning a fortress that he would call "The Moat," outside of Collinsville. The Moat was actually a horseshoe-shaped lake that protected his mansion. The house had a number of elaborate additions made to it, including a steel plated roof (in case it was ever attacked by helicopter) and a luxurious steam bath, made possible thanks to Buster's connections to the

The "Moat" around Wortman's house outside of Collinsville

Steamfitter's Union. He moved into The Moat with his second wife and lived there until his death. The mansion still exists near Collinsville today.

In 1962, the IRS vendetta against Buster Wortman came to a head when he was convicted for income tax evasion. He was sentenced to five years in prison, but the verdict was later reversed on appeal and he was found "not guilty" in the second trial. In December of that same year, Wortman's chief lieutenant, Elmer "Dutch" Dowling, along with another soldier named Melvin Beckman, was found murdered near Swansea, Illinois. Curiously, a napkin was found in Dowling's pocket and scrawled on it were notes about discussions that the jury in Wortman's income tax evasion trial held behind closed doors. An investigation was launched into possible jury tampering but nothing ever came of it. The murders of the two gangsters remained unsolved. Strangely, two months later, Wortman was brought to St. Mary's Hospital

On March 3, 1962, the bodies of Elmer "Dutch" Dowling and Melvin Beckman were found sprawled on the highway, north of Belleville. Dowling had been Wortman's right-hand man and Beckman was a bodyguard in Wortman's organization.

in East St. Louis with a bullet wound. Wortman described the shooting as an "accident."

What may have actually happened is unknown, but there is every reason to believe that Wortman avenged the death of Dutch Dowling and Melvin Beckman. Their deaths obviously upset him and he told reporters at the time that "this really hurts me. Elmer was as close to me as my brother, Ted." The name that kept coming up in connection to the murders was that of Virgil "Doc" Summers, a tough member of the former Shelton gang. Later in the spring, after Buster was treated for the bullet wound, Summers was found shot to death in front of his apartment building in East St. Louis.

Buster Wortman remained the top gang boss in the area until his death in August 1968. He had gone into the Alexian Brothers Hospital in St. Louis for an operation to repair a lesion on his larynx and died while in intensive care. Wortman was only 63 years-old but also suffered from a liver ailment that had been caused by heavy drinking. His death brought about the slow demise of organized crime in East St. Louis, which was by this time crumbling into a city that was unrecognizable to those who had lived there for years. Many say that when the mob moved out of East St. Louis, they abandoned it to whatever came in its wake.

The city would never be the same again.

Farewell Illinois...

And with that, we leave the land of Lincoln behind and head across the Mississippi River to Missouri. Coming soon, more books in the "Weird Highway" series will take Route 66 readers on toward California. The books will include:

* Missouri & Kansas
* Oklahoma & Texas
* Arizona & New Mexico
* California

BIBLIOGRAPHY

Special thanks for this book goes to **Mark Moran** and **Mark Sceurman** of *Weird N.J.* and *Weird U.S.* fame! I was lucky enough to get to be part of their "weird empire" starting back in 2004 and lucky enough to get to do *Weird IL*, as well as help out on another state or two, as well. I've learned a lot from them about what makes road tripping so much fun and how to find the truly "weird," whether at home or out on the open road. So, this book is definitely for them!

I'd also like to thank **Kathy Weiser** for her hard work and dedication with **Legends of America** over the years. She's a true aficionado of Route 66 and the American west and, while we have never met in person (although I hope to correct that one day), I have known and been inspired by her for at least a decade. We'd hoped to get to pull off some sort of project like this together one day, but could never work it out to make it happen. But thanks for everything, Kathy!

And thanks to radio legend **Steve Dahl** (and sons **Patrick, Matt,** and **Mike**) for their live broadcasts from Route 66 in the 1990s. The daily shows were hilarious and fun and while they never made me want to pack up kids in an RV and travel from California to Chicago, they certainly inspired me to take the trip again!

Anderson, Warren H. – *Vanishing Roadside America*; 1981
Antonson, Rick – Route 66 Still Kicks; 2012
Baeder, John – *Gas, Food, and Lodging*; 1982
Butler, John L. – *First Highways of America*; 1994
Crump, Spencer – *Route 66: America's First Main Street*; 1994
Eichar-Jett, Cheryl – "Revisiting Legate's Curve," *Buzz Monthly*; September 2015
–––––––––––––– – "The Route Through Granite City," *Buzz Monthly*; August 2015
Hinckley, Jim – *Ghost Towns of Route 66*; 2011
–––––––––––––– – *Illustrated Route 66 Historical Atlas*; 2014
–––––––––––––– – *Route 66 Encyclopedia*; 2012
Knowles, Drew – *Route 66 Adventure Handbook*; 2006
Margolies, John – *Home Away from Home: Motels in America*; 1995
Olsen, Russell A. – *Route 66: Lost and Found*; 2011
Patton, Phil – *Open Road: A Celebration of the American Highway*; 1986
Repp, Thomas Arthur – *Empires of Amusement*; 1999
Ross, Jim, with art by Jerry McLanahan – *Route 66: The Map Series*; 1990

Snyder, Tom – *The Route 66 Traveler's Companion;* 1990

Taylor, Troy – *Mysterious Illinois;* 2006

----------------- – *Weird Illinois;* 2005

Voyageur Press – *Greetings from Route 66;* 2010

------------------- – *Route 66 Treasures;* 2013

Wade, Rick – "The View from Elkhart Hill," *Illinois Times;* March 18, 2009

Wallis, Michael – *Route 66: The Mother Road;* 1990

Weiser, Kathy – *Legends of America;* current

Witzel, Michael – *The American Gas Station;* 1992

------------------ – *Gas Station Memories;* 1994

------------------ – *Route 66 Remembered;* 2003

Witzel, Michael Karl and Gyvel Young Witzel – *Legendary Route 66;* 2007

Wood, Anthony and Jenny L. Wood – *Motel America;* 2004

Special Thanks to:

April Slaughter: Cover Design & Artwork

Lois Taylor: Editing & Proofreading

Lisa Taylor Horton & Lux

Orrin Taylor

Rene Kruse

Rachael Horath

Elyse & Thomas Reihner

Bethany Horath

John Winterbauer

Kaylan Schardan

Staff & Crew from American Hauntings

Havva Eisenbaum: Who inspired me to finally get this off the ground

Mary DeLong

Haven & Helayna Taylor

ABOUT THE AUTHOR

Troy Taylor is a crime buff, supernatural historian, and the author of nearly 120 books on ghosts, hauntings, crime, and the unexplained in America. He is also the founder of American Hauntings, which holds tours and events across Illinois and around the country. When not traveling to the far-flung reaches of American in search of the unusual, Troy resides somewhere among the cornfields of Illinois.

U.S. 66 – sometimes called the Main Street of America – not only is one of the most important highways between Chicago and the West Coast, but it is also one of the nation's most rewarding vacation routes. – *Chicago Daily Tribune*, November 24, 1957

CPSIA information can be obtained
at www.ICGtesting.com
Printed in the USA
LVOW01s1615110516

487769LV00007B/120/P